NOTHING IS TOO LATE

NOTHING IS TOO LATE

The Hunt for a Holocaust Swindler

MARK E. KALMANSOHN

Brassey's, Inc.
Washington, D.C.

Library of Congress Cataloging-in-Publication Data

Kalmansohn, Mark E., 1953-
Nothing is too late : the hunt for a Holocaust swindler / Mark E. Kalmansohn.—1st ed.
p. cm.
Includes bibliographical references and index.
ISBN 1-57488-685-1 (alk. paper)
1. Kozminski, Lucian Ludwig. 2. Fraud—United States—Case studies.
3. Swindlers and swindling—United States—Case studies. 4. Fraud investigation—United States—Case studies. 5. Holocaust survivors—Crimes against—United States—Case studies. I. Title.
HV6695.K35 2003
364.16'3'0973—dc22   2003021614

Hardcover ISBN 1-57488-685-1
(alk. paper)

Printed in the United States of America on acid-free paper that meets the American National Standards Institute Z39-48 Standard.

Brassey's, Inc.
22841 Quicksilver Drive
Dulles, Virginia 20166

First Edition

10 9 8 7 6 5 4 3 2 1

*To Hannah Senesh, a hero for all time and all people,
and to the children, the most helpless victims of the Holocaust
and the repository of our faith and hope in the future.*

I see the world gradually being turned into a wilderness, I hear the ever-approaching thunder, which will destroy us too, I can feel the sufferings of millions and yet, if I look up into the heavens, I think that it will come all right, that this cruelty too will end, and that peace and tranquility will return again.

In the meantime, I must uphold my ideals, for perhaps the time will come when I shall be able to carry them out.

—Anne Frank
Saturday, July 15, 1944, Amsterdam, Holland

I am a citizen of a neutral country, but I think it is fair to say that neither I nor my country have ever looked on neutrality as a comfortable, easy way to avoid suffering.

—Raoul Wallenberg
January 1945, Budapest, Hungary

Contents

Acknowledgments

I would like to express my deep gratitude to Arlene Friedman, Lou Kinzler, Menahem Russek, Shlomo Blajman, Simon Wiesenthal, the Honorable Suzanne Conlon, Andrea S. Ordin, the Honorable Stephen S. Trott, the Honorable David V. Kenyon, Dr. Tony Chari, Ann O'Neill, Peggy Holter, Tom Tugend, Frank Coonis, Anita Stephan, several German restitution agency officials, and all the victims in the case who had the courage to persevere, particularly Jacob Weingarten, Max Wolman, Molly Schimel, the late Theodore Seidman, Ella and Stefan Mandel, and the late Hans Wittner. I also extend my sincere and grateful appreciation to Rabbi David Baron, Charles Ware, Gregg Gibbons and April Morris, Alan Mesher, Dick Cignarelli, Fred Jacobsen, J. Peter Rich, Brian Turner, Henry Holmes, my brother Alan, Max Candiotty, my late friend Albie, the late Adele Kalmansohn, and the late Charles Marion, all of whom were present when I really needed them. I would like to further credit and acknowledge my father, Dr. Robert Kalmansohn, and my late uncle, Dr. Richard Kalmansohn. I likewise recognize the memory of countless others, alive and dead, for providing boundless inspiration for the creation of this book. Finally, I offer special praise to my truly exceptional mother, Dr. Katherine Kalmansohn, both for her enduring values and for her unqualified love and support during times of unbridled joy as well as grief. She in particular always will remain in my heart and close to my thoughts.

MARK E. KALMANSOHN
Santa Monica, California
September 2003

Introduction

Some friends and colleagues remain ambivalent about the publication of this book. They fear that exposure of the cruel acts of a lone Jewish sociopath will reinforce anti-Semitism, prompting a familiar refrain: "What can you expect? Just like a Jew."

What does "just like a Jew" imply? An age-old code, it suggests that Jews are all alike, neither trustworthy nor worth emulating.

But Christ, for one, was a Jew. Belonging to one of several religious Jewish sects of his time, he lived and died as a devout Jew, having embraced the Old Testament, exhorting his followers to keep the Mosaic Ten Commandments, and observing the Passover seder as his Last Supper.

It is true that Christ and his loyal Jewish apostles were betrayed by a Jew, Judas, much as Lucian Kozminski—whom we pursued over three continents and three decades—betrayed his fellow Jews. But from at least a millennium before Christ was born, Jews largely were harmed by non-Jews and non-Jewish institutions.

This long course of suffering is almost as old as civilization itself. Enslaved by Egyptian pharaohs more than three thousand years ago, Jews escaped in a mass exodus to the land of modern-day Israel. During the one and a half centuries framing Christ's brief life (4 B.C.–32 A.D.), pagan Romans brutally suppressed a rash of Jewish rebellions, raping and killing Jews throughout Galilee, Judea, Egypt, and neighboring areas while enslaving thousands of others and casting the remainder into exile.

In the Middle Ages, Jews who survived the Black Plague were blamed for fomenting and dispersing the epidemic, and thousands were killed in riots by their Christian brethren. It was during this dark period of chaos that Jews through much of Europe were ordered by the state and church into cramped ghettos and isolated behind forbidding stone walls for nearly five centuries. The Spanish Inquisition presented an even worse fate. Edicts issued by the Crown presented a stark choice to Jews of Spain: convert, die, or be expelled. Even after the dawn of the Renaissance, and continuing well into the twentieth century, Jews endured centuries of second-class citizenship, exile, forced conversion, state-sponsored riots (or pogroms), expropriation of assets, rape, arson, and carnage.

The reasons for this tragic history are numerous and varied. A misfortune of simple geography, the eternal capital of the Jews—Jerusalem—was often caught in the crossfire of multiple conquering armies and empires. Then there was the matter of competing new religions, as over the centuries elements of the early Church, and later Catholicism and the Protestant Reformation, focused culpability for the Crucifixion on Christ's fellow Jews rather than the Roman Empire. Social and cultural forces buffeted Diaspora Jews, who were both envied for their success in many fields and feared for their distinct and unfamiliar religion, customs, and attire. Despotic regimes often harnessed these sentiments adroitly, deflecting percolating rage from their own oppressive rule.

Consequently blamed for a host of society's ills and discontents, Jews, paradoxically, were maligned as rapacious industrialists and bankers, dangerous Marxist revolutionaries, cheap simple peddlers, degenerate artists and intellectuals, obsequious slaves to State authority, and treacherous betrayers of their country who were secretly bent on world domination.

These canards covered the spectrum of the Jewish experience in the Diaspora, from lands, where Jews forced into ghettos remained devoted to traditional rites, to tolerant societies where assimilated, secular Jews often cleaved to the dominant culture. It remains a supreme irony that Germany, one of the most hospitable of nations for Jews, would prove that absent a homeland, Jews were safe nowhere.

Nazi Germany's "final solution" for the Jews owed its existence to an unholy blend of ingredients. Among them were Germany's bitter defeat in World War I and the draconian Treaty of Versailles; the decadence of elements of German culture in the 1920s, including a cultural strain of anti-Semitism propagated by icons such as Nietzsche and Wagner; and the rise of Fascism, which undermined the fragile democratic Weimar Republic, culminating in Hitler's brutal hijacking of political power.

Citing his perverse racial and genetic theories in *Mein Kampf*, Hitler vilified Jews as "germ-carriers" who made up a loathsome "ferment of decomposition" and designed a plan to "cleanse" Aryan society by extirpating Jewish existence from the planet.

This led to laws banning Jews from professions and universities, to the mass expropriation of Jewish assets, and to the boycotting and ransacking of Jewish businesses. It led to death mills where Nazis gassed Jews by the thousands, cremated their bodies, and extracted their fillings, skin, and hair for personal and commercial use. It ultimately led to the annihilation of as many as six million European Jews, the equivalent of a man, woman, or child murdered every *thirty seconds* for the *six-year* duration of World War II.

Complicity for this genocide does not reside with Nazi Germany alone. The ranks of Hitler's "willing executioners" were swelled both by nations that were conquered by the *Wehrmacht* and by other Axis Power nations. France's Vichy regime actively collaborated with the Nazis, while Romanians, Ukrainians, Slovaks, Croats, Lithuanians, Latvians, Estonians, and Hungarians slaughtered hundreds of thousands of Jews with a zeal that rivaled the Nazi SS. Even *before* a single Nazi extermination camp started operation, local partisans spearheaded the bloodshed as whole communities of Jews in Latvia, Lithuania, and Romania were obliterated in an orgy of mayhem and murder.

After World War II ended and the horrors of the Holocaust were more fully revealed, many Jews remained trapped between the East and the West. The urgency of Zionism was singularly demonstrated by the events of July 4, 1946, in Kielce, Poland, located between the Treblinka and Auschwitz death camps. History records that after a group of bedraggled survivors sought to return to their confiscated homes, scores were savagely murdered in a riot by Polish Gentiles.

Yet Western nations kept their own and other borders tightly sealed. Most conspicuously, Great Britain sank ships full of Jews desperately attempting to enter the Mandate of Palestine and, despite the Grand Mufti of Jerusalem's complicity with Nazi Germany during World War II, secretly armed local Arabs with weapons knowing they would be used in an effort to eradicate the new State of Israel in 1948.

In the end, many have offered apologies for this millennia-old record of Jewish devastation. None has been more profound than the Catholic Church's *Nostra Aetate* (1965), which once and for all "deplor[ed] the hatred, persecution, and displays of anti-Semitism directed against the Jews at any time or from any source."

A lone federal criminal prosecution twenty years ago brought to light and mind the tragic course of anti-Semitism and its toxic incarnation, the Nazi Holocaust. It remains a great irony that this journey was prompted by Lucian Kozminski, a Holocaust survivor who did the unthinkable—cheated fellow survivors. While betrayal remains as old as the story of Cain and Abel, this leaves us to ponder something more: whether the malevolent Nazi regime itself spawned an evil seed within the character of its own victim, leading to untold and enduring consequences.

1

PAST SUFFERINGS AND PRESENT STRUGGLES

The Door to the Past

It was summer of 1996. Set against a cloudless azure sky, the late-afternoon sun cast orange-yellow rays through the silent cemetery, projecting an eerie mix of shadows and light upon the expanse of tombstones surrounding me.

The entire grounds of the vast area were deserted, save for a huddled family placing a wreath of flowers upon a distant grave and a lone caretaker driving an old truck on a meandering road nearby.

Driving slowly through the cemetery, I seemingly neared the end of a long and unexpected pursuit. Several months before, I had reunited with principal victims in a thirteen-year-old case, memorializing their searing and painful journey through the bowels of a virtual hell on earth but knowing nothing about the present status or location of the perpetrator.

I had seen him just once since his conviction and lengthy sentence years before, walking right past me on the streets of Beverly Hills, California, years before Bureau of Prisons' records reported he had been released from continuous incarceration.

Some ten years later, in 1996, I had heard reports of his death in

1993 and had embarked on a dizzying and murky trail replete with mortuaries, death certificates, rumors, curious remembrances, and odd sightings.

This potpourri of evidence and speculation seemed to cast everything into doubt as even the continuum between the past and present merged in a shadowy and indistinct blur of truths, half-truths, and unintended fiction. I wondered: Could a man who had defrauded thousands of Holocaust victims still be alive, despite an official certification of his death years before? Was I the only one who suspected that he could be? And was there a connection to this man's four-decade record of double-dealing, duplicity, and perhaps even complicity with an agency or official of the U.S. government?

Now encircled by the multitude of still and desolate graves, I could sense a buried truth percolating to the surface, prying open the sealed door of the past and death itself, and, in so doing, presenting the distinct prospect of resolving a strange, troubling, and riveting mystery that had begun many years before.

The Challenge

In June 1941, one and a half years after the outbreak of World War II, Nazi troops swept into the western Soviet Union and the adjacent Baltic States of Lithuania, Latvia, and Estonia. But they did not just conquer territory. Employing sealed, mobile "gas vans" and systematically machine-gunning men, women, and children in deep trenches dug by their victims, the Nazis and their henchmen unleashed a furious bloodbath of epic proportions that engulfed nearly one million Jews. Within a few months, even before a single "death camp" had been built, virtually the entire Jewish community in these areas had been decimated.

Although my very existence hinged upon my grandparents' departure from Lithuania decades before the War, it was in other respects an unexceptional journey that led to my eventual immersion into the world of the Holocaust, its survivors, and a most unusual crime whose implications still endure.

Raised in a comfortable suburban neighborhood of Los Angeles, I grew up the son of two doctors in a family that was Jewish by blood but far from religious. While my mother retained a sense of wonder about the spirituality of life, her childhood exposure to male-dominated Orthodox Judaism had turned her away from formal religion. My father, meanwhile, was an atheist pure and simple, the supreme rationalist doctor convinced that religion bears no role in an existence premised upon empirical methods of proof.

My parents nonetheless dutifully sent me to Saturday school, where I eagerly studied stories of the Old Testament and gradually grew to appreciate my heritage. Reading books about the Holocaust with grim interest, growing up with the children of several survivors, and watching with admiration as the "underdog" Israel conquered hostile Arab armies during the Six Day War, I also came to understand the tragedy of the Holocaust and its impermeable link to the birth of the State of Israel.

Yet despite this awareness, the Holocaust still seemed like a horrible and faded nightmare from a distant past, place, and reality.

America, and especially California, stood a world and generation apart from Europe during the War. A blond, blue-eyed athletic boy, I grew up in an assimilationist culture watching *The Jack Benny Show*, *Sea Hunt*, and *Sky King*; playing sports and rooting for the Sandy Koufax–led Dodgers; visiting the beach; and exploring the varied sights and experiences of Southern California. Decidedly casual, carefree, and contemporary, the prevailing atmosphere encouraged new and progressive forms of spiritual expression and personal affiliation rather than reliance upon traditional religion, ethnicity, or ancestry. It was hardly conducive, therefore, to a present sense of connection with the travails of the bygone era embodied by the Holocaust.

In the fall of 1977, after completing law school, I went to Washington, D.C., to work in the U.S. Justice Department's Antitrust Division. Initially thrilled to be walking the same hallways traversed by my teenage hero, former U.S. Attorney General Robert F. Kennedy, I soon learned that the Antitrust Division was not where the action was and consequently applied and was accepted at the U.S. Attorney's Office in Los Angeles.

Under its first female U.S. Attorney, the classy and accomplished Andrea Sheridan Ordin, the U.S. Attorney's Office exuded an air of electricity and excitement and was characterized by a largely youthful group of talented and energetic people.

It was quite a motley crew. Peppered with straitlaced holdovers from the Nixon-Ford administration, the office predominantly featured a succeeding generation of many former antiwar protestors—some of them still distinct renegades, including a veteran surfer who snuck a six-pack of beer into the office each afternoon; a Vietnam veteran who reputedly partook in drug-laced hot tub parties and ended up incarcerated himself; a salty-tongued, gun-toting female attorney; and one diminutive lawyer who smoked unfiltered Camels and regularly punched out plants in the office.

Their diversity and idiosyncrasies aside, these assistant U.S. attorneys spent most days toiling on the front lines of battle, guiding criminal investigations before a grand jury and, upon indictment, prosecuting serious federal offenses including hijackings, espionage, terrorism, narcotics distribution, government corruption, and fraud. Locking horns with criminal defense counsel both little known and renowned, they tried cases alone before federal judges and juries in spacious, imposing courtrooms. All the while, though occasionally tested by the weaknesses of pride, undue ambition, bias, and even fear, most strived to fulfill their duties in the finest tradition of public service.

In my first trial, in the spring of 1980, the defendant was charged with possession of stolen U.S. postal money orders. Suzanne Conlon, a blond, midthirties veteran prosecutor formerly of the Chicago U.S. Attorney's Office, graciously volunteered to lend me guidance, and ultimately her patience, intelligence, and understated humor helped ease me through my baptism by fire.

My star witness was a tall, good-looking black man named Nick, a government informer who took the stand wearing a double-breasted white suit, white hat, and white shoes. Despite his garish outfit and casual demeanor, Nick came through with flying colors. He boldly fingered the defendant without wavering, and the jury evidently believed him, returning a conviction in short order.

SOON AFTERWARD, Suzanne entered my office and, with a somber look, quietly remarked, "I've been asked to investigate a very . . .

unusual suspected crime." Pausing while studying my expression, she continued, "The *defrauding* of Holocaust victims."

As my brain raced at the thought of such a horrific scheme, Suzanne matter-of-factly explained that since 1952, West German government "restitution" agencies had paid Holocaust survivors billions of dollars in *Wiedergutmachung*—literally, "payments making whole"—for documented wartime losses of family, health, liberty, education, and property.

She then reported that the suspect in the new investigation, Lucian Ludwig Kozminski, had claimed he was a counselor officially affiliated with West Germany's restitution program. Incredibly, he was suspected of routinely extracting cash "advance fees" from survivors while *falsely* promising to file claims for their "blood money."

Turning to the pitfalls of the investigation, Suzanne soberly recounted, "I've got to tell you this would be quite a challenge. This guy has operated his business in L.A. for eleven years with impunity. Most of his victims are elderly and don't have any documents. And we're talking about a complex international investigation that'll require extensive coordination with foreign governments."

But then, with a slight lilt in her voice, she quietly added, "Still, even with these obstacles, this could prove rewarding. Very rewarding."

While greatly intrigued by Suzanne's summary, I could hardly have anticipated her final words: "Mark, I'd like *you* to work this one with me. It's a very sensitive investigation, and I think you're the right one for the job."

For a moment I was unsure how to respond. At once surprised and enthused at the invitation, I nonetheless heard my inner voice of self-doubt ask whether I truly *were* up to the challenge. Yet I suppressed this impulse ever so quickly and, remaining reassured that Suzanne would be present each step of the way, decisively replied, "I . . . I'm flattered by your offer, Suzanne, and I . . . I'd love to work this with you."

And so, with this brief and direct exchange, I now was firmly committed as coprosecutor on the investigation of Lucian Ludwig Kozminski.

Beneath the surface, however, my churning emotions still reflected that things were not so simple. A part of me dreaded the prospect of dealing with elderly survivors of the Holocaust, who would undoubtedly recount a disturbing litany of grief-stricken stories of suffering and misery. And a part of me knew, even if someone had cheated these victims, the daunting effort and sheer energy that would be required to prove it. My impulses, in short, suggested that this would be no ordinary investigation and would severely test the emotional mettle of all involved.

My deep-seated reservations aside, the stage now had been set. We were ready to launch this investigation that then appeared nearly futile and would unfold so slowly and unsteadily, never even imagining the result.

The Unusual Suspect

Upon hearing about the man suspected of defrauding Holocaust victims, I assumed that Lucian Kozminski was a Polish Catholic, or perhaps a naturalized German. But when Suzanne and I first reviewed the thick, musty file on Kozminski, we were stunned to discover he was *not only Jewish but a victim of the Holocaust himself.*

While it was difficult to fathom, the cold record now documented that Kozminski had been born to a Jewish family in Lodz, Poland; uprooted by the Nazis during World War II; and incarcerated in several concentration camps before being liberated by the Allies from a camp in southern Germany. But his story did not end there.

After the War ended, unlike the masses of survivors who fled to the United States, Palestine, and other far-flung locations, Kozminski had curiously stayed in West Germany, where he plied an unknown trade and resided for more than two decades. Then, sometime during 1968, he abruptly departed for the United States.

Arriving in Los Angeles on a ninety-day nonimmigrant visa, he had resided here continuously ever since. The Immigration and Naturalization Service (INS) eventually had commenced lengthy proceedings against him but had been trapped in an inescapable Catch-22: While Kozminski was clearly subject to deportation, he could *not* be deported unless another country was willing to *accept* him.

And none was willing to do so. The Germans, quite simply, had deemed Kozminski a stateless refugee, while the Poles had disavowed his birthright and no longer considered him a Polish citizen. Kozminski therefore had illegally remained in the United States for nearly twelve years, cleverly maneuvering in the twilight zone of our immigration laws.

In addition to claims of fraud by dozens of survivors—all of which remained distinctly uncorroborated—Kozminski's file generally referred to several criminal convictions in West Germany, and an extensive CIA dossier on his activities there. Pending our formal top security clearance, however, the contents of any portion of this dossier would remain a mystery to us for several months to come.

THOUGH KOZMINSKI's past was undeniably checkered and unseemly, we were left to ponder the seeds of doubt planted in our investigative file. For the overriding fact remained that Kozminski was a Holocaust victim of Polish-Jewish extraction, who almost certainly witnessed the unspeakable suffering and brutal murder of family members and acquaintances.

Confronted with this stark reality, Suzanne asked in a hushed tone, "How could *anyone* with his . . . experience actually defraud *other* Holocaust victims?"

Her brow furrowed in a look of deep consternation, but I could provide no answers: "I . . . I just don't know. It's certainly *possible,* but I can't explain. . . ."

"Well," Suzanne interjected, almost in a whisper, "I guess we can't discount the possibility that the victims might be terribly mistaken or . . . confused. At least for now."

Nodding in agreement, I replied, "Yes . . . let's just hope our investigation provides the answers. And if he *did* do it, then we can worry about the whys later."

While Kozminski's status as a Holocaust victim would continue to lurk in our thoughts, the mere fact that he was Jewish would not make me more favorably disposed toward him. I had learned long before that criminal suspects came in all colors, ethnicities, and religious affiliations, and demonstrating partiality on any of these grounds was a dangerous, slippery slope.

And this was by no means the first Jewish suspect whom I would confront, even during the pendency of the Kozminski investigation. Through sheer coincidence, I soon would be responsible for prosecuting Jewish defendants in several high-profile cases, leading defense attorney Stan Greenberg to delight in dubbing me the U.S. Attorney's Office's "Jewish Prosecutions Unit."

The real challenge, rather, would be avoiding the appearance of bias *against* Kozminski. For assuming the evidence was borne out that Kozminski was Jewish and had cheated his fellow Holocaust survivors, I knew I would be sorely tempted to abandon caution and stamp out this apparent traitor to his own—and my own—people.

False Starts and Dead Ends

Kozminski's bulky file embodied another area of grave concern: Despite earlier investigations into his activities by the U.S. Postal Inspectors, District Attorney's Office, and Los Angeles Police Department, all three formal inquiries had fizzled rapidly. Suzanne and I now speculated whether these three failed investigations were the immutable blueprint for our own ultimate demise.

When Suzanne and I met with postal inspector "Bookie" Almond, a pleasant-looking, man in his late forties with thinning hair, he quickly donned his reading glasses and skimmed through the investigative file.

"Oh, yeah," Almond remarked while looking up at us, "I remember this one well. It started with a complaint by a Sheila Storm, a former Polish citizen and Nazi concentration camp inmate. She and her husband paid Kozminski $100 cash to file restitution claims, but neither received the $2,000 in restitution they claimed he promised. Well, they didn't give me any documents or anything, but I decided to meet with Kozminski once to check their story out."

Suzanne queried, "Only once?"

Almond replied, "Yes, only once. I felt it was enough."

We then listened silently as Almond, known as an intelligent and experienced investigator, recounted his meeting.

He remarked, "Well, this guy Kozminski came on pretty strong. I mean, he boasted that he had 'extensive experience in Europe,' where he had served as 'president of a Jewish federation.' He acknowledged he had operated as a restitution counselor for five years but claimed he accepted only the most 'difficult cases,' you know, those that had been rejected by restitution authorities."

Almond drew a deep breath before continuing: "Well, then he turns on the victims. He sort of flips through a very thin folder, waves his hand in the air, and says, 'The Storms? They gave me false and insufficient papers. In fact, I'm done with their claims unless I get better information.' And—"

Suzanne interjected, "And you closed the file?"

Almond responded, "Yes. I really believed the guy. So I rejected the claim that he operated an 'advance fee' scheme and concluded—let's see what I wrote—'[i]t is evident that it is to [Kozminski's] *benefit* to try to have the claims adjudicated.'"

I then asked, "And what's your impression of him now?"

Shaking his head, Almond concluded, "Well, this guy's good. I mean, he could snow you at the *equator*. So if he's a crook . . . well, then, I guess he's *really* good."

This single inquiry showed how the cards in this deck would be stacked—and who held all the aces.

For we now knew we would be contending with a confident, persuasive, and manipulative subject. These same skills would surely make mincemeat of any reliance upon his oral promises to victims, many of whom were elderly, infirm, and less than fluent in English. Yet our other major investigative option also appeared foreclosed: Nearly all victim documents were contained in claim files reposited at none other than Kozminski's own offices.

The district attorney's investigation was equally discouraging. The file reflected that Deputy D.A. Stephen S. Trott commenced an inquiry in June 1975, shortly after receiving a phone call from a director of the local Jewish community service center.

Advising that Kozminski was reportedly "*gouging* $125 out of [Jewish Holocaust victims] and apparently *holding their passports* as . . . economic ransom," Trott pointedly noted that the local West German consul had termed Kozminski "a crook." In concluding that these people are "easy prey for this type of thing and somewhat inexperienced in the ways of the law," Trott reported enduring fears that "this is nothing more than a *gigantic rip-off.*"

But despite Trott's dire warning, the investigation had been closed just *eight days later.* In his summary report, the assigned investigator tersely concluded that "the victims in this case were contacted by [the] DDA [Deputy District Attorney]. . . . They have *withdrawn* their complaint and *refused* to discuss the matter." (emphasis added)

As if the Postal Inspector's collapsed investigation were not enough, this inquiry now exposed a new area of abiding concern: the victims themselves. For Kozminski's clients may indeed have been "very easy prey," but they were also survivors of the most extreme exercise of state authority. While they understandably might prove reluctant to cooperate with us, incriminate another Jew, "jeopardize" their restitution claims, or testify amid the swirl of public exposure, our investigation would be doomed from the outset without their active assistance.

The LAPD's "bunko" probe was also short-lived, focusing upon survivors' charges that Kozminski extracted "advance fees" but never filed their restitution claims. The absence of documents and the prospect of a complex, multinational investigation proved too much, leading to a swift termination of the inquiry.

Just as daunting as these three failed inquiries, we still had no idea exactly what we were investigating. Plagued by this uncertainty, we pondered: Was Kozminski—as most victims suggested—purposefully coercing their payments through a "naked" *fraudulent* promise to file restitution claims? Was he actually *filing* claims and then secretly pilfering the ensuing restitution payments? Or was he a misunderstood and marginally competent restitution counselor who was innocent of any crime?

Perhaps as an excuse to relegate this horrible chapter to the history books, I again wondered: Would our effort really be worth it? Was this all just a terrible mistake? And if not, how many victims were out there, anyway? Ten? Fifty? Or could there be more?

Dead in the Water

Rather than the FBI or another federal agency, our investigation was assigned to the U.S. Postal Service. Because many Postal Inspectors were adept at ferreting out the most complex of mail-fraud crimes, we remained confident despite the substantial hurdles we faced. This optimism, however, would soon fade abruptly.

We met as planned in Suzanne's office with Postal Inspector Michael Parry, a brown-haired man in his midthirties who had interviewed several survivors and examined subpoenaed records from Kozminski's known bank account.

Casually noting the deposit of a West German restitution payment that the victim apparently never received, he quickly added that nothing else in Kozminski's account appeared suspicious. But Inspector Parry was far from done.

Proceeding to open a brown folder and read from its contents, he matter-of-factly recounted his interview with another survivor, Jacob Weingarten.

Parry began, "OK. This guy Weingarten apparently was interned during the War in some labor camps and concentration camps. He was liberated while on a forced death march in May 1945 and came here a few years later."

He continued in a monotone, "Let's see, in July . . . 1972, Weingarten first met with Kozminski, who told him he had a 'good [restitution] case' for medical disability. So he signed a power of attorney authorizing Kozminski to keep 15 percent of any restitution payment and also gave him a $100 money order as a 'nonrecurring fee.' The file shows that Kozminski continued to request fees, and Weingarten claims to have paid him some $1,500 in cash over the next five years."

Pausing while shuffling through the file, Parry went on, "OK. Now, Weingarten says he heard nothing about his claim until July 1977, when Kozminski sent him a letter advising that he had been awarded about $3,800 in restitution. Kozminski told him in the letter that 'this amount is at your disposal at any time' and then advised that because of the difficulty of the case he was entitled to 'an additional [fee] of 25 percent.' "

Pulling a document from the file, Parry went on: "A few months later, this Weingarten guy still hadn't received his restitution, so he contacted the West German consulate general. He claims they advised him that his restitution payment had been transferred to Kozminski's bank account in September 1975, nearly two years before."

Slowly closing the file and peering at us, Parry concluded, "Wein-garten, I guess, got pretty pissed off and confronted Kozminski. The suspect responded by offering a share, I'll admit a very small one, of the award. But Weingarten rejected the offer and stormed out. Now he complains that Kozminski never paid him anything."

We were struck by the postal inspector's evidence, which flatly refuted the notion that Kozminski's operation was just a naked "advance fee" scheme, limited to cajoling dribs and drabs of cash payments from victims. Rather, something far more sinister seemed to be afoot, for we now knew that Kozminski actually proceeded to *file* claims and, at least in one instance, had *obtained* and *fraudulently converted* a restitution award. Indeed, the propriety of Kozminski's entire operation now had been cast into doubt.

The investigating postal inspector, however, somehow had reached an entirely different conclusion. Rising from his seat, Parry paced through the small, cluttered government office while launching into a carefully rehearsed explanation.

First he provided an assessment that, while unduly pessimistic, was not unwarranted, remarking, "I've got to tell you, I think this case is a real loser. The victims just won't cooperate. I mean, they don't want to have *anything* to do with us."

Continuing apace, he now adopted a troubling prospective defense that we presumably would be hard-pressed to refute, "And this Weingarten thing, Kozminski probably just misplaced the payment and then got put off when the guy blew up at him. I don't think he committed any crime other than keeping sloppy files."

But Parry still was not done. His voice rising, he boldly pro-claimed, "Based on my observations, I've concluded that it's the *victims* [not Kozminski] who are *greedy* and *untrustworthy* and who have committed *larceny* in their hearts."

Pausing for effect, he added, "If you have *any* case, it's against them."

With that final pronouncement, Parry slumped back into his seat flashing a small and nervous smile, searching for a hint of our approval. But none was forthcoming.

Suzanne and I instead abruptly turned toward each other and

locked eyes in silence, both absolutely appalled and disgusted, neither believing what we had just heard.

It was one thing, after all, to examine evidence of guilt skeptically or play the devil's advocate. But it was quite another for the *case investigator himself* to point an accusatory finger at the *victims*, most of whom were poor and elderly, as the true perpetrators of fraud and deception in this matter.

While suppressing a deeper instinct to bolt across the room and squeeze my hands around his throat, I now groped for an explanation, privately wondering: Did Parry belong to an extreme right-wing group? Or was he simply a garden-variety anti-Semite?

Despite these initial impulses, I later realized that a more benign interpretation also may have existed, reflecting more about Parry's self-confidence than any innate prejudice. His own evidence had converted a relatively straightforward "advance fee" probe into a far more serious and extensive investigation. Perhaps believing he was in over his head, Parry may have sought a convenient excuse for shirking this formidable challenge: blame the victims.

Yet regardless of the explanation—assuming a rational one even existed—all the signs were abundantly clear: This inquiry was stalled in place so long as Parry remained our assigned investigator.

Refraining from engaging in a futile exchange over Parry's skewed perspective, Suzanne literally bit her lip and muttered, "I think we've heard *enough*, Inspector Parry. Thanks for your report . . . and you're welcome to leave . . . *now*."

An uncomfortable silence fell over the room. Parry looked at me, but I averted my eyes. He looked back toward Suzanne, who was flushed red with anger, barely controlling her Irish temper. No one uttered a word as Parry self-consciously rose and stepped from the room, quickly shutting the door behind him.

The door had barely closed before Suzanne was on the phone with Parry's supervisor, indignantly reporting his outrageous comments. She brusquely concluded by demanding, "I want this son of a bitch off our investigation *now*."

After profusely apologizing, the supervisor stammered, "Don't worry, Ms. Conlon. We . . . We'll get you a replacement . . . *immediately*."

While greatly relieved that Parry had been "smoked out" and removed at such an early stage, we now faced the harsh reality that an unpromising investigation had become even more difficult. I now anxiously speculated: Were we dead in the water before we had begun? And would—or could—Parry's replacement really make any difference?

The German Factor

His initials were L. K., but he assuredly was not named Lucian Kozminski. Christened Lothar Fritz Kinzler, he preferred to be called Lou. He was also the new postal inspector assigned to our case.

Born near Berlin during World War II and raised in Germany, Kinzler lived for years in a house he later learned had been confiscated from a Jewish family. When Kinzler was a young child, his father died on the Russian front during World War II, following in the footsteps of his grandfather, who died on the Western front during World War I.

Eager to make a new life, Kinzler came to the United States at the age of nineteen, soon afterward joining the U.S. Army and departing for the war in Vietnam. Escaping that encounter unscathed, Kinzler obtained his U.S. citizenship and a college degree and soon afterward was hired as a U.S. postal inspector.

Brown-haired and sporting a small mustache and thin-rimmed glasses, Kinzler was tall and skinny with a concave chest, his body slightly twisted by early years of malnutrition during World War II. He sometimes seemed almost uncomfortable in his own skin, blinking nervously and occasionally hunching his back. He could snap defensively at a moment's notice. And yet, Kinzler was earnest and intelligent with a quick sense of humor, and he spoke several languages fluently. He exuded a certain dignity.

Kinzler came to us with a mixed reputation. Suzanne Conlon had worked with him on a prior fraud case, and while she found him hardworking and dedicated, she also believed him a maverick who sometimes resisted direction.

Aside from Suzanne's persisting doubt, we both speculated how

the victims would react to Kinzler and how he would
Would they be fearful and less cooperative when a
postal inspector called them for an interview? Would Kinzler harbor
some of the same hidden feelings as Parry?

The victims were not the only ones. I suspected it would feel
strange and uncomfortable working on this investigation next to a
former German citizen. Deep down, I wondered if I could trust his
instincts or even trust him as a person. Could he really be the right
person for the job? And even assuming he was, would my own judgment always be clouded by Kinzler's indirect association with the
very perpetrators of the Holocaust?

That said, I was greatly cheered during our initial meeting with
Kinzler in Suzanne's office. Like a breath of fresh air after our dis-
mal experience with Inspector Parry, virtually the first words out of
Kinzler's mouth were, "So, guys, how are we going to *nail* this
scumbag?"

Smiling ever so slightly at Kinzler, even despite my misgivings, I
knew at that very moment that he would represent a refreshing and
dramatic improvement.

When Kinzler replaced Parry in September 1980, we had reached
a critical crossroads. We all strongly suspected Kozminski was perpetrating a venal fraud. But now we had to develop the right strategy
to catch him.

Slingshot With Two Stones

We now turned to the plan for our investigation, one we would scrupulously follow during the ensuing nine months despite persistent
difficulties and frustration. With Suzanne mired in her office preparing for a trial in another matter, Kinzler and I laid the foundation
for this strategy over lunch in nearby Chinatown, shortly after he formally joined the investigation.

Facing Kinzler over platters of steaming chow mein and vegetables, I recounted our dilemma, "Really, it's sort of a Catch-22. The
only way we're going to get substantial evidence of Kozminski's guilt
is by seizing all his files. On the other hand, the *only* way we get his

files is by showing fraud in the first place. And that's going to be tough, certainly based on what we've seen so far."

Kinzler, sipping a cup of tea, paused and then slowly responded, "Well, what are we going to do? What's the plan?"

"I don't think we have much choice," I replied. "We've got to focus on *quality* of proof to get that warrant. It's got to be airtight, I mean *irrefutable* fraud, because we're sure not going to have a lot of evidence."

Kinzler queried, "Well, what about the Weingarten claim, for example?"

"Not good enough," I interjected. "Remember, Kozminski actually offered to pay some of Weingarten's restitution, even though it was two years later. He may have some sort of argument there, however implausible, and we just can't take that chance. Because if our warrant gets shot down later on, we lose *all* the evidence from our search . . . and we're right back to square one."

"OK," Kinzler muttered, swallowing a mouthful of noodles. "I get you. So tell me, just how many examples of *irrefutable* fraud do we need to find?"

Holding up my two chopsticks for emphasis, I swiftly replied, "Two. We need *two*. Put it this way: Based on what we've seen, any more than two will be a bitch. And if we only come in with one . . . well, someone may chalk that up to mistake or oversight. If the judge buys *that* argument, we're dead. *No* search warrant, *no* case."

Pausing, Kinzler then remarked with a slight smile, "So you're telling me we need a slingshot with two stones to bring Kozminski down? Boy, this is making me feel like David versus Goliath."

"It's even worse than you think," I responded. "Because we've got to rely upon our existing group of complaints. And they're *not* very promising."

With a look of consternation, Kinzler now queried, "Then why not just *publicize* our investigation and get more victims? I mean, I'm sure they'd come out of the woodwork like . . . well, like termites."

"Yeah," I remarked, "even though your analogy was lousy. But remember, Kozminski finds out about it too, and then our evidence may go up in smoke. Or he may just vanish into thin air, along with his assets. Then what do we have?"

Nodding his head in agreement, Kinzler soberly concluded, "I see what you mean. Well, I guess we've *really* got our work cut out for us."

KINZLER WAS RIGHT, and soon things became more difficult. Swamped with a massive fraud case already scheduled for trial, Suzanne simply could not devote sufficient time to other matters and had decided to remove herself from our investigation. Lou Kinzler and I understood but knew we would sorely miss her.

This was particularly true for me. For the departure of Suzanne—an experienced and intelligent prosecutor—had hit a very deep nerve.

Still relatively new in office, I harbored serious doubts as to whether I possessed the experience, the savvy, or even the competence to handle this investigation alone. Part of me simply wanted to roll into a ball and hide while the investigation somehow disappeared quickly and quietly.

But I knew that was not a viable option. The only other choice was clear: I would have to see this thing through to the end, seeking out Suzanne for occasional advice and, however reluctantly, drawing closer to and relying upon Kinzler throughout the entire process.

And so I mustered up my strength and, along with Kinzler, embarked on a critical round of victim interviews. One of the most memorable was with Theodore Seidman.

A pleasant, white-haired man, Seidman warmly greeted us at the door of his simple Westside apartment, ushered us inside with a stooped back and limp, and then proceeded to relate the extraordinary saga of his wartime experience.

IN 1939, at the age of twenty, Seidman lived with his mother in Sosnowiec, Poland, near the German border and a few miles north of a nondescript Polish town named Oswiecim, the future site of the Auschwitz death camp. On September 4, the calm of peace was suddenly shattered as masses of German troops invaded the town.

While the ground literally thundered from the onslaught of Nazi soldiers, tanks, and artillery, a bewildered Seidman instinctively sought refuge in a long, dark tunnel, where he hid for several nerve-racking hours. After an eerie stillness seemed to prevail outside, Seidman finally ducked his head out in unrestrained curiosity.

In a single instant, the quiet was broken by the screaming, sound of oncoming bullets fired by a nearby German tank. Whistling next to Seidman's neck, the bullets "felt like a sharp wind" as they narrowly missed their target.

Terrified at his brush with death, Seidman abandoned his hiding place and scampered home in a frantic dash. But home provided little refuge. Soon after destroying the Great Synagogue of Sosnowiec, the SS forced Seidman and all other Jewish males into a cramped room at the city hall where they were randomly assigned a number from one to ten. As the others looked on in terror, all men designated tens were promptly lined up along one wall.

Facing the tens were a group of Nazi soldiers, who slowly raised their rifles and upon a command barked in German, fired in unison. The Jews contorted briefly in pain and then crumpled silently to the ground, all dead in the mere passing of a moment.

Gazing at the blood-splattered carnage before him, a trembling Seidman knew he had barely eluded the Nazis' grasp of death. His assigned number was nine.

The surviving Jews then were transferred to an enclosed marketplace, and while soldiers fired rounds of bullets into the air, they were ordered to remove all belts, watches, and jewelry, which the Germans voraciously gathered. The black-uniformed SS next called in each prisoner for an "interrogation," administering severe beatings and kickings in the process. But that was the lighter punishment, for those provoked into responding to insults such as "your mother is a bitch" were shot dead on the spot. This nightmare continued for the next three days as the Jews were kept prisoners in this torture chamber, starved and forced to sleep on a cold, dank cement floor.

By the end of this torment, Seidman was convinced he had entered a virtual hell on earth. But little did he know that his gruesome wartime ordeal was far from over.

The scene of terror then shifted as the Jews were sent to the local jail, recently left deserted by escaping prisoners. A skilled locksmith, Seidman was tasked with repairing the prison's damaged bars and locks. Promptly escorted by two bayonet-toting Germans to a local shop for tools, he tried to contain his silent horror as they passed the rotting, twisted corpses of ten Jews hanged on makeshift crossbars in a public square.

In order to humiliate Seidman and his fellow Jews, the Nazis later ordered them to perform menial tasks in public, such as sweeping city streets. As the Jews slaved away at gunpoint, many of the non-Jewish *goyim* Poles, some of them Seidman's own acquaintances, gathered around and cheerfully ridiculed them, taunting, "Good for you. You're *finally* doing some work in this town."

Later, when Seidman was inexplicably sent home at night for a short period, his family advised him that the Nazis were transporting young Jewish males to an unknown but ominous destination and urged him to flee toward Russia. Seidman reluctantly agreed and later slipped onto a train bound for Kraków. But the Nazis soon caught him and several other Jews, forcing them off the train and detaining them in a bare room for three days before abruptly releasing them.

Granted this reprieve, without hesitation Seidman fled north to Przemysl, now controlled by the Russians after their joint Polish land grab with Germany.

Upon arriving at his destination, Seidman was spared the murderous impulses of the Nazis but became a slave laborer for the Russians. He worked day after day in a dank electric plant for nearly two years, and at times it seemed it would never end. Then, one fateful day, after Seidman heard ominous reports that the Russians were forcibly shipping all Jews by cattle wagon to Siberia, he decided to leave.

With the impermeable walls of two evil empires now closing in from both sides and desperate to learn the fate of his family, he promptly departed Przemysl and headed home, back into the teeth of the ever tightening grasp of the Nazis.

But the Seidman family reunion would be distinctly short-lived. Not long after Seidman's return to Sosnowiec, the Nazis forced all 28,000 local Jews into the enclosed ghetto of nearby Srodula. Food and medical supplies were reduced to a trickle, and hundreds soon died from starvation and disease. Then, just when it seemed that the horror could not worsen, the rail transports from the ghetto began.

Physically separated from his family by bayonet-toting troops, an anguished Seidman watched helplessly as his mother, brother, sister, and young niece were rounded up and forced into cattle cars at the nearby rail station. The slow-moving cars soon departed with their doomed hostages and headed toward the beckoning gas chambers and crematoriums of the nearby Auschwitz death camp.

And then it was the distraught Seidman's turn, as he was transported the other direction, to a forced-labor camp at Waldenburg and an entirely different fate.

For nearly a year Seidman toiled at backbreaking work in an ammunition factory, surviving only because it was under the control of the German army *(Wermacht)* and a civilian foreman, not the dreaded SS. His emotions, his memories, and even his life all seemed suspended in this purgatory of work, fitful sleep, and a near-starvation diet.

Then, one day in early 1945, Seidman's wartime ordeal suddenly ended as hordes of Russian troops swarmed noisily into the area. The Nazis beat a hasty retreat, leaving their dazed and emaciated prisoners behind, free at last though barely clinging to life.

The cessation of hostilities, however, would prove less than a joyous occasion for Seidman. Disoriented and exhausted, he trudged for days through the countryside alone, sleeping in the dark forest and consuming grasses and shrubs for nourishment.

At last he managed to find his way home. But he soon realized the awful truth: His entire family was gone, never to return. Now a Polish gentile resided in the Seidman family's apartment, and he greeted the returning survivor with a wrathful threat: "Get the hell out here. It's *mine.*"

Homeless and stripped of his family, Seidman now joined the Haganah, a Jewish group dedicated to shipping weapons to the Jewish underground in Palestine and resettling Jews there. Nearly boarding a ship called the *Exodus* bound for Palestine, he delayed departing upon hearing that his brother-in-law had returned to town.

Seidman soon had a bittersweet reunion with him in Sosnowiec's kibbutz, or temporary Jewish communal living quarters, as they both shed tears of grief for their loss and joy for their survival. At the kibbutz, Seidman also met a diminutive brunette girl named Anna, like Seidman, an orphaned and traumatized Holocaust survivor. The two formed an instant kinship, one that would endure for more than fifty years.

Later, upon the Haganah's instructions, Seidman and Anna tore up all their identification papers, disguised themselves as Greeks to avoid capture by their "fellow" Poles, and set off on a perilous train journey ending in Stuttgart. It was there that upon reuniting with one of his brother's friends, Seidman finally learned the fate of his brother.

As it turned out, Seidman's brother somehow survived Auschwitz, but his travails were far from over.

With the Russians closing in from the East near the end of the War, the Nazis abandoned the camp and marched Seidman's brother and other emaciated survivors day and night toward Germany. As the death march eventually snaked across the border and deeper into Germany, his brother soon became sick with dysentery. He suffered from diarrhea and grew ever weaker. Despite desperately trying to maintain the inexorable pace, Seidman's brother finally became immobilized, and when he stayed behind to rest his fate was sealed. A Nazi soldier shot him in the head and killed him just two days before liberation.

While in Stuttgart, Seidman and Anna remained fiercely devoted to the creation of a Jewish homeland in Palestine but secretly dreamed of life, liberty, and the pursuit of happiness in America. Married by a rabbi, they later managed to obtain immigration papers and board a ship filled with refugees bound for the United States. But even this last leg of their pilgrimage was not without incident.

At one point the aging ship almost sank, pitching so drastically that passengers were ordered to cling perilously to one side of the vessel. Almost too exhausted and seasick to go on, a joyous Seidman finally caught a glimpse of the Statue of Liberty, and at that defining moment his sickness instantly disappeared.

After recounting this tragic journey, Seidman paused, quivering slightly and eyes filled with tears. I glanced at Kinzler, who appeared nearly shaken to his roots, his brow furrowed in sympathy and his eyes slightly moist. I must admit that something inside me actually felt reassured that Kinzler was so visibly touched, and I now sensed we just might develop a working rapport together.

But this was not my only reaction, as for a moment I wondered why we were even there listening to this poignant, gut-wrenching saga.

Derived from another place and time, Seidman's account seemed entirely removed from our jobs, daily existence, and present reality and appeared to embody something far beyond our experience and even our comprehension. I now wondered: Was there anything Kinzler and I could undertake, anything our investigation could accomplish, that might affect this man's life in a meaningful way?

But even as I struggled with these thoughts, it was Seidman who drew the connection between his past ordeals and our present purpose. In the scheme of things, this connection might well be considered slight, but I vowed never to lose sight of it.

After a brief interlude, Seidman now turned to the sequel: his futile attempt to receive some sort of compensation for all his suffering and grief. For this purpose Seidman had turned, beginning in 1971, to Lucian Kozminski to initiate a medical disability claim arising from his incarceration and beatings.

Seidman remarked, "Nine years later, I still hadn't received my restitution. All I did was pay *him* money. A total of some $400 in cash for a 'nonrecurring fee,' for things like 'handling,' German Supreme Court fees and postage."

"Finally I was very frustrated," Seidman continued in an understated tone, "so I told him I wanted my file back. But he said, 'You've got to be kidding. You're about ready to get your restitution. Why would you want to do such a foolish thing?' But, of course, my money never came."

After recounting his disappointment with Kozminski, Seidman softly muttered, almost with resignation, *"He took my blood money."*

He then looked at us plaintively with his bespectacled brown eyes, as I gazed back silently, trying to digest his story and assess him as a prospective witness.

The more I reflected, the less impressed I was. Seidman's wartime account had admittedly been heartrending. But he had seemed almost meek, even matter-of-fact, in his description of Kozminski's conduct. While I wanted to observe at least a hint of visible rage or anger, his bearing had reflected a notable absence of either.

Yet even as I privately questioned Seidman's suitability as a compelling witness, Kinzler and I knew the truth: The evidence in Seidman's account simply did not embody the *clear-cut* fraud we needed for our warrant. And with that simple judgment we decided to file this one away, never suspecting that new evidence on Seidman's claim later would prove critical to our efforts.

LACK OF VISIBLE indignation was not the issue with Arthur Reich. A man in his early sixties with salt-and-pepper hair, a stooped back, and nervous affect, Reich was plagued by a spotty memory and clearly reluctant to testify. Ushering Kinzler and me to a small dining room table, Reich sat us opposite him and his wife, a small gray-haired woman who tried to calm her husband's alternate nerves and occasional bursts of anger as he recounted the twisted course of his claim for restitution.

Reich began, "For ten years before I ever met Kozminski, I got a 40 percent disability pension from Germany—due to my health problems from the camps, you know. But when I first met Kozminski in 1969, he said, 'Arthur, you should be getting a much larger pension. Here, sign this power of attorney—you'll see my fee's only 10 percent—and I'll get it for you.' So like a fool I signed."

Reich shook his head in disgust before continuing: "Well, he was just beginning. Every three or four months, he asked for cash. Thirty dollars here for lawyer's fees, $50 here for lawyer's fees, cash for his secretary, all sorts of things. But each time I gave him the money. It ended up at some $600, more or less."

As it turned out, after Reich remarried in August 1977, he and his new wife bumped into Kozminski at a local bar called the City Slicker, which they heard Kozminski owned.

Digging into her purse, Ms. Reich removed a letter from West Germany about her pension benefits and asked Kozminski to translate it. According to Ms. Reich, who actually knew full well the contents of the document, Kozminski blatantly lied about it and insisted she come to his office for a "consultation." It was then that she concluded Kozminski was "a crook."

Meeting with the Reichs several months later at his office, Koz-minski demanded another $35 and execution of a new power of attorney to "continue" with Reich's claim. When a suspicious Ms. Reich asked to read the document, Kozminski quickly grabbed it and snapped, "People like you, I have *buried* already and don't need any-more," and then contemptuously ordered the Reichs out of his office.

Reich now remarked, "Finally I was finished with him. I wrote directly to the Berlin Restitution Office and told them I had fired Kozminski. Done with him. *Kaput.* But in early 1978, they wrote back and said, 'We're sorry, Mr. Reich, but we already awarded you $1,000 and sent it to Kozminski's bank account three years ago!' "

"Needless to say," Reich continued angrily, "I took the letter, went straight to his office, and showed it to him. And you know what he said? He said, 'Arthur, Arthur, I knew all about that, but the money got lost coming over on a ship.' Such nerve. Of course, he didn't explain why he asked for $35 and a new power of attorney two and a half years *after* my restitution was awarded."

Reich added, "Well, lo and behold, a few weeks later, an envelope arrived. No letter or anything inside. Just a check . . . for $403.50. And he kept all the rest, something like 56 percent of my restitution award."

Now MAKING a tight fist for emphasis, Reich clearly remained furi-ous at Kozminski. Glancing toward his wife, who nodded in assent, he remarked, "My wife *knew* he was a crook, and as she likes to remind me, I should have listened to her."

But the enraged Reich still remained distinctly uncomfortable about cooperating with our investigation, pointedly noting to us, "Despite what he did, it's over and done. And I don't want to relive all the memories."

At least for now, however, we knew that Reich's reluctance was of no moment. For despite persuasive evidence of fraud, Kozminski possessed a palpable if strained defense, having claimed Reich's resti-tution payment was misplaced and eventually having remitted part of it, however belatedly. Reich's claim therefore, like Seidman's, still did not represent the *irrefutable* fraud we so urgently needed for our warrant.

So again we continued our elusive hunt, this time buoyed by the knowledge that our next interview held out great promise for our faltering investigation.

The Delicate Thread

A few days later, we met with Stefan and Ella Mandel at their modest apartment in West Los Angeles. Both in their midfifties, Stefan was a pleasant-looking stocky man with wavy gray hair, while the soft-spoken Ella had reddish brown hair and large, expressive brown eyes.

After ushering us into the living room, the warm and gracious Stefan grasped my hand tightly and looked straight into my eyes with an unfiltered gaze, remarking, "I'm so glad you finally came. We've been waiting a very long time for this."

My reaction was nearly spontaneous, for at that moment I felt a strong bond with this seemingly earnest and genuine man and sensed it would endure for years to come.

The doe-eyed Ella was distinctly less enthusiastic about our appearance. Beneath her pleasant veneer she seemed emotionally fragile, acutely self-conscious, and reticent. For a while she barely uttered a word. But as the subjects of our conversation became more intimate during the ensuing hours, Ella's reluctance subsided. In the end, she would join her husband in recounting a harrowing story of tragedy, fate and survival.

RAISED ON THE Baltic Sea near Danzig, Poland, Stefan and his siblings often whiled away the hours playing "Indians" with bows and arrows in the nearby forest. During those carefree days, Stefan knew little about his native religion and began studying Hebrew only when he was sent home from school during Catholic religious hour. But he soon would learn the harsh and fateful lesson taught to virtually all Poles of Jewish extraction.

In September 1939, when Stefan was twelve years old and residing in Lodz, the Nazis abruptly stormed into Poland. Later enclosing the old city of Lodz behind steep walls and barbed wire, they ordered all

Jews to relocate into the newly created ghetto. At first eluding the Nazi dragnet, the resourceful Stefan regularly disguised himself in a Hitler youth uniform and managed to escape to the city outside the walls.

Upon liquidation of the ghetto four years later, however, Stefan was caught in the throes of the mass transportation of Jews eastward. Despite the Germans' incantation of *"Juden raus!"* (Jews out!), most Jews wanted to believe Nazi propaganda of "a new life" in a "promised land" and obediently packed their pots and pans, valuables, and other belongings. Shipped on freight trains to the Auschwitz death camp, Stefan and his fellow Jews immediately noticed the ring of electrified fences and the haunting, strange smell wafting from the large chimneys beyond. But most still stubbornly clung to hope, refusing to acknowledge the stark symbols of death now encasing them.

Several weeks after arriving at Auschwitz, Stefan was unexpectedly sent with a select group of one thousand men to Hanover, Germany, to toil in a stone mine. For most, however, this merely changed the setting of certain and impending death. Day after grueling day in the sooty, stifling darkness, Stefan stuffed dynamite into holes bored for blasting, and after eight long months of insufferable labor on a near-starvation diet just sixty men remained alive.

This grueling ordeal ended only when the SS, fearing for their own lives, rounded up the haggard, emaciated group of survivors and marched them toward the Bergen-Belsen concentration camp, away from the advance of Russian troops from the east. For even as Nazi Germany now faced certain defeat, the SS would relentlessly continue its separate war against the Jews, Stefan's group being no exception.

The first night, the prisoners were shoved into barns where the SS beat them with fists and clubs ceaselessly, prompting a cacophony of bloodcurdling screams of terror until daybreak. Aware by the second evening that he simply could not endure any more, Stefan spontaneously chose a course that was fraught with peril but the only one consistent with survival.

Frantically digging a hole under the barn a short distance away from his captors, he managed to squeeze underneath and pull himself through the narrow opening. Moments later he was running in the darkness of night outside, a hail of bullets screaming in the distance behind him. Fully prepared to meet his end with a bullet entering his back, Stefan continued to sense his legs pumping and his heart racing, but it would be several minutes before his mind realized he had escaped unharmed. Eventually his body gave out, and Stefan collapsed in utter exhaustion in a distant field, falling into a deep slumber.

Hours later he was startled out of his sleep by Polish farmers, who shook him awake and excitedly asked whether he had seen the *English* soldiers in the vicinity. Hardly believing his own ears, a jubilant Stefan now knew the Allies were victorious and the War had ended. But even in this singular moment, he would not let his guard down: Acutely aware of the likely consequences, he dared not inform these "fellow" Poles that he was Jewish.

Days later, Stefan befriended a Jewish American G.I. who, taking pity on this bedraggled survivor, valiantly commandeered a jeep to take him to Bergen-Belsen to search for his sister.

Incredibly, Stefan found her there amid a twilight stench of rotting corpses and death, emaciated but still clinging to life. And that was not all he found. For it also was at Bergen-Belsen where Stefan met the frail but lovely Ella Joskowicz, whom he would marry the following year.

ELLA WAS BORN and raised in a small city called Zdunska-Wola, about twenty-five miles from Lodz. When she was barely thirteen, the Germans invaded Poland and swiftly herded all Jews of Zdunska-Wola into a congested ghetto.

But Ella's nightmare had just begun as, one by one, her loving family would be torn from her side by the Nazis' claws of death. In 1941, machine gun-toting Nazi henchmen abruptly took away Ella's younger sister Lola, and spirited her off to an unknown location. Lola, in all likelihood, had been enslaved to serve at the unholy delight of one or more German officers, only to be eventually discarded and replaced by another doomed young prisoner. Though Ella would never see Lola again in the flesh, her sister would come to her each night in a series of fitful dreams, vivid nightmares that would be exceeded only by new and unforeseen living horrors.

Later the same year, the terror shifted to another location, as Ella and the rest of her family were forcibly resettled in the cramped, squalid Lodz ghetto, now renamed Litzmannstadt.

Because the Germans were sending all men away to an uncertain fate, Ella, her mother, and her remaining sister, Zosia, carefully hid her father in a small space behind a wall. But this earnest effort eventually proved doomed, as long after ghetto food supplies were reduced to a trickle, Ella's father met a silent and desolate death by starvation. Ella discovered his emaciated remains and experienced a searing, horrible sense of loss that would endure to the present.

The following year the Nazis liquidated the Lodz ghetto and transported Ella, her sister, and her mother to Auschwitz in dark, stench-filled cattle cars. The rail cars were so densely packed that men, women, and children all stood during the entire journey, some sobbing uncontrollably, others defecating in place, and yet others meeting a silent death.

Immediately upon arriving at the sprawling camp, Ella and her sister Zosia were forcibly separated from their mother, who disappeared in the teeming mass of humanity, never to be seen by her loved ones again.

Night after night, the teenaged Ella and Zosia huddled together in their bare, lice-infested barracks, surrounded by starved, diseased, and despondent inmates. Soon hearing rumors that Jews were being killed in large gas chambers, they peered in horror at the camp's tall crematoruma chimneys bellowing a dark, ghastly smoke throughout each day. Though dearly hoping for a miracle, the two sisters now realized their mother's likely fate. And they wondered how soon they would join her.

As the Allies inevitably closed in during February 1945, the Nazis endeavored to complete their murderous task by sending Ella, Zosia, and other Auschwitz prisoners on a forced death march to Bergen-Belsen. The sisters somehow survived this seemingly interminable trek during the dead of winter. But emaciated with malnutrition, shortly after arriving at the camp Ella contracted typhus and Zosia, tuberculosis.

Almost deaf from her numbing affliction, Ella one day heard a faint chorus of yells. For once, however, these were prisoners' screams of joy, not terror, as French troops arrived to liberate the camp. Ella was so drained of emotion, so numbed by her losses, that she simply did not know how to react to this momentous occasion. Nor, as it turned out, did most of the liberating troops.

For upon entering Camp 1 at Bergen-Belsen, horrified Allied soldiers found a sickening mass of near-dead and dead humanity: 41,000 skeletal prisoners and 13,000 unburied bodies within an area measuring one mile by four hundred yards. Barely believing their own eyes, the troops quickly burned every disease-ridden corpse, rag, and shrub and frantically tried for to care for the living and the dying.

The troops soon made a nearly equally appalling discovery just two miles away, where they found eight hundred *tons* of food meticulously stored at a Nazi military facility. But this abundance was too late for many of the survivors, whose diseased, emaciated bodies were irreversibly decomposing even while still alive. Allied troops watched helplessly as another 13,000 inmates died within one week of liberation and several thousand more in the weeks thereafter.

Now fearing the Red Cross would take her sister away forever, Ella hid Zosia and desperately tried to care for her, carefully feeding her rations of food and hot soup. But her tireless efforts were all to no avail.

In a cruel and cold twist of fate, Zosia died nearly six years after the Nazis invaded Poland and just one month after Bergen-Belsen was liberated and the War ended. The two inseparable sisters finally had been forcibly parted. Suddenly bereft of family and wracked with nagging guilt in this living nightmare, Ella secretly yearned to die with her beloved sister. But ever so slowly one excruciating hour passed, and then one day. And she somehow survived to tell her story.

FOR A SMALL recompense for their incalculable suffering, both Mandels had filed several restitution claims through Lucian Kozminski and paid him $757 in fees over an eight-year period. In 1974, Stefan actually received a restitution payment for one of these claims, amounting to some $1,000 for loss of jewelry.

But we were concerned about Kozminski's handling of another

claim which, according to subpoenaed records, had resulted in direct payment of $932 to Kozminski's bank account more than five years before. We now pointedly asked Ella if she had received this payment, or any part of it.

Looking at us with a blank stare, Ella paused and then nervously muttered, "No." We asked her if Kozminski ever told her about the restitution award, and Ella again quietly muttered, "No. Not a word."

As Ella's voice trailed off and she gazed into the distance, an irate Stefan interjected, "I can assure you she never got a cent. This is *unbelievable*. I should have known that bastard was a crook."

With these clear disavowals, Ella Mandel's deceptively small claim appeared to constitute our first irrefutable instance of fraud.

There would be no quibbling about the permissible percentage of Kozminski's fees, and it would be difficult to argue the money was misplaced. The evidence was clear: Kozminski simply failed to remit restitution or even acknowledge receipt of Ella's award for five years, continuing to the very day of our witness interview.

Now that we had finally located a compelling claim, we faced an entirely different problem. Understandably protective of his wife, Stefan did not want Ella to publicly recount the trauma of her wartime experience and absolutely would not permit her to sign a declaration or testify.

We earnestly tried to assure the Mandels. They would not be alone. We would locate another victim with testimony more essential to our search warrant and seek to admit our evidence strictly through Stefan's statements rather than Ella's.

At least for the moment, however, the Mandels remained unconvinced.

As Ella intoned, her voice quivering with emotion, "I'd like to help you, but I just can't do it. I do not want to . . . I won't . . . relive the . . . suffering."

The horrors of the past now seemed to touch a nerve in Ella, who abruptly stood up and silently walked into the kitchen.

As Ella gazed through a window into the distance, Stefan leaned forward and quietly remarked in an earnest tone, "Listen, Mr. Kalmansohn. I'm furious at Kozminski. I will do whatever I can to cooperate. But I have to protect my wife. She is fragile and cannot go through all this."

Stefan's words only increased my budding admiration for this evidently decent and honorable man. Kinzler and I meanwhile would heed Stefan's wishes and, despite the tenuous state of our investigation, vowed not to press the issue, at least for now.

But we were more inspired than ever to press on with the investigation.

As we pulled out of the Mandels' driveway in Kinzler's white government-issue sedan, I remarked, "Well, between you and me, Lou, I'm convinced this guy's a crook. I mean, the victims' stories are too similar and the pattern is too consistent. I think he's been ripping these people off."

Kinzler, glancing at me while turning the steering wheel, soberly concurred, "Yeah. No doubt about it. And he's stealing a lot more than money."

I stated, "You mean. . . ."

"Well," Kinzler interjected, "at first I thought, God, after what these people suffered through, what's a few dollars—even thousands of dollars—decades later?"

"Yeah," I remarked, "I *was* wondering about that. . . ."

Kinzler then went on, "Yeah, but all you have to do is listen to *these* people. I mean, they get even *more* emotional talking about Kozminski. It's like he stripped away something, some chance to ease . . . the memories."

"That's true," I responded. "And worse yet, as they all point out, a fellow Jew and Holocaust survivor."

"I gotta tell you," Kinzler added, "no matter how many victims there are or how much money he stole, this thing is important, *real* important."

"I think you're right," I replied, relieved that Kinzler had reached the same conclusion I had weeks before. "And we've really got to get a move on. This guy's advertising throughout the world, reaching tens of thousands—maybe hundreds of thousands—of survivors."

"Yeah," Kinzler responded. "If we don't move quickly he'll continue to cheat survivors day after day, with absolute impunity."

"And besides that," I added, "most of our victims are pretty

elderly and don't have very good memories as it is. This clock is tick-
ing . . . faster every day."

"Well, I sure hope the Mandels come around," Kinzler concluded.
"I think we're going to need them. They're like a delicate thread in
all this, and without them . . . I . . . I'm just not sure we'll have
enough. . . ."

And with that final thought, we drove on in the silence of the
night, both contemplating the challenge that lay directly ahead.

So WEEK AFTER WEEK, we continued our protracted search in
extensive meetings and calls with Holocaust survivors. Even while
these interviews progressed, a subtle reality slowly began to emerge.

These people were shaken to the core, traumatized, and understandably skittish about cooperating or examining any part of their
past suffering. Yet through all the fear and pain they retained a quiet
dignity, a humanity, even an elusive sense of faith. We knew, as a
result, that we just might be able to reach them.

Armed with this hope, we now approached our next interview,
confident that it could hold the key to unlocking the Pandora's box
of Lucian Kozminski.

The Telltale Postscript

For decades the Fairfax District had served as the virtual hub for the
community of Holocaust survivors in Los Angeles. Extending down
a ten-block stretch of Fairfax Avenue, this district was marked by a
string of delicatessens, bakeries, Jewish religious shops, Kosher restaurants, small motels, newspaper stands featuring Yiddish and
Hebrew periodicals, and the teeming Farmer's Market—a sprawling,
partially enclosed complex featuring a potpourri of produce, meats,
and goods amid a competing blend of old-world aromas.

On any given day, the streets of this community were filled with
people from all corners of Europe and all strains of the Jewish religion, from the black-garbed ultra-Orthodox to the less devout hailing
from largely assimilated Western Europe. The languages, customs,
cultures, and cuisines may have varied, but the denizens of this area

shared some important things. Largely elderly, many were Holocaust survivors, and virtually all of them were Jews.

It was this common experience that drew the community together. Tight-knit and often insular, where word could travel fast and furious, this community remained adjacent to, but a world apart from, society at large: While the Holocaust was already a historical fact, in this bygone era—long before *Schindler's List*—awareness of the tragedy remained distinctly limited and muted in most quarters.

AT THE HEART of the Fairfax District stood Wittner's, a long shop stocked with cigars and filled with the sweet, pungent aroma of tobacco. On a sun-drenched afternoon, Kinzler and I went there to meet Hans Wittner, an upbeat, vibrant man in his midseventies with silvery gray hair, beaming brown eyes, and a ready smile.

When we entered the shop, we immediately spotted Wittner standing behind the counter before a large display of cigars. Motioning us over, he greeted us warmly, stating, "Come in, come in. I've been looking forward to meeting both of you."

After we approached and stood facing him across the counter, Wittner slowly leaned over and remarked, "I've got something you gentlemen should find *very* interesting. I think we're finally going to get this guy."

And with that intriguing introduction, he launched into his story, blending a variable tone of zest and melancholy.

BORN IN BERLIN, Wittner labored in the German lumber industry for more than eight years. All that changed in 1933 when Hitler and the National Socialist Workers Party ascended to power on the crest of a virulently anti-Semitic tide, and Wittner made a difficult and fateful decision.

At the time, most German Jews were passionate and dedicated patriots who refused to believe Hitler constituted a real threat either to them or to their nation. But the rise of the Nazis posed a genuine sense of foreboding to Wittner and several of his relatives who decided to take a drastic step.

Quitting their work and leaving their families, friends, and belongings behind, they promptly fled Nazi Germany to an uncertain fate. They departed just a few years before the Nazis forced Jews from their jobs and homes, relegated them to second-class citizenship, and began rounding them up for eventual deportation.

Wittner and his relatives first traveled due east, eventually arriving in Poland. Seeking to put down roots there, they soon found Poland a less than hospitable place for Jews, particularly foreign ones. Many Polish gentiles were anti-Semitic, while a substantial portion of Polish Jews themselves were black-garbed traditional Hasidim, a stark contrast to the assimilated Western-oriented Wittners.

So in 1937, the Wittners once again packed their belongings and departed, this time only two years before Germany invaded Poland and forcibly herded Jews into ghettos on the path to extinction. Shortly after that, the Wittner family settled in England. But Wittner, still restless, would continue alone to France, where he again found the adjustment difficult and feared that rising tensions with Germany could thrust the entire region into a bloody war.

Again his bags were packed, and this time he managed to escape to Cuba shortly before the Vichy regime handed 90,000 French Jews to the Nazis for extermination. Finally, in July 1941, one and a half years after Hitler initiated his conquest of Europe, Wittner emigrated to the United States, settling in California. Although uprooted and displaced like the age-old wandering Jew, Wittner had somehow stayed one step ahead of the cruelest and deadliest march of fate.

WHILE WITTNER recounted his story, I realized that his experience had been markedly different from most of the other victims. For despite his extensive travails, he had never been incarcerated in a concentration camp. Momentarily distracted, I could not help but wonder whether this could account for a certain lightness in his step, a lilt to his voice, and his ebullient bearing, or whether some other more pedestrian explanation existed.

As Wittner turned to the subject of restitution, his ensuing reference to Kozminski prompted a loud groan from his feisty gray-haired wife, Sarah, who had just entered the shop and rapidly approached.

Her finger wagging as she arrived at our side, Sarah excitedly remarked, "*That crook*? Listen, as a rule I like people, but I *hate* him."

Kinzler and I looked at her quizzically, and after pausing for effect, she eagerly launched into her own story.

Sarah reported that, over the years, Kozminski and her husband occasionally spent some time together socially. Kozminski eventually pleaded with Hans to borrow $2,000, and Sarah's accommodating and trusting husband charitably complied. Many months later, however, Kozminski had repaid nothing on the loan.

While still in debt to Hans, one day Kozminski paid a social call to the Wittners at their apartment. This was Sarah's opportunity. Swiftly entering the kitchen, she grabbed a long butcher knife and stepped into the living room where Kozminski sat with Hans. As Sarah rapidly approached, she pointed the knife at Kozminski and demanded that he make payment on the loan.

At first seemingly unconcerned, Kozminski flippantly responded, "This is not your apartment. It's your husband's."

But Sarah wielded the knife more tightly and came even closer, bringing the blade next to Kozminski's body.

Trembling slightly, Kozminski now knew Sarah's warning was genuine. Fumbling for his checkbook, he hastily wrote a check for $1,000. A triumphant Sarah immediately grabbed the payment and threatened, "Now, if I see you again, I'll kill you."

Obediently heeding the warning, Kozminski stood up and left abruptly, never to return.

Hans chuckled good-naturedly as Sarah completed her story, but his smile rapidly faded as he now turned to the twisted tale of his claim for restitution.

WITTNER BEGAN, "Well, I first went to Kozminski's office in June 1978, and after we chatted for a while—we always spoke German—I told him I wanted to file a claim for loss of employment in Germany before the War. Kozminski became very excited and told me I was entitled to a large restitution award. So I signed a power of attorney and gave him $125 cash as he requested."

Glancing at some notes on the counter, Wittner went on, "In November 1979, he told me my claim was 'progressing' but asked for another $53.85 cash for 'postage,' so I paid him. *Oy*, if I had only known. . . ."

Now shaking his head with regret, Wittner continued, "It was about eight months later when he came into this shop again. He said, 'I've got very good news, Hans. Your claim has been settled. Only one thing remains. The Germans are demanding that before you collect, you pay $488.89 for back payment of unemployment stamps.'"

Visibly wincing, Wittner now added, "And, of course, he said, 'You can make the check out to me and I'll forward it directly to the German Social Security office. Remember, I've got a power of attorney.'"

Pausing briefly, Wittner then explained, "So thinking I was about to get my restitution, I gave him the check."

Drawing a deep breath, he continued, "But three weeks later, Kozminski again came back, and this time he said, 'I'm sorry, Hans, but there's been a slight miscalculation. The Germans now request that you send another $156.11 in order to collect your money. I hate to bother you with such a small amount, but it's required. Of course, you can make the check payable to me again.' Like an idiot I paid him."

Sarah groaned loudly, but Wittner went on, "Believe it or not, he came to me again a little while later. This time he said I was about to get a monthly pension and some $20,000 to $30,000, but I had to make a 'final' payment of $86 cash for 'secretarial expenses.' So guess what I did? Would you believe it? I paid him again. Still, of course, I didn't receive my restitution."

"Some six months later," Wittner now explained, "I had had enough and decided to confront him. So I went to his office and told him I wanted proof that my $645 was sent to West Germany. Kozminski knew I was really mad, so he said, 'Calm down, calm down, Hans. Look, I seem to have misplaced those two check stubs. But I'll look for them and send you copies as soon as I find them.'"

"But three months later," Wittner advised, "he still hadn't sent them. So I went to his office again. This time I said, 'Listen, you *goniff*, if you don't give me evidence that you sent my $645 to Germany, then I want all of my money back. And I swear on my mother's grave, I'll go right to the authorities.'"

While Sarah cackled at her husband's description, Hans continued, "Listen, I really meant it, and I think he got scared. He said, 'OK, OK. Don't worry. I promise I'll send you the proof. Just give me couple of days.'"

"Sure enough," Wittner intoned, "he sent me a letter all right. It was a carbon copy of a July 20, 1980, letter to the Berlin Restitution Office. And it had a postscript that read . . . it read in German, 'Enclosed cashier's check $645 for backpayment for six years.'"

Wittner now pulled a letter from his coat pocket and placed it before us. Pointing to it, he remarked, "But I knew something was very strange. See, *look* at the postscript. The whole letter is a carbon copy, but the postscript is *original* typing!"

As Kinzler and I perused the document, we were startled to see that Wittner's description was absolutely accurate. The postscript was, quite unmistakably, different typing from the rest of the letter.

With an exuberant tone, Wittner went on, "You see! Well, anyway, I decided to write directly to the Berlin Restitution Office. And guess what they answered? They told me that Kozminski never sent them *any* money on my claim. Nothing."

"So now I was really angry. I wrote Kozminski a letter and enclosed a copy of the letter from Germany. I told him, 'Please explain.' I figured I had him."

"But you know what he did?" Wittner implored. "He had the *chutzpah* to write me back and tell me he was tired of my complaints and my contact with the Restitution Office. He said, 'Don't bother me again until your restitution comes at the end of the year.' And then he said that I still owed him money!"

Shaking his head, Wittner added, "And, of course, I heard nothing. I never got my restitution, and I never got my money back from that swindler."

Inhaling deeply having concluded his detailed account, Wittner now looked at us, winked, and playfully remarked, "Quite a *goniff*, huh?"

But playfulness aside, he also was incensed and only too happy to cooperate with our investigation.

As Wittner slipped cigars into our pockets before we departed, his expression suddenly grew serious as he emphatically stated, "I will do whatever you want, cooperate in any manner. There is an important principle at stake. And this man must be stopped."

And we knew we may have found the way to stop him. For while deceptively modest, Wittner's claim seemingly represented none other than our second smoking gun against Lucian Kozminski.

As we stepped out of the shop, several black-clad *haredim* Jews scurrying by, Kinzler exuberantly remarked, "I think we've really *got* the scumbag now. I mean, he induces Wittner to give him $645, falsely promising it'd be sent to Germany to 'release' a restitution payment."

"Right," I replied. "Then, when he learns Wittner had contacted Germany directly, he *compounds* his fraud by forging a postscript 'proving' he sent the money to Berlin. Talk about covering your tracks. . . ."

"Well," Kinzler remarked through gritted teeth. "We're about to expose his tracks. If the original of that letter doesn't have a postscript . . . then his goose is cooked."

"Yeah," I replied, "and we've got our warrant."

ORDINARILY, we were not supposed to contact the West German government directly. But we simply had to know the truth.

Casting caution to the wind, on September 23, 1981, Lou Kinzler promptly called West Germany and reached a Ms. Trilse at the Bundesversicherungs Office (Social Security agency) in Berlin. Reporting that she was familiar with the Wittner file, Trilse immediately located it and found Kozminski's July 20, 1980, letter.

Quickly and silently scanning the document, she exhaled deeply and then delivered her unequivocal report, "Mr. Kinzler, I can assure you that this letter contains *no* postscript, *no* reference to $645, and *no* reference to a 'back payment.'"

Now aware of its undeniable import, Kinzler eagerly requested the original letter, but Trilse cautiously responded: "I cannot send this to you straight away. I first must obtain approval from German authorities, and then we must route the document through the West German Consulate in Los Angeles." The process would take months.

Having confirmed Hans Wittner's suspicions, we now would be certain that when the original undoctored letter arrived, we were ready to act. At long last, it finally appeared we were on the verge of cracking this investigation wide open.

Tip of the Iceberg

In order to obtain a search warrant, the government must show through affidavits and exhibits that, more probably than not, evidence of a crime exists at a particular location. But its burden does not end there: Even if probable cause has been established, the government also must demonstrate that the nature and scope of the proposed search and seizure are entirely consistent with the evidence in support of the warrant.

As I remarked to Kinzler while we sat in my office, formulating strategy on our prospective search warrant, "You know, Lou, we've really got to make this airtight. We can't ask for *any* evidence that doesn't relate to his restitution business."

Kinzler replied, "Well, why don't we just ask for everything at his office, seize it all, and sort it out later?"

Shaking my head, I responded, "I'd like to do that. But God knows, that would probably include some personal stuff, and the warrant or the search later could be ruled illegal. And you now what that means. . . ."

"Yeah," Kinzler interjected, "The whole kit and caboodle gets suppressed. All the victim files. Everything. Even if we could move forward, we'd probably be left with just a handful of claims. And it may look like we're picking on poor Kozminski."

"Right," I answered. "Hey, if we were in Great Britain, the worst you would get is an administrative reprimand. Here, *all* the evidence goes out. *And* everything 'tainted' by our search. So we better apply our scalpel here. . . ."

Mindful of these crucial issues and corresponding pitfalls, we now turned to preparation of the warrant itself.

The first decision was relatively easy. Foregoing the prospect of searching Kozminski's home, we instead would focus exclusively upon his Wiedergutmachungs-Office, Restitutions (BEG), at 347 South Ogden Drive, Suite 208, in Los Angeles.

REGISTER — EINSCHREIBEN

NOTE NEW ADDRESS
L. KOZMINSKI
347 SOUTH OGDEN DR. #208
LOS ANGELES. CALIF. 90036
TEL. (213) 937-3409

VERSICHERUNGSANSTALT
ANGESTELLTE
...verwaltung
... Reinickendorf

...str. 2

... GERMANY

den 20. Juli 1980

Antrag auf Leistungen aus der deutschen Angestelltenversicherung
Hans WITTNER, geboren 27. April 1909
Vers. Nr.: 5 3 2 7 0 4 0 9 W 0 3 9
BKZ 5565
Mein Schreiben vom 22.12.79

Sehr geehrte Herren,

...meines Mandanten verweise ich auf die eidesstattliche des Herrn
Walter BOHM von 29. Juni 1978

...Bohm erklärt, dass mein Mandant bis Anfang 1932 in Kattowitz und Zednia (Polen)
...tätig war. Die diesbezüglichen Unterlagen waren infolge Kriegseinwirkung
...den gekommen.

...Rente wegen Berufsunfähigkeit

...liegt ärztliches Attest bei.

Mit vorzüglicher Hochachtung

L Kozminski

...ich ausgefüllten Fragebogen
" ärztliches Attest
eidesstattliche Versicherung Walter Bohm

Anliegend Kaschscheck fuer $645.00 Nachzahlung fuer 6 Jahre

645.00
488.89

1161

L Kozminski

*Kozminski's July 20, 1980 letter on Wittner claim (copy of authentic original
with forged postscript referring to enclosure of $645)*

Though several victims had already provided a fairly detailed description of that location, we left little to chance.

WHILE AWAITING West Germany's forwarding of the undoctored Kozminski letter on the Wittner claim, Kinzler and another postal inspector had paid Kozminski an unannounced undercover visit, posing as a victim's relatives with inquiries about a restitution file. Our objectives were twofold: to obtain a precise description of the layout of Kozminski's office and, if we were extremely fortunate, to record any incriminating statements for our warrant. Kinzler, as a result, had carefully strapped a body wire inside his shirt before embarking on this delicate mission.

When the postal inspectors arrived at the South Ogden location and knocked on the door of the large office, they were greeted by none other than Lucian Kozminski. As he peered at the middle-aged man facing him, Kinzler immediately was struck by Kozminski's distinctive appearance. For in sharp contrast to his victims, he some-how *looked* the part of a shady crook. With a long thin nose, black mustache, and thick glasses, Kozminski was short and bald with a dark fringe circling the back of his head. Kinzler's first impression would endure, and from that moment on he invariably referred to Kozminski, simply, as the Weasel.

Kinzler was also struck by Kozminski's intuitive reaction to the inspectors' unannounced visit. For as Kinzler peered into Kozminski's skeptical eyes, he strongly sensed that Kozminski was not buy-ing into the cover story and instead suspected the postal inspectors were neither Jewish nor actually interested in a particular victim's file.

Ever so nonchalantly, Kozminski then went through the motions. Briskly leading Kinzler and the other postal inspector to his victim files, he briefly rummaged through one cabinet before remarking that he was unable to locate the file on Kinzler's "relative."

Impatiently slamming the cabinet drawer shut, he turned back to Kinzler, stating with irritation, "I'm really too busy for this interrup-tion. I have work to do." And with that and a dismissive wave of his hand, he quickly escorted both agents out, tersely ending the exchange without having uttered a single incriminating statement.

It hardly mattered in the end, as we soon discovered that Kinzler's body wire had malfunctioned and was virtually inaudible.

Now THAT WE had managed to obtain a detailed description of Kozminski's office, we turned to the substance of the warrant. Crafting it with as much particularity as possible, we described the items subject to search and seizure as follows:

> [A]ny and all records . . . referring or relating to Wiedergutmachungs-Office, Restitutions (BEG), including but not limited to, letters and documents relating to customers and individuals solicited by the . . . business; correspondence of Lucian Kozminski with associates in Germany and with German Restitution Agencies . . . telephone bills and records; lists and files of . . . customers; financial books and records . . . safes . . . typewriters, [and] employment personnel files.

While properly insulating an assortment of private documents and materials, we believed our description would permit us to seize almost anything relating to Kozminski's restitution business, amply serving our purposes.

We next turned to the evidence justifying the nature and scope of our proposed search and seizure.

With our two irrefutable instances of fraud—embodied in Ella Mandel's and Hans Wittner's claims—we were confident we possessed sufficient probable cause. However, to gain access to all of Kozminski's files, correspondence, and records, we would have to persuasively demonstrate that the Mandel and Wittner claims actually represented the "tip of a fraudulent iceberg" permeating Kozminski's entire business.

In order to make this critical showing, we would rely principally upon the affidavits of three people: Hans Wittner, Stefan Mandel, and Lou Kinzler.

Shortly after I completed Hans Wittner's affidavit, he cursorily reviewed and signed it, boldly remarking, "I can't wait to testify against him in open court."

Though Ella was the true victim, we then finalized Stefan Mandel's affidavit in an earnest attempt to shield her from testifying.

Ten months after our first interview with the Mandels, we tentatively presented our proposed affidavit to Stefan in the living room of his home. We did so knowing that if the Mandels would not cooperate, we would be reduced to a single irrefutable instance of fraud and, in all likelihood, would have to delay seeking a search warrant indefinitely.

After I explained to Stefan that we had located another key witness to Kozminski's fraud, had carefully prepared an affidavit for Stefan's signature, not Ella's, and would seek an order sealing affidavits in support of the warrant, I silently studied his face for a reaction. A long moment passed as Stefan ruminated, eyes turning inward.

Then his face suddenly brightened and, eyes slightly moist, he remarked, "I can't thank you enough for what you've done to protect Ella. We realize there are no guarantees, that Ella still might have to testify. But I think we owe you this much."

Reaching down to the table before him, he picked up a pen and promptly signed the affidavit. Now peering up at Kinzler and me, voice quivering with emotion, he quietly stated, "I don't care about the money. I *do* care about all the other survivors. Now you go get him."

Greatly relieved that we had finally broken the ice and secured the Mandels' cooperation at this critical stage, we next tied all the pieces together in Lou Kinzler's affidavit. Methodically detailing the trail of the payment that Ella Mandel never received, Kinzler went on to describe the forged postscript in the letter presented to Hans Wittner. He then proceeded to demonstrate that, consistent with the pattern in many sophisticated frauds, our evidence probably constituted just the tip of the iceberg.

Specifically, Kinzler reported that the postal inspectors' files reflected that more than one hundred people in the United States and Canada had paid Kozminski "non-recurring fees," and then were lulled into remitting additional fees by "promis[es] that their money would arrive shortly from Germany." Estimating that 95 percent of Kozminski's clients never received a restitution award, he surmised that even when restitution was awarded Kozminski kept all or a substantial portion, far in excess of any agreed-upon fee. In the end, he concluded that Kozminski was operating a scheme to defraud and requested permission to search and seize the extensive materials described in our warrant.

We were ready to move.

On December 15, 1981, some three months after our initial request, the West German consulate in Los Angeles finally received and forwarded from Berlin the authentic Kozminski letter, which bore no postscript. Two days later, after attaching the letter and the corresponding forged copy to Kinzler's affidavit, we requested that Magistrate Joseph R. Reichmann issue a warrant.

In his chambers, Reichmann, a former criminal defense attorney, sat at his desk reviewing our papers, scanning the three affidavits and carefully studying Kozminski's fraudulent postscript. Kinzler meanwhile stood next to him, silently awaiting Reichmann's decision. Shaking his head in disbelief, the Magistrate muttered something under his breath. Then he picked up his pen and executed the warrant, handing it to Kinzler.

Glancing at the document, Kinzler reassured himself that our long-sought judicial signature actually appeared on the warrant. Now smiling ever so slightly, he carefully folded the document, placed it inside his breast pocket, and headed for the door.

So at last we had completed the first critical stage in our journey. After long months of effort and patience, we finally had arrived at the threshold of Kozminski's door. Still the knawing question remained: What would be inside?

A Time to Search

Like the deceptively tranquil eye of a hurricane, executing a search warrant in a complex fraud case can be an oddly prosaic and yet suspenseful experience. Unlike a search for illegal weapons, narcotics, or stolen goods, agents remain completely unaware whether documents they seize contain evidence of a suspect's guilt or innocence. As such, at once momentous and anticlimactic, the search becomes a seemingly routine procedure simultaneously fraught with critical implications.

On December 18, 1981, bearing our signed search warrant, Kinzler and three armed postal inspectors headed for their rendezvous with the eye of the storm swirling around our suspect. Upon arriving outside the designated suite, they faced a brown formica door with a simple nameplate reading, "Wiedergutmachungs-Office, Lucian Kozminski, Counselor." Kinzler promptly stepped forward, knocking loudly several times.

Reaching down, he unfastened a holster strapped to his side and placed his right hand on a small black revolver. He was taking no chances that Kozminski, perhaps tipped off to the search, might take matters into his own hands. After a few long moments, the door was slowly opened by Lucian Ludwig Kozminski. Unarmed and wearing a sport shirt and slacks, he stood silently.

Kinzler was face-to-face with Kozminski. For a moment it all seemed so surreal.

During many long months, Kozminski had seemed like an elusive ghost, freely and flagrantly operating his business while Kinzler and I toiled away, painstakingly grasping at bits of incriminating evidence. Kinzler had experienced one brief, largely futile undercover encounter with Kozminski while wearing his body wire. But this was all very different, as the tables had dramatically turned: Kinzler now faced him, armed with a search warrant, ready to assume the upper hand, at least Kinzler fervently hoped.

Flanked by his fellow agents, Kinzler now eyed Kozminski, who stared back with a hint of recognition. Before Kozminski could utter a word, however, Kinzler flashed his credential and perfunctorily advised that the agents were there to execute a search of his office. Kozminski's deadpan expression remained unchanged as he opened the door wider to let the agents inside. Removing the search warrant from his pocket, Kinzler stepped toward Kozminski and brusquely handed it to him, remarking, "This is for you."

Kozminski glanced briefly at the document and, suddenly looking up with an ingratiating smile, slapped Kinzler on the back and spontaneously asked, "So, Inspector, how would you like a drink?" His eyes darting to the side, he motioned to a cabinet along one wall containing several bottles of partially consumed hard liquor.

Wincing at the thought of consuming alcohol so early in the day,

Kinzler instinctively declined the offer. But he knew he had just witnessed a telling glimpse of one facet of Kozminski's personality.

As a veteran postal inspector, Kinzler was mindful that fraud defendants typically possess a special charm and charisma that enable them to fleece their victims and drop their gregarious mask only when cornered. Kozminski was apparently no exception. Agents were about to seize his files and shut down his business, but he seemed unconcerned and almost jovial, as if this jarring event were all according to *his* plan.

Diverting his attention from the suspect, Kinzler briefly surveyed Kozminski's office and was immediately struck by its unkempt condition. A variety of papers were strewn about, apparently randomly, on a dusty cigar stand, a rickety wooden table, a nearby brown sofa, and a secretarial desk in the corner. Magazines, telephone books, and an assortment of other materials also were scattered indiscriminately, and the office furniture was old, worn, and dusty.

For a moment he wondered whether Kozminski's reported alcoholism or unstable mental state could account for this unruly mess, but he quickly dispelled the notion. The agents were there simply to do a job, and he would see that it was done correctly.

WHILE THE AGENTS went about their business over the next three hours, Kozminski flitted about the office, at times acting charming and at other times watching silently, occasionally pointing out "personal" materials not subject to seizure, intoning, "That's mine. That's mine. You can't take that." For long stretches he disappeared out of the agents' sight into the rear of the office, apparently privately taking stock of this tumultuous and unforeseen invasion.

All the while, the agents methodically executed their task, hewing closely to the warrant and selectively seizing Kozminski's restitution materials while leaving several unrelated items behind. A massive volume of victim files, found in the same row of cabinets identified during Kinzler's undercover stint, would account for the bulk of seized materials. The other most conspicuous items were two old typewriters, which Kinzler ordered seized to compare with the fraudulent postscript on the Wittner letter and "modified" fee provisions in several of Kozminski's powers of attorney.

In the end, despite the mess of materials and the pervasive inter-mingling of personal and business matters, the agents conducted their search carefully and discretely. Strictly limited to items named in the warrant, their seizure yielded a final quarry of thirty-one sealed boxes of evidence.

Aside from having apparently crippled his ability to operate, we now possessed proof that eventually might bring Kozminski to jus-tice. Though hardly lacking in incentive, we would often recall his final words moments before the agents departed: Grinning broadly at Kinzler, Kozminski shook his hand, winked, and boldly proclaimed, "Listen, Mr. Inspector, when *you* figure all this out let *me* know."

As Kinzler left, accompanied by his boxes of evidence, he indeed wondered whether he could figure it all out.

Would the victims' accounts be borne out, or would he discover a largely legitimate business plagued by sloppiness and mistakes? Did the agents, in short, possess a veritable gold mine—or nothing more than fool's gold?

The Inner Search

Even as the fate of our search remained sealed within the confines of several nondescript boxes, Kinzler and I embarked on an entirely different type of probe. Prompted by our recurring exposure to the travails of Holocaust survivors, we were virtually compelled to explore our own disappointments and uncertainties, however trivial they seemed by comparison.

In his early forties, Kinzler was beset with a distinct restlessness and an intangible lack of fulfillment. He had felt somewhat like a duck out of water for quite some time. He had never known his father, who died in World War II, and always felt a certain hole in his existence as a result. After arriving in the United States, he had often stood out conspicuously, as the German-American serving in Vietnam and the German-American postal inspector. He was socia-ble but never really one of the boys.

Now seemingly approaching the pinnacle of his career, Kinzler nonetheless questioned whether any case ever could inspire him equally, and he remained unsure about the direction and course of his professional future. Though sincerely devoted to his wife and children, Kinzler wondered whether something greater existed, whether life had more to offer than the merely conventional route. Faced with the unexplored territory of the shrinking path before him, he remained plagued with doubts about his present existence as well as his capacity to achieve a sense of inner peace.

I, on the other hand, had felt the pain of several tragic and unexpected deaths in my family over the previous decade. I also had watched in horror as my idol as a youth, Robert F. Kennedy, was shot dead just days after I had grasped his hand at a local temple. And then, groping for a piece of relative stability and contentment in life, I had found the apparent incarnation of the woman of my dreams.

It was a vision, however, that would slowly but surely slip away like so many innumerable grains of sand. Marked by a final breach of trust, it was finally over, and I knew I would have to pick up the pieces and move on, struggling daily with the challenges of personal growth beneath a stoic and unrevealing professional facade.

The more time Kinzler and I spent together, the more we would lapse into dialogue about our internal searches. What did we really want from our careers? What did we have to look forward to in life? And how could we draw upon and evolve from our personal pain and disappointments?

While poised at these personal crossroads, Kinzler and I invariably turned to the task at hand, only to witness an unexpected synthesis between our public and private searches: Thrusting ourselves with renewed dedication into the looming challenge, baring our senses with fewer inhibitions than normal, we would both immerse ourselves in our expanding investigation.

Perhaps, in so doing, we were seeking to defer some of our present turmoil and even needed self-examination. But at least we would try to do something right.

2

THE FAR-FLUNG QUEST

Needle in a Haystack

Kozminski's facetious challenge still ringing in his ears, Kinzler now faced a mountain of tens of thousands of poorly organized documents, most in foreign languages including German, Yiddish, Polish, French, Hebrew, and Russian. So he began the daunting process of reviewing our seized materials, trying to make sense of Kozminski's apparently careless and indiscriminate handling of survivors' claims.

As the review dragged on for weeks, our concern slowly deepened. Despite finally obtaining Kozminski's files and discovering substantial corroboration of "advance fee" payments, we could find no evidence that he actually pilfered any of the victims' restitution monies. In short, there was apparently no smoking gun.

At times we feared the worst, speculating that we might never decipher these documents, a foreboding specter that presented two unpalatable scenarios. On the one hand, the case could shrivel up before our eyes, reduced to a truncated battle on a few hotly contested claims. Or yet another and possibly the last investigation of Kozminski simply might fold and collapse unto itself.

While we struggled, Kozminski remained cocky as ever, complaining to Stefan Mandel that the postal inspectors had "ripped up his office like Nazis" but would "find nothing." Seemingly so certain of recovery on Mandel's pending claim, he boastfully offered, "If you want, I'll buy you out right now."

We nonetheless vowed, as we had before, that we simply would not quit. If necessary, we would methodically piece this puzzle together by carting *all* the documents to West Germany and lugging them to each and every restitution agency. With this force of conviction, Kinzler continued to persevere undaunted by our lack of progress, tirelessly toiling over his quest for a hidden vein of gold.

At times, levity managed to crack our anxious state. Kinzler showed up at my office one day with a few prized seized items. One was a black-and-white photograph of Kozminski taken years before: With a black mustache and a black fringe around his bald head and sporting sunglasses, Kozminski wore a black suit with a large red-white-and-blue pin reading, NIXON NOW. Releasing the tension, Kinzler and I glared at the picture and chuckled, both remarking that it took one crook to know another.

Kinzler also produced a cheaply designed black nameplate prominently reading, LUCIAN KOZMINSKI—COUNSELOR, which he promptly positioned squarely on my desk with a mischievous wink, remarking, "Just where it belongs."

But we both knew this was no laughing matter. Kinzler had struggled vainly for weeks, rummaging through Kozminski's unruly pile. At times he would call me in sheer frustration, lamenting that maybe the Weasel was too smart for us. Maybe he had squirreled incriminating evidence away. Maybe there was a madness to his apparent disorganization. Or maybe, somehow, Kozminski had been tipped off to our search.

A conspicuous doubt, even self-doubt, began to creep into Kinzler's tone. He invariably would mutter disconsolately, "Mark, I'm just not sure I can figure any of this out. And if I can't, then what do we do?"

I realized this represented the whole ball of wax, and there was nothing I could do but offer encouragement. Many of the key documents in Kozminski's files were in German, and while Kinzler spoke and read it fluently, I could not read a word. At this critical stage of the investigation, it would all come down to Lou Kinzler. If it meant anything, I retained full confidence that if the evidence existed, he would find it.

AT LAST, Kinzler's efforts paid off. Hidden amid the massive heap of seized materials, he found two plain-looking manila envelopes, one of which bore the telling handwritten inscription, ERLEDIGT, ABER NOCH NICHT BEZAHLT, meaning *"finished, but not yet paid."*

Kinzler hardly could believe his own eyes. Inside these envelopes he discovered neatly organized records relating to about forty victims. Each file reflected an actual restitution award and subsequent payment to Kozminski, including deposits to his personal bank account, in most instances several years old and some dating back as far as 1975. In reviewing this astonishing find, Kinzler realized that if Kozminski failed to remit these payments to his clients, he had unwittingly provided the blueprint for his own criminal indictment.

Selecting one representative file for a victim named Mordka Wolman, Kinzler noted a restitution agency award of $3,738 on May 31, 1978, and payment transfer to Kozminski shortly afterward. Now, nearly four years later, Kinzler telephoned "Max" Wolman at his local television repair business.

After briefly introducing himself, Kinzler queried, "Now, Mr. Wolman, we've discovered from our files that you were a . . . client of Lucian Kozminski. Is that information correct?

Wolman tersely replied in a monotone, "Yes."

Then, bracing himself, Kinzler fired the $64,000 question, point-blank, "OK. Now, Mr. Wolman, can you tell me whether you ever received a restitution payment of some $3,800 from Lucian Kozminski?"

A long moment of silence ensued before Wolman quietly responded, "No. Not a cent. Why, *should* I have?"

Soon afterward a shaken Wolman arrived at Kinzler's office and was seated at a small table facing the postal inspector. A burly, crew-cut man with brown saucer eyes protruding from his pleasant round face, Wolman began by soberly recounting the basis for the restitution claim that led him to the doorstep of Lucian Kozminski.

WHILE HE was just an infant, Wolman's family emigrated from Lodz, Poland, to France and resided for years near his father's bakery in Paris. These were halcyon yet exciting times for the young Wolman, who loved the sights and sounds of the cosmopolitan, bristling City of Light. But the family's tranquil Parisian existence was shattered when Wolman was barely twelve.

On May 10, 1940, German *panzers* and infantry launched a massive invasion into France, shocking the French army by circumventing the heavily fortified Maginot Line and punching gaping corridors through Luxembourg and the Ardennes forest. French troops immediately fell into a pell-mell retreat, and just one month later, the largest European standing army before the War collapsed in ignominious defeat.

The shame of France's capitulation to Germany was only compounded during the ensuing Nazi occupation. While German forces directly controlled northern France, they ceded command over unoccupied southern France to the collaborationist Vichy government headed by the popular Marshal Pétain. At the Nazis' behest, the Vichy regime enthusiastically imposed restrictions on Jewish immigration; set up several internment and labor camps; excluded Jews from government, the army, professions, and businesses; confiscated Jewish property; and assisted in the arrest of Jews in both the occupied and the unoccupied zones for eventual deportation to the death camps, where nearly 90,000 French Jews perished, including 6,000 youths under the age of thirteen.

Wolman, his mother, his brother, and his two sisters followed the path of fully half of Parisian Jews, fleeing soon after the Nazi invasion. Not wishing to place all her eggs in one basket, Wolman's mother sent one son and daughter to a farm run by Polish immigrants and escaped with Wolman and his remaining sister to another farm run by a sympathetic French Christian in Courtry, about one hour from Paris.

For five years they lived a surreal existence, sleeping in a primitive log cabin tucked in the wilderness, while each day Wolman—under the assumed identity of Marcel Deschamps—trekked to the nearby farm and toiled on the land, planting and picking strawberries, corn, and potatoes. Though uprooted from his home and wracked with anxiety about his siblings and father, Wolman eventually adjusted and actually grew to enjoy life close to the land.

Wolman's father, Moshe, was not so fortunate. Ordered by the Nazis and French *gendarmes* to report to a central processing center, he was promptly arrested and interned at the Beaune-la-Roland camp, located due south of the French capital.

Wolman and his family managed to visit Moshe once, peering at him in the muddy squalor of the camp through a tall wire fence. Moshe had sought to assure Wolman, quietly remarking, "Don't worry, son. Soon this will be over and we will see each other again." That day, however, would never arrive.

Sometime during 1943, Wolman's father was deported to Auschwitz, where he contracted typhus and soon afterward was gassed and cremated at the age of forty. But he was not alone, for most of Wolman's extended family eventually met the same fate.

After the Nazi surrender to the Allies on May 8, 1945, Wolman and the surviving members of his family reunited and returned to Paris. But life would never be the same, as they would never leave their brush with the Nazi-Vichy death trap entirely behind.

Upon his return to Paris, Wolman had the good fortune of becoming reacquainted with Dyna Fyszel, born in Brzezing near Lodz, Poland, and raised in Wolman's neighborhood in Paris. Childhood sweethearts, Dyna and Wolman were separated for five years by the perils of war. While Wolman hid in the French wilderness, Dyna was sheltered by a Christian family outside Paris until forced to flee to Grenoble, where a fake identity card bearing the name Denise Aimard allowed her to pass freely, albeit nervously, as a non-Jew. There she lived on a virtual tightrope, aware that just one slip would cast her into the web of the Nazi death machine.

Although Dyna survived the War, her father and uncle faced an entirely different destiny. Under threat of retaliation against their families for noncompliance, shortly after the Nazi invasion they were ordered to report to the authorities for identity papers. First incarcerated at the French transit camps of Beaune-la-Roland and then Pithiviers, before long they were shipped on the inevitable journey to Auschwitz. Dyna's uncle died ten days after arrival, a naked corpse in a freezing Nazi torture chamber. Her tall, strapping father, Elje, survived the horrors of the Auschwitz, Mauthausen, and Ebensee death camps in name only, returning to Paris after the War a hunched-over shell weighing just seventy pounds.

Shocked at the sight of this virtual ghost, Dyna and her family cared for him and sought to nourish him back to life, but he was already a broken man, physically, emotionally, and spiritually. He died nine years after the War, at the age of forty-four.

At last together after the War, Dyna and Wolman married in 1948 and moved to the United States twenty years later. But like ghosts that return in the still of the night, Wolman's memories of his war-time experience in France remained. Permanently traumatized with lifelong health problems, he would remain most haunted by the murder of his father, visions of which recurred nearly every night during his fitful sleep.

SEEKING RESTITUTION for the death of his father, Wolman first visited Kozminski's office in 1977, paid him $50 cash, and signed a power of attorney authorizing a 15 percent fee. Upon Kozminski's demand, Wolman later paid an additional $295 in three separate cash payments. And then he had heard nothing.

Facing Kinzler, Wolman now stared in disbelief at the deposit slip to Kozminski's bank account, the award from West Germany, and the date on each document. An ashen-faced Wolman muttered, "I can't believe it. He got my money *four years ago?*"

After Kinzler then showed him a power of attorney "authorizing" a *35 percent* fee, Wolman grabbed the document and, glancing at it briefly, intoned, "I swear to you, Mr. Kinzler, he *added* 20 percent after I left his office. His fee was supposed to be just 15 percent. This really is *unbelievable.*"

Pausing while ruminating, Wolman added, "And now that I think about it, did you know that I gave him two more cash payments *after* he had already deposited my money? The crook, he said they were to 'ensure the success' of my claim."

Wolman's fury now grew by the moment. His face turning crimson, he recounted, "When I was living in France many years ago, someone once cheated me out of a lot of money. And you know what

I did? I grabbed the thief and held him by his ankles outside a window until he promised to pay. And you know what? It worked."

Before Kinzler could respond, an incensed Wolman proposed a simpler solution for Kozminski, bellowing, "I'm going to kill that *goniff!* I'm going to take that little snake in my hands and *crush* him!"

Squeezing his fists tightly for emphasis, Wolman glared at Kinzler as the room fell silent. Truly alarmed by this fulsome outburst, Kinzler simply was unsure how to respond. Then, finally choosing his tack, he tried to reason with Wolman, admonishing, "If you kill Kozminski, you'll go to jail for a long time."

But Wolman would hear none of it and continued ranting, tears welling in his eyes. "I don't care. I'm going to *kill* him. That money was for my father's suffering . . ." He stood abruptly as if to leave and accomplish this mission at once.

A frustrated Kinzler paused, looked up at Wolman and, desperately grasped at his final straw, spontaneously remarking, "If you walk out of this office and kill Kozminski, *I'll* never . . . I'll never *speak* to you again."

During the tense moment of silence that followed, the two men stared at each other, eyes locked in a battle of wills. Then, ever so slowly, Wolman visibly calmed and almost sheepishly responded, "Well, I . . . I guess I don't want *that* to happen."

With that sudden change of heart and the threat at last dispelled, Kinzler heaved a huge sigh of relief and smiled reassuringly at the distraught but subdued victim.

When Kinzler called me moments after Wolman had left his office, we immediately realized the potential import of this new development, for if Kozminski also failed to remit payment to the other victims in these select files, his actual, sordid intent would be unmasked: to outlive each of them and retain their money forever.

Survivors Revisited

While targeting claims that were "finished but not yet paid," we vowed to contact every possible victim. We were determined that, at the least, these people would know someone understood their plight and earnestly sought justice for them.

So, beginning with the claims that were "finished but not yet paid," we initiated a round of interviews with Kozminski's newly revealed victims, the living embodiment of the Holocaust nightmare. Most aged beyond their years, survivors daily recounted the Nazis' brutal beatings and murder of their loved ones; the horrors of quantum gassings; the crematoriums for "efficient" disposal of bodies; the filth, disease, and starvation; the enduring mental anguish and trauma; and, in the end, Kozminski's failure to remit restitution for a negligible but symbolic portion of this untold suffering.

Kinzler and I both knew this was no ordinary case. But I still had not expected that these tragic and searing accounts would strike so deeply into my own humanity, accompanying me home every evening, quietly seeping into my stray thoughts, into my unconscious, even into my deepest dreams.

THERE WERE Morris and Pesla Littwin, a small gray-haired couple who recounted in trembling voices how the Nazis herded them into cramped ghettos and later shipped them on freight trains to concentration camps in their native Poland. After they met Kozminski in 1968, he callously extracted some $400 in fees during a ten-year period. On one occasion, after Pesla questioned his demand that they sign documents with blank lines, he angrily retorted, "You don't trust me or something?" and petulantly ordered them to leave. Kozminski, however, never advised them that on February 15, 1978, the Berlin Restitution Office awarded Pesla $970.69 for hardship and loss of jewelry or that he deposited that sum on June 1, 1978, nearly three and half years before our interview.

There was Zesa Starr, a disabled concentration camp survivor, now residing in Denver, Colorado. In his high-pitched plaintive voice, Starr related that he first met Kozminski in 1969 and paid him nearly $600 in cash during the ensuing twelve years. But Kozminski never advised him that on June 16, 1975, the Berlin Restitution Office awarded Starr 2,400 Deutsche marks (about $931) and 2,000 Deutsche marks (about $775) on two separate claims, or that he soon deposited and retained those sums.

There was Fela Fuchs, a frail silver-haired woman in her late sixties, who suffered greatly while incarcerated in Langenbielau, a subcamp of Gross-Rosen, and other Nazi concentration camps. She and her late husband, Moritz, first contacted Kozminski in 1969 and paid him $50 to handle her claim. When Fuchs visited Kozminski's office in 1980 and again the next year, he promised he would prepare a letter "explaining" the status of her decade-old claim and each time demanded $65 more for "stamp costs." But Kozminski never sent the promised letters or advised them that several years earlier, on May 26, 1978, Fuchs was awarded 2,130 Deutsche marks ($1,029), which were directly deposited into Kozminski's bank account.

There was Edith Teitman, a stately black-haired woman in her midforties who met with Kinzler and me in the living room of her comfortable home. Her brown eyes slowly turning inward, she described her desolate experience as a frightened young girl, hiding for years in a convent while the Nazis systematically liquidated her family and friends.

Thirty years later she met Kozminski, who filed claims for Teitman's loss of freedom, loss of education, and continuing damage to health, all the while extracting $800 from her over a two-year period. Some two years later, in September 1977, Kozminski called Teitman to his office, advised her that her case was settled, and, after demanding an additional $100, insisted she sign papers proving she was still alive. When Teitman attempted to review the documents he had presented for her signature, Kozminski snapped, "Don't you *trust* me?"

Rudely rebuffing her husband Abraham's attempt to intercede, he then angrily remarked, "You *never* saw so much money as you will see" and promptly told them both to "shut up or you'll get *nothing*."

On March 17, 1979, Kozminski finally sent Teitman a check for $10,379.70, which, after bouncing twice, at last cleared. Yet he never advised her that she had actually been awarded $32,690 on July 1, 1977, nearly two years before.

There was Hela Suchecki, an elderly heavily accented woman whom we interviewed over the phone from Jerusalem, Israel. She duly reported that in October 1971, she met with Kozminski at his office and signed a power of attorney, enlisting him to file several claims relating to her husband, Schapsa, who died in 1966. These included loss of consortium associated with Schapsa's nervous and medical disorders and ensuing death, all of which were caused by his internment at Auschwitz and other Nazi concentration camps where he was shot in both the heart and the forehead.

But during the entire period from 1974 to 1982, Kozminski never advised Suchecki that on September 19, 1974, the Munich Restitution Office had awarded her 30,584.19 Deutsche marks (about $12,754) or that after authorizing his West German attorney-contact to deduct 25 percent of the payment for fees and an unrelated debt to the Pantl-brau brewery, he received and kept $9,363.63. Kozminski rather represented that Suchecki's claim remained unresolved and regularly extracted more fees for his "continuing" representation.

On and on. Victim after victim. The stories were entirely different, but the twisted ending always remained the same. Every one of the forty or so "finished but not yet paid" files revealed the same conclusion: Kozminski's outright theft of the victim's restitution payment. And now that we had cracked Kozminski's files, we suspected this might just be the tip of the iceberg.

While some losses were for hundreds of dollars and others were tens of thousands of dollars, we tried to approach each file with equal gravity. After all, we had already seen that some victims lived relatively comfortably, while others had to borrow change to take the bus to the U.S. Attorney's Office. Particularly in this most unusual investigation, we decided it was not for us to determine whether a victim could "afford" his or losses: We would simply treat theft as theft.

Especially in comparison to our early months of early struggle, it now seemed that time and events were moving faster and faster. My emotions swirled like a maelstrom, engendered by near daily contact with Kozminski's newly found victims. Forging new and deeper bonds with several of them, I was rapidly losing my distance from the case and my capacity to view Kozminski as anything other than a demonized traitor to his—and my—people. Incriminating evidence, meanwhile, was mounting, and our investigation rapidly expanding.

And yet, hidden beneath it all, the gnawing questions still persisted. I continued to ponder: Just who is Lucian Kozminski? What motivates him? And why does he treat Holocaust survivors this way?

I often ruminated over these critical questions, sometimes for hours in utter silence. But at this moment, I again deferred them, hoping that our growing pool of evidence would provide some clues, if not some concrete answers.

Kinzler, meanwhile, was experiencing his own reaction to our barrage of newly found witnesses, observing that when he interviewed them, "they shook like leaves." Several victims had candidly attributed their reaction to Kinzler's being an authority figure, not his German background. But for Kinzler, there was no escaping his heritage. He repeatedly brooded over the fact that his "forefathers did their damnedest to wipe these people out and came very close to doing it." Again and again he was plagued by the same disturbing thoughts: What if the War had turned out differently? What would his role in this have been? Perhaps to ease his pain and guilt, amid it all, Kinzler took to reading Heinrich Heine, the famous German-Jewish poet, and citing his favorite passages.

In these and other ways, rapidly unfolding events in this investigation were causing both of us to dig deeper inside ourselves, exploring our personal connections to the Holocaust as well as formulating new approaches to our query. In the midst of all this, we turned to a most memorable and inspiring witness interview, with a man who had had the courage to take on Lucian Kozminski alone.

Heart of a Lion

A proud-looking man in his early sixties with white hair and blazing blue eyes, Jacob Weingarten was a person on a mission. Submitting one of the earliest complaints in this investigation to Postal Inspector Parry and later commencing one of the few civil suits against Kozminski, he had remained in dogged pursuit of justice. When we met with him in my cramped office, Weingarten sitting next to Kinzler while facing me, the reasons soon became evident.

Weingarten was raised in the eastern part of Czechoslovakia, near the borders of Hungary and Romania. Established as a nation after World War I, Czechoslovakia was unusually tolerant of its Jews, even permitting the ultra-Orthodox to serve in the Czech army without having to shear their telltale locks. But all that soon changed.

In September 1938, fresh from his bloodless *Anschluss* with Austria featuring the obsequious "capitulation" of Germany's like-minded neighbor to Nazi forces, Hitler turned his eyes upon the vast Czech munitions industry located in the predominantly German-speaking Sudetenland. After the Nazi Führer slyly coupled blustery threats with conciliatory gestures, that vital region was unilaterally ceded to Germany by British Prime Minister Neville Chamberlain and the European Allies in exchange for "peace in our time."

Rather than gaining lasting peace, however, the Allies bought a mere six months while unwittingly fueling the Nazi war machine. In March 1939, Hitler brazenly breached the Munich Pact by invading the Czech provinces of Bohemia and Moravia and erecting a puppet Fascist state in Slovakia. Soon afterward, during August 1939, Weingarten watched in fear as hordes of German troops and planes traversed the country and massed at the eastern border. Then, on September 1, the Nazis launched their pulverizing *blitzkrieg* of Poland.

Great Britain and France now compounded their appeasement of Hitler by failing to come to Poland's defense despite formal declarations of war. Likewise, in spite of the Nazi juggernaut's conquest of Poland, Denmark (April 1940), Norway (April 1940), Belgium (May 1940), the Netherlands (May 1940), Luxembourg (May 1940), France (May 1940), Yugoslavia (April 1941), and Greece (April 1941), the United States remained unmoved and officially neutral until virtually dragged into the War by Japan's bombing of Pearl Harbor on December 7, 1941.

Meanwhile, Hitler rewarded Hungary for joining the Axis Powers by giving it the eastern part of Czechoslovakia and portions of Romania and Yugoslavia. Now designated a Hungarian "citizen," along with several hundred thousand other displaced Jews, on October 18, 1940, Weingarten was drafted into the Hungarian army to fight alongside none other than German troops.

But his tour of duty with the Axis Powers ended abruptly three months later. After German foreign minister Joachim von Ribbentrop ordered the Hungarians to purge Jews from business, professions, and the government, the six Jews in Weingarten's unit were directly removed and dispatched to a Hungarian forced labor camp. Virtually overnight, Weingarten was forced to exchange his uniform of the Hungarian army for the rags of a Hungarian prisoner.

At the camp, Weingarten toiled under the watchful eye of armed Hungarian guards thirteen hours a day, building roads, rail lines, and airports for military use. Every day, prisoners were fed one pound of bread and watery, bloody soup "not fit for a dog's consumption." They were awakened each day at dawn and returned to their exhausting duties. After several months of this oppressive duty, Weingarten and his fellow inmates were tasked with carrying large boxes of ammunition to the front. Each box of bullets weighed more than 160 pounds, and after six torturous weeks, the men were exhausted.

The nearly emaciated prisoners then were transferred to German jurisdiction, under the command of a general of the German air force (*Luftwaffe*). This particular officer, not a member of the SS, was appalled at the prisoners' condition and soon ensured that they were fed the same food he and his pilots consumed. Existing under these improved conditions, Weingarten and his fellow inmates worked on construction of the general's new airport until the end of 1941.

But then, much to his dismay, Weingarten was transferred back to Hungarian jurisdiction, back to the daily meals of bloody soup and harsh treatment from cruel, virulently anti-Semitic Hungarian guards. Shipped some two hundred miles from Budapest, he spent the next one and a half years building more military airports. During the ensuing year, he helped erect another airport near the Austro-Hungarian border and, in 1943, was transferred closer to Romania, where he labored on the construction of several rail lines. Sent out once again months later, Weingarten was tasked with building pontoons for the Hungarian marines.

But the end still was nowhere in sight. Despite Weingarten's nearly four years of grueling forced labor on a near starvation diet, the larger swirl of events soon catapulted him into an even more gruesome appointment with destiny.

By the spring of 1944, the German war effort was doomed. On March 19, after the Miklos Horthy–led Hungarian government sought to negotiate a separate armistice with the Allies, the Nazis invaded Hungary and installed a puppet regime headed by Dome Sztojay. At the Nazis' behest, during the next several months 440,000 Jews under Hungarian jurisdiction were transported to the death camps for accelerated "disposal." As Hungarian Jewry teetered on the brink of extinction, the mass deportations were suddenly halted in July, when Horthy engineered a return to power and soon afterward entered into an armistice with the Soviet Union.

But Eichmann would not be deterred from his master plan. The Nazis summarily arrested Horthy and shipped him to Germany, instated a Fascist Arrow Cross regime under Ferenc Szalasi, and proceeded to culminate their Final Solution of the Hungarian Jews. During the next few months, half of Budapest's 200,000 Jews were butchered by Arrow Cross Fascists or rounded up and shipped to Auschwitz-Birkenau for extermination. Only the heroic efforts of Raoul Wallenberg, Swiss diplomat Carl Lutz, and other "neutral" officials averted the total annihilation of remaining Jews in Hungary.

Though the Hungarian government finally entered into a permanent armistice with the Soviet Union in January 1945, the Germans still retained large portions of Hungarian territory. Two months later, a black-uniformed Gestapo general arrived at Weingarten's labor camp and advised the officials there that the Jews now "belonged" to the Germans and would be "protected" by them. But the veil of this cruel propaganda hoax was soon lifted as Weingarten and his fellow Jews were swiftly deported in sealed cattle cars to the notorious concentration camp at Mauthausen, Austria, away from the advance of the oncoming Soviet army.

When Weingarten arrived at Mauthausen in April, the War was almost over, but the prisoners hardly knew it. The camp seemed like a hellish Hieronymous Bosch painting, replete with barbed-wire fences, vicious trigger-happy SS guards, and emaciated hordes of Jews barely clinging to life, many with flesh barely draping a protruding skeletal frame.

Weingarten had a short, bittersweet reunion with one of his brothers, who was gravely ill with typhus and unable even to walk. Just days after this tearful meeting, a horrified Weingarten watched helplessly as a Nazi soldier raised a Lugar pistol to his brother's head and fired. Blood squirted from his brother's head as he fell dead in a heap.

This cold-blooded murder was not unusual. In addition to Nazi doctors' barbaric use of inmates for pseudoscientific experiments involving phenol injections, lice infestation, and tuberculosis, during the Mauthausen camp's existence the Nazis gassed or worked to death more than 70,000 prisoners.

In early May, after somehow emerging from this death mill alive, Weingarten and others were forced out of the camp on a westward death march to elude the ever advancing Russians. As most of the emaciated prisoners trudged on for mile after mile, those who straggled behind, or simply collapsed into a heap, were summarily shot on the spot. This bedraggled procession into hell finally ended when their Nazi captors abruptly scampered away into the distance.

Relieved but still disoriented with exhaustion, starvation, and trauma, the prisoners randomly wandered about the forest for several hours. Then after a brief rumbling sound in the distance, troops from the American army arrived. Though Weingarten and his fellow survivors were drained of virtually all emotion, their liberators were not. Many wore horrified, shocked expressions at the sight of the emaciated survivors, some retched spontaneously, and others simply cursed the Nazis for their inhumane deeds.

Three months later, Weingarten discovered that his other brother, Sam, had been incarcerated at Mauthausen during the same period and eventually liberated by the U.S. 11th Armored Division on May 7, 1945. While Sam ultimately would recuperate from a severe bout with typhus, he would never recover from the murder of his wife, Fanny, and their four children at Auschwitz. A forlorn and broken man, he would ask in bewilderment whether anyone had seen them for decades after the War.

Weingarten also learned that his sister, Sarah, had survived the Holocaust by a matter of days. While incarcerated at Auschwitz, she had been stationed for months directly across from the crematoriums, undertaking the ghastly task of removing jewelry and other valuables from the clothing of prisoners who had been gassed and were scheduled for cremation. Just before her ninety-day assignment there was

slated to end with her own visit to the gas chambers, Sarah was transferred to Bergen-Belsen, from which she was later liberated.

After the War, Weingarten was hospitalized for months at the
Mayo Clinic in Rochester, Minnesota, where doctors finally diag-
nosed a severe infection in the nerve lining of his stomach that ren-
dered him incapable of digesting solid foods. This incapacitating
condition was merely one symptom of the ravages of war from which
he would suffer for decades.

SITTING FACING ME in my small office, Weingarten briefly glanced
at Kinzler next to him and paused, emitting an almost involuntary
plaintive sigh. Kinzler and I were speechless. My stomach was raw
and contorted in knots, and yet I knew I could not even begin to feel
the searing losses he had suffered.

Sensing it was time to switch topics, his blue eyes watery but still
shining, Weingarten remarked with a lilt, "And now I'll tell you
about that crook Kozminski."

Weingarten then revealed further details about his swindled restitution payment of $3,747.62. He remarked, "That crook, did you
know he also botched my claim? It's the truth. You see, after I
became suspicious, I went to the court in Stuttgart, you know, in Germany. And you know what they said? They said his papers were
defective. And it was *too late* to correct them."

His eyes filling with tears of frustration, Weingarten continued,
"But the court said it took pity on me and still awarded me 10,000
Deutsche marks. And can you believe it? *That's* the money he later
stole from me. But that *still* isn't everything."

Inhaling briefly as if to steel himself, he went on: "Well, it turns
out my sister took a trip to Stuttgart in 1977. So she calls Kozminski's
local attorney there . . . I think his name was Ludolf Lerman. Anyway, Lerman says that my restitution payment should have come
through his office. He was supposed to deduct his fees and send the
rest to Kozminski. But Lerman says he never got anything."

Kinzler and I looked at Weingarten quizzically as he concluded:
"Well, the next day Lerman calls my sister back. He says Kozminski
had secretly requested two years earlier that my payment go right to
his bank account. And sure enough, that's what happened. So then

Lerman gets really mad on the phone and screams, '*Ein Schwindler!*'"

After later futilely confronting Kozminski, Weingarten had not relented. He had retained a lawyer to file a civil suit against Kozminski. His lawyer had taken Kozminski's deposition and aggressively pursued discovery.

As Weingarten explained to Kinzler and me, defiant tears in his eyes, "After all I and my family went through, Kozminski stole my payment. And, of all things, for the medical disability that I suffered from the Nazis. No one should get away with that. Ever."

As THE DETERMINED, indomitable Weingarten again told his story, I was reminded of the chasm between these survivors and other humans who lead relatively normal lives. Sitting before me was an ordinary-looking man, his blue eyes often shimmering with optimism, dignity, and life. He had survived unspeakable suffering and trauma but was neither dour nor bitter.

It was almost unfathomable. I doubted whether I possessed the same capacity and wondered if any explanation existed. Was it the person, the experience, or both? Could this demonstrate the true capacity of the human spirit trapped within all of us?

The Dark Inner Sanctum

Among the most important records postal inspectors seized were checks payable to a non-Jew of German descent: Marguerite Schneider, Kozminski's former secretary, who provided our only glimpse from within the bowels of his operation. It was not a comforting sight.

A black-haired, plain-looking woman in her midfifties, Schneider met with Kinzler and me for a lengthy session in my office. Occasionally donning reading glasses with a long metal chain, she recited her story in English with a strong German accent, punctuated with seemingly inappropriate nervous chuckles.

Schneider began, "Well, I worked for Kozminski on and off for about five years. Mainly as a part-time secretary to type letters, you

know, to West Germany and to clients. But it was never easy. He—
He disgusted me so much that I quit twice. Each time he begged me
to come back."

Wincing in remembrance, Schneider continued, "I mean, he spat
at his clients, swore at them, yelled at them, hung the phone up on
them. He would shove them and kick them out of his office. Once,
he got so angry he threw an old man with crutches to the floor." She
nodded her head with a furrowed expression of pity.

And then she went on, "But of course that wasn't all. He got these
poor people to sign *blank* powers of attorney that gave him a 15 percent fee. Then, after they left the office, he ordered me to insert *additional* percentages, you know, like another 25 percent or 30 percent."

"Of course, if any restitution came, he usually didn't tell the victims. No, instead he'd ask them for more money. And you should see
him when that money came from Germany. I mean, his hands would
tremble. They would shake uncontrollably."

Repulsed by Kozminski's conduct, Schneider often objected that
he was "taking money from [his] own people," but he dismissed her
protests out-of-hand, usually retorting, "It's not your business. They
[the victims] are *senile* and *stupid*."

On another occasion he snapped, "Hah, *mompitz*. They are *crazy*."
Still other times when she objected, Kozminski simply told her to
"shut up and follow orders." Finally, after Schneider warned a client
not to sign a blank power of attorney, an enraged Kozminski actually
threatened, "Shut up or you're going to get hurt."

Yet Schneider persisted, frequently warning Kozminski, "One day
they will catch you." Kozminski would invariably grin in response,
point to his head, and flippantly proclaim, "They will *never* catch me.
I'm too smart."

Shortly before she quit, Schneider finally accused Kozminski of
acting "worse than the SS." Unfazed, he quickly retorted, "Ah, you
know, the SS were *not* so stupid. Did you know I slept with the camp
commandant's wife?"

Kozminski further boasted that after the War, he became president of a Jewish group in Germany (the self-proclaimed "King of
Jewelry") and later arrived in the United States with one suitcase full
of money and another full of liquor.

Though fees from Kozminski's thousands of victims worldwide generated abundant cash flow for years, Schneider could not figure out where he stashed his funds. She advised us, however, that he purchased a restaurant for at least $25,000, bought two cars, and regularly sent substantial sums of money to his sons.

Toward the end, Ms. Schneider grinned and wagged her finger at us, remarking, "You better be very careful. This Kozminski may have a problem with alcohol, but he's very intelligent and clever. And don't think for a moment he's crazy. You're going to have quite a fight."

As she concluded her vivid account, Schneider visibly relaxed. Appearing relieved to have finally divulged this unseemly story, she chuckled one last time and then studied Kinzler and me silently.

I BRIEFLY RUMINATED about Schneider's fairly colorful description of Kozminski. It was one thing, after all, for Kozminski to methodically cheat his clients. But now he also appeared quite odd, absurdly boastful, unusually abusive toward his fellow Holocaust survivors, and strangely benign toward the SS. I flashed on an image of a Picasso-like portrait of a twisted, broken soul with disjointed, jagged edges. For a moment I wondered if Kozminski were not just an alcoholic but also psychotic, or nearly so. And I speculated whether these very misgivings about his mental state could form the basis of Kozminski's prospective defense against criminal charges.

Now I redirected my attention to Ms. Schneider, who continued to gaze silently at me. For a moment I wondered: Had she lived in Germany during the War? Had she been a Nazi sympathizer? Did she suffer herself? Or did she witness suffering, perhaps that of Jewish neighbors or acquaintances? And how did she feel working for a man who, by her own account, cheated victims of the Nazi regime?

Owing in part to Schneider's sensitivities, I knew that some of these questions would be deferred to the eve of any trial and others would simply never be broached. For now, however, as I studied Schneider carefully, she seemed to strike me as an unaffected, fairly simple woman who had been relatively straightforward in her account.

I was all too aware that Schneider's statements could have been self-serving and prompted by fear of her own culpability in Kozminski's sordid operation. The facts, however, suggested otherwise. Aside from her notable failure to request immunity from prosecution, Schneider's account of Kozminski's brazen conduct was corroborated by several victims. Hence, her statements appeared entirely credible and consistent with her repeated admonition to Kozminski, "I will never lie for you."

Her motives aside, Schneider's prospective testimony was undoubtedly critical. By providing indispensable evidence of Kozminski's intent and willfulness, she could undermine any contention that he had misplaced or lost control of his files, or that he "would never do this to his own people." In short, as long as Schneider did not recant her statements or collapse on the stand, she would remain our unmistakable ace in the hole.

WHILE THE FRUITS of our search of Kozminski's offices were paying off handsomely, fulfilling our brightest hopes, our work was far from complete.

Before we could consider proceeding to a grand jury for indictment, we had to confirm that our evidence of restitution awards and payments was authentic and admissible in court. We also had to ensure that officials from several restitution offices would come to the United States to testify at trial and that Kozminski's West German attorney-contacts would not attempt to whitewash his conduct or otherwise shield him from liability.

Because the United States government could not subpoena foreign documents or compel foreign nationals to testify, Kinzler and I departed on a sensitive and critical mission to the very source: Germany.

Return of the Native

For two weeks in April 1982, Lou Kinzler and I embarked on a whirlwind trip through West Germany. We conducted no fewer than fifteen interviews in nine cities and visited an additional eight locations before we were done.

No stranger to West Germany, I had traveled there extensively after my college graduation eight years before and visited a girlfriend in a town near Nuremberg, the birthplace of laws ostracizing Jews from German society. I remember the unsettling feeling I had while vacationing in this beautiful wooded country that had spawned the genocide of my people and the destruction of an entire continent. I remember secretly wondering whether each man I encountered over the age of fifty had served in the German army or SS during World War II. I remember the eerie sensation I felt riding on German trains when the compartment door suddenly slid open and a stern-faced uniformed officer asked, in guttural German, to check our passports. Finally, I remember my small, hidden feeling of relief when we eventually crossed the border and departed the country.

On the surface, this trip appeared to be quite different. Bearing a brown-jacketed diplomatic passport, I traveled through West Germany as a federal prosecutor officially representing the United States of America. Yet even in formal meetings, my mind often wandered to the prevailing irony of our purpose.

There I sat, a Jewish American whose grandparents the Nazis certainly would have liquidated, interviewing cordial Germans (primarily males over fifty) about a Jewish refugee from concentration camps and postwar Germany who appeared to be defrauding victims of the Nazi Holocaust! Thrust into the fulcrum of this unlikely intersection of lives, I bore reluctant witness to the silent, hidden portals of fickle and unyielding fate.

Yet, while profound for me, the experience for Lou Kinzler was altogether transforming. As he now recounts in an understated manner, "It has left a lasting impression on me."

Here was a man, born during World War II and raised in Germany, a U.S. army veteran married to a black American woman, who had returned to Germany to investigate none other than a Jewish Holocaust survivor. Kinzler stood in a solitary and surreal twilight zone, freely conversing with Germans who carried his blood in their veins and the bloodstain of millions on their hands and who were neither his compatriots nor his true kin. Struggling to reconcile this complex reality, as the trip progressed, he became ever more indignant at imperfect justice as well as the caprice of destiny itself.

It was not surprising, then, that as Kinzler and I traveled on this journey together, almost imperceptibly we drew closer on several levels. We both realized that no matter what the future held, we would always retain this special bond and enduring memory.

Red Tape and Black Boots

Despite our status as U.S. government employees, Kinzler and I enjoyed no formal diplomatic standing. We could neither compel prospective foreign witnesses to meet with us nor conduct an official investigation on foreign soil. Mindful of these constraints, the State Department and West German government established ground rules for our West German trip, which were communicated to us shortly before our departure.

These rules contained a set procedure for all our interviews. Specifically, Kinzler and I would not pose any questions directly to prospective witnesses, and the witnesses would not answer us directly. Rather, a member of the West German police (*Polizei*) would attend each interview and serve as a conduit. We would advise the *Polizei* of our question, and he would duly turn to the witness and repeat it. After the witness answered the inquiry, the *Polizei* would reiterate it to us.

This precise procedure, the State Department soberly advised us, would avoid our direct "contamination" of foreign nationals while maintaining West Germany's inviolate sovereignty. The process also promised to be extremely cumbersome and ineffective. More than doubling the length of our interviews, it increased the risk that questions and answers, twice filtered in German, would be lost in translation, as well as provide recalcitrant witnesses greater opportunity to form ambiguous or evasive responses. This represented, in short, the typical establishment response we encountered during our investigation, with bureaucratic niceties purposefully exalted over people laboring in the trenches.

Kinzler and I were thoroughly miffed. Deeply concerned that our interviews would prove unproductive and degenerate into confusion, we resolved to evade this diplomatic minefield whenever possible.

Taking the initiative and posing questions directly to witnesses, we would grope for a stopgap solution if and when the *Polizei* objected and interceded.

We were fortunate in the end. The *Polizei did* attend most interviews, and when we began interrogating witnesses directly some *did* question whether we were using proper procedures. But we always reacted nonchalantly, frequently with humor, as Kinzler typically smiled and responded, "Come on, now. You don't *really* want to repeat every question and answer while we sit here, do you?" The *Polizei*, slightly embarrassed, would invariably grin and reply, "Of course not. Go ahead with your questions."

There was one notable exception. When we came to Munich, Kinzler and I were immediately notified that our interview with Dr. Karl Pokorny, one of Kozminski's attorney-contacts, would take place within the confines of the Munich police station.

Later arriving for that appointed session, we were formally greeted by Rudy Pecher of the *Polizei,* a middle-aged man with black hair and a stern reddish face. Wearing a gray uniform and shiny, tall black boots with a holster strapped to his side, Pecher was an imposing presence eerily reminiscent of Germany's recent past. Now gruffly muttering that we should follow him, he abruptly turned and marched away.

Moments later we entered a drab interview room where Pecher introduced us to Pokorny, a white-haired man with a regal, pompous demeanor. We knew from our files that Pokorny was Kozminski's attorney-contact on the claim for a Magda Winkler, who was reportedly awarded a substantial restitution payment that Kozminski secretly deposited and retained.

When Kinzler began questioning Pokorny about the Winkler file, Pecher abruptly cut him off, reprimanded him for following improper procedures, and insisted that we filter all questions and answers through him. This time our humor did not work. Refusing to relent, Pecher instead boldly launched into the contorted procedure set by our respective bureaucracies.

After seven or eight laborious questions and answers, however, he realized the process was utterly futile. Turning to Kinzler and me, Pecher tersely instructed *us* to proceed with questions, advising us that he would remain to ensure the interview was conducted "properly."

But our small victory was fleeting, as inquiries soon revealed that, emboldened by Pecher's apparent disdain toward us, Pokorny was extremely uncooperative. Although all witnesses had been expressly advised that our trip was confidential, he admitted that he had *told* *Kozminski* about our scheduled interview. In a condescending tone, Pokorny remarked, "I must tell you, all the information in the victim's file is confidential, so I cannot produce any documents for your examination. *No one* will gain access to any of *my* files."

After this unproductive session continued for several minutes, Pecher had finally heard enough. His eyes bulging and his face beet red, he stood up, stepped briskly to the desk where Pokorny sat, and abruptly slammed his palm down, sending papers flying into the air.

Glaring at Pokorny, Pecher heatedly barked, "You *will* cooperate. If you don't, I will go over to your office right now, seize *all* of your files and shut you down. Do you understand?"

Pokorny, his pompous visage now shattered, meekly nodded his assent.

From that moment on, the tone of the interview changed dramatically. Much more forthcoming about the victim and her file, Pokorny even agreed to testify at the trial. By then, however, he was a lost cause. Because we knew Pokorny could not be trusted on the stand, Magda Winkler simply would not be named as a victim in our indictment.

AFTER OUR INTERVIEW concluded, Pecher escorted us into his office and sat behind his desk, facing us. Now his hard, cold exterior was thawing. He laughed about his treatment of Pokorny and, with genuine interest, asked several questions about our investigation. Finally, his guard completely down, Pecher savagely ridiculed the interview procedures adopted by our two governments.

Pausing with the wink of an eye, Pecher suddenly reached into a drawer and pulled out a bottle of hard liquor. Taking a long midmorning swig, he nonchalantly offered the bottle to us. Kinzler and I, at first startled, politely obliged. As we drank facing our gracious, smiling host, we realized that even with the *Polizei*'s Rudy Pecher, things are not always what they seem.

Water From a Rock

After landing in Frankfurt, Kinzler and I had stayed one night in Hofheim, a timeless, charming town on the Rhine River, and then moved on to the comfortable city of Wiesbaden, which lies on the north side of the Rhine directly opposite from Mainz. There we began our slate of interviews with Hans Rock, one of Kozminski's longtime attorney-contacts in West Germany.

Kozminski enlisted his attorney-contacts by necessity, not by choice. Some West German restitution agencies and courts simply did not permit him, as a nonlawyer and foreigner, to correspond with them directly. Others permitted him to file claims but prohibited him from receiving his clients' restitution payments. These restrictions compelled Kozminski to enter into formal arrangements with lawyers in several West German locales, some of whom actually processed Kozminski's claims with restitution agencies and courts and others of whom merely received restitution monies and forwarded them directly to him.

Most of these lawyers were genuinely unaware of Kozminski's fraudulent scheme. They were not present when he extracted cash payments from victims and were generally oblivious to the ultimate disposition of restitution payments forwarded to Kozminski. Nonetheless, a few were contacted directly by victims about missing restitution payments, while others experienced Kozminski's duplicity in their own dealings with him. Most attorney-contacts, as a result, strongly suspected Kozminski was unsavory and clearly were embarrassed by their association with him.

We knew our lack of subpoena power would be most pronounced with these prospective witnesses, who, unlike restitution agency officials, were not West German government employees and could not be compelled to cooperate. Forced to employ a carrot-and-stick approach, we hoped the German government and *Polizei* would pressure these lawyers while we earnestly cajoled and sweet-talked them.

Suppressing doubts about the integrity and even the culpability of some, we remained focused on the prevailing objective, fully aware that our business and jurisdiction were strictly limited to Lucian Kozminski.

OUR DOCUMENTS revealed that, at least in some cases, Hans Rock had deducted excessive attorney's fees from victims' restitution payments, signaling greater complicity in Kozminski's scheme than that of any other German attorney. We therefore knew we would have to approach this particular witness gingerly and in a nonaccusatory manner.

When we entered the anteroom of Rock's offices, we immediately noticed that the *Polizei* were conspicuously absent, only later learning that his unseemly reputation had prompted them to bypass his interview entirely.

After a few minutes of waiting silently, we were suddenly ushered into a dusty wood-paneled office stocked with law books and files, with assorted papers casually and haphazardly strewn about. Silhouetted against a panel of shuttered windows, Hans Rock sat facing us from behind his desk, slowly puffing on a long black cigarette holder as curls of smoke wafted through the air. A fidgety, eccentric-looking man in his late fifties or early sixties, Rock was bald with unkempt white hair circling the back of his head. His uniquely expressive face was partially illuminated by the late afternoon sun streaming through the closed but porous shutters. Facing this peculiar man as we sat enshrouded in the musty, yellow-orange hue of our shadowy setting, I could not dispel the recurring notion that somehow we were strangely removed from both our case and our home.

Struggling to maintain my focus, I posed a litany of questions, and as Kinzler translated and supplemented my inquiries, Rock responded almost exclusively in German. As our interview continued, Rock dramatically recounted his relationship with Kozminski, growing more expressive and enraged until he eventually ranted and raved with his brown eyes bulging maniacally.

At the onset, Rock remarked, "First, you gentlemen should get one thing straight. I was never a . . . an attorney on Kozminski's cases. I just . . . processed documents with restitution agencies." Pausing, he glanced at us as if to gauge our reaction.

Then he went on, "And the claims he sent? Absolute garbage. Ninety-nine percent were unworthy, and to make it worse, he offered me chicken feed—25 Deutsche marks [about $10] for each case. I told him these fees could not even cover my expenses, but then he simply didn't pay me anything."

After some insistent questioning, Rock conceded that part of that debt was finally relieved when, at Kozminski's specific direction, he deducted $6,000 from Edith Teitman's restitution payment despite never having worked on her case.

As we turned to Rock's prospective appearance as a witness, he completely balked. Loudly proclaiming that he wanted nothing more to do with Kozminski, he remarked, "I am appalled that you would propose wasting my time at this trial."

Back and forth we went, consuming well over an hour. When Kinzler passionately appealed to his sense of morality, Rock glared at him with bulging eyes and retorted, "Morality? Hah, *what* morality? I *lost* my morality as a young man on the Russian front."

Finally, I decided to appeal to Rock's self-interest, remarking, "Now, Mr. Rock, Inspector Kinzler and I would *never* try to accuse *you* of any . . . wrongdoing. But if you don't testify, then, God knows, Kozminski may try to blame *you* for his crimes. And his . . . accusations would remain unrefuted on the . . . official trial record."

This apparently struck a responsive chord. For the first time during the entire interview, Rock grew silent, staring at us with a confounded expression, his eyes glazed over and lost in thought. Finally he relented, ever so slowly replying, "OK, OK. I'll bring those files—what are they, Teitman, Seidman, and Wittner? And I'll testify if you insist."

Thus, after an excruciating and prolonged session, we had at last secured Rock's grudging cooperation. Now having completed his harangue, a spent Rock flashed his odd smile and cordially invited us to dinner. But I, for one, had grown somewhat weary of Rock's company and politely declined, and Kinzler and I soon departed the office.

Warter From Bonn

The next day we headed to the capital city of Bonn and there met amid a plaza of stately government buildings with Hans Warter, a foreign ministry consular officer designated our expert witness on the procedures and policies of the West German restitution program.

Warter was a distinct contrast to Hans Rock. A short bespectacled man with a white oval face and impeccably dressed in a dark suit, he presented a distinguished, almost Churchillian bearing. Thoughtful and reflective, almost tranquil, he spoke with an understated eloquence in nearly flawless British-accented English. Kinzler and I fell silent as he presented a near soliloquy of his experiences.

At the onset of our meeting, Warter recounted, "You know, as a young man I served in the German army. And shortly after the . . . war, I came to learn about the horrors of the Holocaust. A terrible thing. So I was inspired by this—I guess you can call it weighty knowledge—and decided to work for the new West German restitution program. Now I've been here for twenty-five years."

Warter explained that whereas the program was coordinated by the central government, each autonomous West German state maintained an office where Holocaust survivors could apply for restitution arising from four general categories of losses. One category was "loss of liberty," which included incarceration in concentration camps and forced labor camps, as well as forced emigration. The second category was death or injury, which provided restitution for injured survivors and relatives of the millions of Jews murdered in the Holocaust. The third category was damage to health, which allowed recovery for long-term illness or other medical conditions associated with the Third Reich's reign of terror. The fourth category was "loss of economic basis." During the Holocaust, the Nazis stripped Jews of their professions, deprived them of education, and confiscated countless billions of dollars in Jewish businesses and industry, as well as money, state pensions, jewelry, art, and other personal valuables, leading Himmler to boast, "The wealth [the Jews] had we have taken from them." These manifold deprivations were addressed by the fourth restitution category.

Warter reported that depending on the claim, victims could be eligible for a lump-sum payment, a pension, or both. Two substantial hurdles, however, had to be cleared before benefits were awarded.

He explained, "Well, you see, first survivors must submit independent documentation of loss. Now, many victims understandably possess limited records, so this often leads to denial of their claims. At least those that the Nazis' own meticulous records cannot save. Now, we also apply an income ceiling on applicants. This ensures that only the most needy received available benefits."

Even aside from the impediments cited by Warter, we also were aware that victims faced a jumble of frequently revised rules and regulations, as well as a cadre of German bureaucrats who often assumed victims were trying to cheat them and occasionally were "small-minded, arbitrary, insensitive, and malevolent."

Yet despite the categorical rejection of virtually tens of thousands of claims, Warter noted that to date the West German government had paid more than $25 billion in restitution to Holocaust victims.

As our interview progressed, it soon became evident that Warter assumed his responsibility with keen interest and the utmost gravity. He soberly related intricate details about the particular Allied army that liberated each concentration camp; Jewish patterns of migration throughout the world; the historical differences between Ashkenazi Jews, Sephardi Jews, and other Jewish subgroups; and the continuing, unremitting plight of most Holocaust survivors. In the end, we knew that rather than a mere occupation, Warter's position was no less than his life's work.

Still, I had mixed feelings. This man, after all, was a middle-aged German. He had served in the German army during World War II. He may have killed American soldiers, civilians and perhaps even Jews. And though he had since become an expert on the West German restitution program for Holocaust survivors, he almost seemed *too* clinical, *too* composed, *too* bureaucratic. Deep inside, part of me wondered whether—in another time and place—this type of man could have dutifully and meticulously monitored the progression of trains to Auschwitz.

When our interview finally concluded, Warter matter-of-factly advised us that his testimony would be coordinated through the foreign ministry, while testimony of other West German witnesses would be arranged through the U.S. Departments of Justice and State, on the one hand, and the German states and West German embassy, on the other. Aware of the daunting bureaucratic process we faced, Warter graciously offered to help in any way possible.

IN THE END, Warter's clinical diagnosis of restitution programs—and the entire post-Holocaust effort to make survivors whole again—brought to mind the searing passages in Dan Pagis's "Draft of a Reparations Agreement":

> ... Everything will be returned to the place,
> paragraph after paragraph,
> The scream back into the throat.
> The gold teeth back to the gums.
> The terror.
> The smoke back to the tin chimney
> and further on and inside
> back to the hollow bones,
> and already you will be covered with
> skin and sinews and you will live,
> look, you will have your lives back,
> sit in the living room, read the evening paper.
> Here you are. Nothing is too late.
> As to the yellow star: immediately
> it will be torn from your chest
> and will emigrate to the sky.

Interface, Interdiction, and Interlude

One by one, witnesses fell into line. Restitution agency officials proved uniformly cooperative, and with few exceptions, even Kozminski's attorney-contacts patiently reviewed files with us and agreed to testify at trial.

Eventually heading to the northwest beer-producing center of Düsseldorf, we met with Walter Heeren, *Regierungsoberamtsrat* (chief) of the Landerentenbehoerde Nord Rhein-Westafalen (Düsseldorf restitution agency), while a Ms. Fricke of the *Polizei* routinely and quietly observed. The gruff-voiced Heeren, a bearded, bespectacled man in his late forties, readily agreed to bring the Wolman file and testify, and then spontaneously revealed a new twist in Kozminski's convoluted course of deception.

Heeren explained, "Our agency awarded restitution of some $4,000 to Wolman, not for the death of his father—which was the only claim filed by Kozminski—but as an automatic back payment on a monthly health pension. The award of that pension had long predated Kozminski's . . . involvement in this case."

Glancing at the file, Heeren continued, "Well, shortly before we issued the payment, Kozminski sent us a power of attorney for Wolman. It was purely a coincidence, but it compelled us to send these monies directly to him. It's a shame."

Shaking his head, Heeren concluded, "I guess stealing this money wasn't good enough, because Kozminski kept demanding more money for Wolman's pension. And now you tell me Wolman didn't even know about it. This is very . . . improper."

While miffed at this evidence of further duplicity and double-dealing, we nonetheless took solace that *we* had witnessed Heeren's account rather than Wolman, whose combustible rage toward Kozminski otherwise may well have been rekindled.

Hours after bidding farewell to Heeren, we passed stately Roman ruins gracing ancient Trier and soon arrived at the wooded Alsace town of Saarburg. There, the congenial Wolfgang Momper, *Regierungsdirektor* (agency director) of the Bezirksamt für Wiedergutmachung (Saarburg restitution office), dutifully consented to bring the Teitman file and testify. Promptly heading next to the verdant city of Stuttgart, we met with Kozminski's former attorney-contact Ludolf Lerman, who solemnly pledged his full cooperation on the Weingarten claim. And so it went.

Amid this flurry of interviews, our encounter with Otto Gnirs, *Präsident des Landesamts für die Wiedergutmachung* (Stuttgart agency president), was notable for reasons other than his consent to bring the Seidman, Weingarten, and Reich files and testify at trial. Gnirs stood as a bold and refreshing exception to German officials' propensity to follow the rules by rotely acknowledging Kozminski's formal powers of attorney.

We met with the soft-spoken Gnirs, a chubby, bespectacled man in his midfifties with brown hair and a chalky round face, in the silent presence of a young *Polizei* officer named Joachim Rueck. Initially noting his continuous service as a restitution agency official since 1957, Gnirs advised us that he long had been suspicious of Lucian Kozminski's activities. Citing the Reich file as a notable example, he carefully traced the dubious course of a prolonged cat-and-mouse game between Kozminski and his agency.

Gnirs said, "It all began in the early 1970s. Sometime after Reich already was receiving a restitution pension, Kozminski sent us a *vollmacht,* you know, a power of attorney, authorizing him to represent Reich. So when the agency announced that a backpayment linked to inflation would issue, sometime in 1973, we routinely mailed the notice to Kozminski."

Gnirs glanced at us, wincing slightly, and then continued, "But I didn't expect Kozminski's response. He wrote back insisting that the funds be sent directly to *him*. Of course, I knew that he had nothing to do with this automatic pension increase, so I ignored his request and sent the payment directly to Reich."

Winking at us almost playfully, he went on, "Well, the same thing happened the next year. The agency sent Kozminski a notice advising that another back payment would be issued. One month later, Kozminski wrote us again, demanding that the payment be sent to him. But I again mailed the funds directly to Reich. He tried the same thing again two years later, and I ignored him once again."

Gnirs concluded, "Well, I reached the end of the line when Ludolf Lerman, Kozminski's Stuttgart attorney, told me Kozminski had embezzled Jacob Weingarten's restitution monies. Now I knew he was a cheat. So on June 22, 1979, I ordered my agency to refuse to honor Kozminski's *vollmachts*, prohibit filing of any claims that he forwarded, and cease all contact with him. I thought we were finished with him."

But despite this forthright directive, the resourceful Kozminski simply would not be denied. Cunningly engineering an end run around Gnirs's blanket prohibition, he secretly enlisted Hans Rock to file all future restitution claims with the agency, and as a result, he remained strategically placed to fleece Theodore Seidman and dozens of other victims out of their rightful restitution.

As they progressed, these interviews seemed nearly surreal, as if occurring in a purified air chamber. The West German restitution agency officials had been cooperative, but everything seemed to be reduced to musty old documents and files. The restitution claims appeared detached from their very genesis: the suffering and torture of our victims that had been perpetrated by the Germans. In its own way, the entire process felt disconnected from the flesh and blood of humanity.

I was not alone in my feeling of dissonance. A slow rage seemed to be building inside Kinzler, both toward the Germans' unpardonable acts of genocide and toward the German bureaucrats' matter-of-fact approach to the entire matter. He often muttered asides to me on these topics during our interviews and later recounted his frustration to me when we were alone. The more we traveled through Germany, the more intense these feelings became.

THE WEEKEND brought a brief respite from our far-flung interviews as Kinzler and I headed to four nearby locations.

We first went to the sleepy university town of Heidelberg, where on a crisp April Saturday, sunlight sparkled amid small flurries of snowflakes during our trek to the ancient castle overlooking the Neckar River. This surreal vision of light and snow still remains deeply etched in my memory and in a curious way has come to symbolize our entire trip.

After next visiting the venerable walled town of Rothenburg, we drove through Wertheim, the town of Kinzler's early years. As we briefly stopped outside his childhood home, Kinzler peered at the aged structure silently, his thoughts apparently focused upon a distant time and memory.

Minutes later, we headed to nearby Würzburg, where Kinzler also spent part of his childhood days. While we drove through the small town, quaintly nestled in rolling hills dotted by church steeples, Kinzler again ruminated and stared almost forlornly into the distance.

Finally, he quietly remarked, "It seems like another lifetime. I . . .

I almost can't believe that I used to live here, and that now I'm back
. . . on this case, of all things."

The Glass House

Restitution agency officials whom we interviewed worked daily with
files of Holocaust victims, routinely approved substantial restitution
for survivors, and now were fully aware that Kozminski had brazenly purloined payments issued by their agencies. Yet during our
meetings, they virtually all expressed grave and abiding concern
about the same aspect of their prospective testimony.

These officials worried that at trial Kozminski and his counsel
would depict *them* as the perpetrators of fraud and suffering. They
would be roundly accused of providing misleading information to
Kozminski, unfairly rejecting victims' claims, and callously delaying
restitution awards. They would be fingered as citizens of Germany,
the nation that imposed the evils of the Holocaust upon Kozminski
and his fellow Jews, and ultimately would be characterized as a cabal
of unreconstructed Nazis plotting to embarrass, vilify, and, at last,
destroy Kozminski.

I still remember the reaction of one official who breezily recounted
facts from a victim file before turning to the prospect of his trial testimony. Almost casually, he inquired, "You don't really need me to
testify, do you?" When Kinzler responded in the affirmative, the
bureaucrat's facial muscles contracted and his pleasant demeanor
changed as he pleaded, "But it isn't *really* necessary, is it?" When
Kinzler again responded in the affirmative and carefully explained
why, the now crestfallen and perplexed prospective witness replied,
"But, you know, we're *German*. And we're supposed to testify *against*
Kozminski?"

We repeatedly tried to assure these officials that no reasonable basis
existed for attacking any of them at Kozminski's trial. They could
not even arguably be implicated in Kozminski's personal scheme to
defraud. Any attempt to stain them with the brush of Nazism would
prompt my vehement objection and almost certainly would be dis-

allowed by the court. In the end, they truly had nothing to fear from either Kozminski or his defense counsel.

But our earnest assurances were not entirely effective, as these officials' reluctance seemed immune to rational thought or discourse. Often expressed in hushed, self-conscious tones, their concerns simply would not dissipate. Clearly arising from something deep-seated and almost impenetrable, their fears were apparently the product of a tangled web enmeshing the distinctive German nationality, daily exposure to survivors' files, the lingering residue of anti-Semitism, Kozminski's past suffering, the echoes of the Holocaust, and personal and collective guilt. Despite our sustained effort, we knew that at some level, we never could untangle these hopelessly knotted strands of the psyche.

Ashes and Whitewash

Little did Kinzler and I know that among a series of important interviews in Munich, our meeting with Dr. Otto Betz would be a harbinger of a most unusual and troubling day.

It all began the morning after our memorable encounter with Rudy Pecher of the *Polizei* and Dr. Karl Pokorny, when we met Pecher as arranged in front of the Munich police station. Again wearing his holster, gray uniform, and prominent black boots, he tersely introduced us to Volker Schaaf, a thin-haired *Polizei* officer in his late forties who greeted us amiably.

Reverting to a more formal posture in Schaaf's presence, Pecher gruffly barked that we should follow them to the home of Dr. Betz, another of Kozminski's local attorney-contacts. After the two *Polizei* hopped into their car, Kinzler and I got into ours, and we all set off in tandem.

As we navigated the winding road toward Rottach-Egern, less than an hour outside Munich, manicured suburban terrain gave way to a lush forest, glistening with mildew from the early-morning fog. Eventually reaching a clearing in a dense grove of trees, we drove next to the placid blue waters of crystal-clear Lake Tegernsee, a light mist hovering over the surface in wisps of gray and white.

Moments later, Pecher pulled into a long, steep driveway and headed toward a large wood-and-glass home facing the lake. Kinzler and I dutifully followed and, after parking behind the *Polizei* sedan, joined Pecher and Schaaf at the front door.

Upon several authoritative knocks by Pecher, the door was slowly opened by Dr. Otto Betz. A dignified-looking man in his midsixties with a shock of white-gray hair, he curtly invited us inside, seating us in a large wood-paneled study.

As soon as Pecher announced our purpose and Kinzler matter-of-factly removed a victim file from his briefcase, we knew our subject would be less than forthcoming. Sitting opposite us with a defensive glint in his eyes, Betz visibly stiffened and, despite his apparently considerable mental faculties, experienced a curious and pronounced loss of memory.

When we displayed the file for the victim in question, Louis Konitz, Betz responded; "I . . . I've never heard of him. And let's see, I guess those are my signatures and my letterhead on the documents, but I don't remember any of these papers. You must understand, gentlemen, I've handled thousands of restitution cases since 1947 and several hundred more just in the last decade."

But that was just the beginning.

When we turned to the topic of Lucian Kozminski, Betz's eyes glazed over and he seemingly drew a complete blank. He then remarked adamantly: "I can tell you I've never even heard of him. You see, I worked with some . . . . oh I would say thirty . . . . American colleagues on these claims. Why should I remember him?"

Stunned by Betz's complete disavowal of Kozminski, we quickly displayed several letters between them. But his recollection still would not be refreshed, and now facing a prospective witness with no memory, we had hit a veritable impasse.

Far more restrained in the presence of his colleague than he had been the previous day, Pecher stood up and slowly paced, his eyes bulging slightly in frustration. Stopping for effect, he glared at Betz with skepticism and queried incredulously, "You mean you *worked* with Kozminski and you don't even remember his *name?*"

But Betz, unperturbed, simply shrugged and shook his head no.

Now sizing him up one last time, Pecher seemed to realize the cause was hopeless and quickly relented, sitting down in silence.

Though Betz finally agreed to appear at the trial, we knew his testimony would be virtually worthless, flawed by his notable inability to recall either the victim's file or Kozminski himself. And so we departed the exquisite home of Dr. Otto Betz, erected largely upon the fees of Holocaust victims, with our own hands conspicuously empty.

After we joined Pecher and Schaaf for a convivial breakfast, Kinzler and I were left to ponder whether we had witnessed a deliberate, convenient loss of memory or a simple denial, an unconscious attempt to forget an unseemly or painful subject. While the verdict on Betz would remain unresolved, our next witness's blanket and strained denial would soon be transparently evident.

LATER IN THE AFTERNOON, still accompanied by Rudy Pecher, Kinzler and I met with Joseph Thalmayr, the *Regierungsdirektor* (agency director) of the Bayerisches Landesentschaedigungsamt (Munich restitution agency). A man in his midforties with brown hair and a pasty face, Thalmayr perfunctorily reviewed several victim files with us and then, without warning, suddenly pulled out the file of another concentration camp survivor: Lucian Ludwig Kozminski.

Now reading aloud from the file, Thalmayr matter-of-factly recited the litany of Kozminski's gruesome experience. From May 1943 to August 1944, Kozminski was interned at the Auschwitz death camp, prisoner #111770. From August 1944 to February 25, 1945, he was incarcerated at the Gross-Rosen and Flossenbürg camps in northern Bavaria, prisoner #82332. From March 26, 1945, through April 22, 1945, Kozminski was imprisoned at Ohrdruf, an outpost of the Buchenwald concentration camp, prisoner #137507. Finally, on April 23, 1945, Kozminski and other inmates were moved toward Weimar, in what was then East Germany, and liberated by American troops in late April or early May.

Kinzler and I glanced at each other with the same expression, both aware that we had been administered another harsh dose of reality, and I again sensed that odd feeling about the uneven edges of fate. We were, of course, intimately aware of the details of Kozminski's incarceration in several concentration camps. But there was something very unsettling about hearing these facts coldly recited by a middle-aged German bureaucrat while we were visiting Germany investigating the theft of restitution for losses incurred in the Holocaust. For a moment, my reality was distinctly skewed, as Kozminski seemed to become the victim and Thalmayr the oppressor.

I sensed this was symptomatic of a truer reality: Much as we condemned Kozminski's greedy acts, his own experience as a victim appeared inextricably woven into the dense fabric of our expanding investigation. Kozminski was, after all, not just a human being but also a victim of Nazi persecution.

PERHAPS AWARE of our reaction, Thalmayr verbalized a sentiment captured in the rare unguarded look or subtle intonation of other restitution agency officials, calmly explaining: "You know, like the camps at Bergen-Belsen and Dachau, Buchenwald absolutely was not an extermination camp."

Continuing unabated, he pointedly added, *"No one* was *killed* in these camps. Rather, they *all* died of starvation and disease."

Kinzler and I both stared at Thalmayr, utterly speechless. My mind immediately raced to the teenage Anne Frank who died at Bergen-Belsen in March 1945, along with 45,000 others in that year alone. To tens of thousands slaughtered and incinerated at Dachau, reportedly prompting the mayor of the adjacent city to complain about the pervasive smell of burning flesh. To gruesome pictures of emaciated inmates, flaccid skin hanging from their bones, in the notorious Buchenwald camp where the SS killed thousands by phenol injections and nearby "euthanasia" disposal.

Thalmayr's description was absurd and thoroughly incredible, for aside from deliberately murdering tens of thousands of inmates in these camps, the Nazis controlled all conditions and carefully manipulated the death rate from starvation and disease with an avowed goal of "destruction through work" (*Vernichtung durch Arbeit*).

But now Thalmayr went even further, confidently proclaiming, "Of course, the only death camps during the War were located in Poland and run entirely by Poles."

Then, pausing for effect, he concluded forcefully, "And you should know that the Germans played absolutely no role in the mass extermination at these camps."

Thalmayr somehow ignored the Nazi Order Police and *Einsatzgruppen*'s massacre of nearly one million Jews even before a single extermination camp was built. He also disregarded the SS Economic and Administrative Main Office's precise instructions to commandants of Dachau, Buchenwald, Auschwitz, and other camps in 1941: A "medical commission" would soon visit to select prisoners for code 14f.13—"special treatment." This diabolical Nazi plan culminated with mass deportations, largely of Jews, to death camps at Sobibor, where 250,000 people were killed; Chelmno, where 350,000 were killed; Belzec, where 600,000 were killed; Treblinka, where 800,000 were killed; Majdanek, where 360,000 were killed; and, Auschwitz-Birkenau, where more than 1½ million were killed.

Again we stared at Thalmayr, our minds racing in confused disbelief. Here was a man who directed the Munich Restitution Agency and processed claims of Holocaust victims daily. Here was a man who presumably would be aware, even more than ordinary Germans, of his nation's sordid complicity in mass murder. Yet all we heard was unsolicited, blanket denial with truth the inevitable casualty.

Biting my lip, I strained to remember our singular goal of securing Thalmayr's cooperation and persuading him to testify at Kozminski's trial. So I remained silent. Kinzler, however, would not be similarly restrained. In a firm but measured tone, he responded, "Mr. Thalmayr, I . . . I'm surprised you say that. It doesn't really matter *where* the camps were located. You must know that they were invented by the Nazis for their master plan of extermination and were just a . . . a part of the slaughter of millions elsewhere, including in Germany."

After Kinzler completed his blunt response, Thalmayr looked at him blankly, shrugged, and routinely stood to shake our hands goodbye. While Rudy Pecher, seated next to us, abruptly stood and eyed Thalmayr with a glint of contempt, Kinzler and I instinctively smiled politely and shook Thalmayr's hand.

Accompanied by Pecher, we then swiftly departed, knowing we always would remain worlds apart.

NOT QUITE READY to leave Munich, Kinzler and I later drove a short distance to the Dachau concentration camp, adjacent to the thousand-year-old city of Dachau. When American troops arrived there just thirty-seven years earlier, hardened combat veterans found a true vision from hell. At one satellite camp, they were sickened by the putrid smell of burnt flesh and soon learned that the camp commandant had ordered the liquidation of four thousand surviving prisoners shortly before their arrival. The horrified soldiers then found a string of forty railway cars leading into the main camp, each filled with emaciated, bullet-riddled, and decomposing corpses. Compounding the shock from these atrocities, the anguished troops watched helplessly as the remaining starved, diseased prisoners died at the rate of one hundred per day during the ensuing two weeks.

Kinzler and I quietly walked together through the deserted camp, stopping to look at Nandor Glid's bronze sculpture of gaunt, gnarled bodies of Holocaust victims and ruminating over the bold lettering on a nearby stone wall, which read, PLUS JAMAIS . . . NIE WIEDER . . . NEVER AGAIN.

Later, at the crematorium ovens, we both wept silently. As Kinzler says, "I imagined, looking through the windows, that I could see hands clawing at the glass. Mark and I didn't have to say a word. We saw and felt the same thing."

In the end, Dachau's silent echoes of suffering came to symbolize the larger meaning of our investigation and would continue to serve as a chilling reminder of the deceptively short passage between the distant past and the often illusory present.

Reunion in the Divided City

Driving on an insulated East German highway specially designed with no exits, we headed due north toward West Berlin, a city that had been blockaded by the Communists in 1948 and later separated from its eastern counterpart with a large concrete wall and no-man's land featuring barbed wire, watchtowers, and guard dogs.

As we traversed the East German countryside on our eight-hour journey, the visible spectrum of colors gradually dissipated to somber hues of gray, brown, and black. The terrain was harsh and bleak, the polluted sky sooty and dark, and the buildings in the villages and cities we passed were drab, nondescript, and often dilapidated. Our mood, meanwhile, correspondingly grew darker as Kinzler soberly cited instances where East German–born tourists, like him, were forcibly apprehended at the border, treated as citizens of the Communist state, and not permitted to return to the West.

Twilight gave way to the still black of night, and with a hint of trepidation in Kinzler's eyes, we soon arrived at the heavily fortified checkpoint and took our place in a long line of cars. When we finally reached the front of the queue, two armed East German guards approached our car, and after we dutifully displayed our brown-jacketed diplomatic passports, grabbed them and examined them with evident suspicion. Moments later, the guards looked up, motioned us to the side of the road, and tersely instructed us to wait.

Sitting alone in the darkness as car after car cleared the nearby checkpoint, Kinzler and I waited and continued to wait. Now lamenting that we had driven rather than flown to Berlin, Kinzler noted that the lengthy distance separating us from West Germany precluded turning around and attempting a wholesale retreat.

Finally, after more than an hour of lingering suspense, the guards marched toward our car, silently returned our passports, and waved us through the checkpoint. Pulling back on to the highway we set off, soon entering the welcome environs of West Berlin.

RESUMING OUR hectic pace upon arrival, we conducted seven more interviews in the next three days, each securing another vital building block for our case.

We needed no introduction to Helga Trilse at the *Bundesversicherungsanstalt Für Angestellte* (Social Security agency), who had confirmed by telephone Kozminski's fraudulent postscript the previous September, creating the breakthrough that led to our pivotal search of his offices.

After greeting us warmly and reminiscing briefly, the agreeable brown-haired Trilse unexpectedly turned to other sordid aspects of Kozminski's deception, as reflected in Hans Wittner's official restitution file. We already knew that after failing to forward Wittner's $645 to West Germany, Kozminski attempted to disguise his treachery by sending a forged letter to Wittner on March 24, 1981.

But now Trilse revealed, "You gentlemen only know part of the truth. You see, Mr. Wittner's claim actually was *denied* on September 15, 1980. Kozminski then sent a letter of appeal advising that he forgot to mention that Wittner was Jewish—a pretty big omission, you must admit—but it was denied on December 10, 1980. Wittner would'd've gotten restitution if we knew he was Jewish, but Kozminski's appeal was too late."

Kinzler and I glanced at each other as she continued, "And from your expressions, you seem to understand what this means. It means that when your Mr. Kozminski gave Wittner 'proof' that $645 was sent here to release a restitution payment, he already knew Wittner's claim and appeal had been denied many months before."

Kinzler and I again looked at each other and winced. While disgusted at this latest revelation of callousness and indecency, we now knew that almost *nothing* Kozminski had done would shock us or even strain credulity.

Shortly after bidding farewell to Trilse, we met with Wolfgang Meineke of the Berlin Restitution Office, which had processed claims for five of our principal witnesses: Ella Mandel, Fela Fuchs, Zesa Starr, Louis Konitz, and Arthur Reich.

A balding man in his early sixties who limped with the support of a cane, Meineke remarked, "You know, I long suspected Kozminski was cheating his clients. But he had those powers of attorney, so I had no . . . authority to stop him. Now, however, I must admit I'm very relieved. I hope you put him out of the restitution business for good."

In the end, we were grateful for Meineke's unqualified support and readily accepted his insistent offer that we join him for dinner.

Upon completing our remaining interviews and before heading to the airport, we decided to cross briefly into East Berlin. This time a stern-looking female guard stood in a small booth at the checkpoint. After silently disappearing with our diplomatic passports for several minutes, she finally returned and brusquely motioned us through.

Relieved after this final brush with East German authorities, Kinzler and I stepped across the border and briefly journeyed into the drab and oppressive surroundings of East Berlin. As this draining but illuminating trip drew to an end, Kinzler and I were aware that we had crossed our own invisible wall and soon would be heading into uncharted territory: preparing formal charges against Lucian Kozminski. An important chapter had concluded while another one was beginning.

Sculpting the Case

Upon returning from West Germany, we moved at a rapid and methodical pace toward indictment. We moved rapidly because we could not permit Kozminski to cause more suffering, tamper with witnesses, or undertake something more drastic, such as fleeing the country. We moved methodically because in order to craft an indictment, we had to fully appreciate and grasp the true nature and scope of all our evidence.

Kinzler, as a result, reexamined Kozminski's files with the benefit of valuable insights reached over many laborious months, including those gleaned from our recent round of interviews in West Germany. This time, as Kinzler and I concluded days later during a lengthy after-hours session in my office, the web of fraud soon became evident.

As we both propped our legs on my desk, Kinzler began, "You know, Mark, piecing together everything we've learned, including in Germany, I can see that we were overlooking the real key all along. It's simple: There's absolutely *no* consistent or predictable pattern to his fraud. He cheated every one of his three thousand clients, in virtually any way and every way possible."

I quickly responded, "You're absolutely right. That *is* the key. At the beginning he'd demand a nonrecurring fee, but then there was always more. Demands for nonexistent West German filing fees, 'reimbursements' to West German attorneys that he had stiffed, and all sorts of other expenses."

Kinzler interjected, "Yeah, and he didn't discriminate. Everyone got hit up for fees, whether their claims were pending, denied, granted, or even filed."

I replied, "Right. And of course, when he actually received restitution awards, sometimes he'd keep the whole thing, and other times he'd throw the victim a few crumbs, relying upon his doctored fee agreements. I guess it depended on his mood that day."

Kinzler nodded in agreement before continuing: "The guy was too clever. I mean, he keeps the victims in the dark about their claims but raises their hopes at the same time, saying, 'Your money's about to come.' After he's done draining them of their funds, he claims the money's stuck in a foreign account or got delayed by summer vacation in Germany or a fire in his office destroyed his files. What a piece of work."

Slipping my feet from the desk, I added, "Yeah, and there was just no limit to this. He advertised everywhere, throughout the world. Wherever Jews lived, anywhere, there were fresh new victims to fleece."

Now that we fully grasped the pervasive breadth of Kozminski's fraud, fully corroborating Ms. Schneider's sordid account, we began sculpting the final shape of our proposed indictment.

While sorely tempted to bury Kozminski under a mountain of charges naming twenty-five or more victims, we determined that the absence of a clear pattern of fraud and the sheer volume of evidence might prove confusing and unwieldy, ultimately miring us in intricate variations of Kozminski's fraudulent themes. Opting instead for an entirely different strategy, we decided to prepare a streamlined indictment naming just ten victims, seven who received no portion of their restitution from Kozminski and three who received only a fraction.

Several persuasive considerations supported this approach.

First, by naming an insular group of victims defrauded in the same manner, our case would be simple and compelling. Second, depending upon resources and strategy, we still would retain the flexibility of calling several other victims as witnesses to Kozminski's "scheme to defraud." Third, a streamlined indictment would allow us to focus our preparation. We knew that most victims had never testified in court, many were elderly with faulty memories, and others might be intimidated by Kozminski's courtroom presence. A shorter indictment meant we could address these concerns by devoting more valuable attention to each of our named victims.

As a result, we meticulously whittled down our massive pile of evidence to a narrow, succinct cluster of charges. At the risk of appearing to minimize the scope of Kozminski's fraud, we endeavored to maximize the likelihood of his conviction.

KOZMINSKI APPEARED clever and slippery in thwarting civil lawsuits and eluding or fending off criminal cases. Aware that he would represent an uniquely formidable foe, before presenting an indictment, we carefully reexamined the one remaining piece of the puzzle: Lucian Ludwig Kozminski.

The Emerging Portrait

Who was this person, Lucian Ludwig Kozminski? We had learned much in painstakingly gathering and assembling our evidence, yet his emerging and often unsettling portrait still remained unfinished.

Though Kozminski's files reflected a peculiar uncertainty over whether he was born in 1916 or 1926, we knew his birthplace was Turek, a small city amid a cluster of villages between the Prosna River to the west and Lodz several hundred miles to the east. While most Jews in that region worked as tailors, shoemakers, and locksmiths, Kozminski's father was reportedly an unlicensed healer (or *felczer*), who administered "medical aid" to patients by cupping glasses and applying live leeches, among other folk remedies.

At a young age, Kozminski and his family reportedly moved to Lodz, Poland's major industrial center, about seventy-five miles west of Warsaw. They there joined a bustling community that included approximately 378,000 Jews, most of them workers or manufacturers, composing 14.4 percent of the city's two million residents and nearly one third of its urban-area inhabitants. A dynamic and vibrant hub of Jewish culture, political dialogue, and social activity before the War, Lodz was home to two Yiddish daily newspapers, three Hebrew secondary schools, and a Jewish library, as well as several Jewish theaters and sports clubs.

We were unaware of Kozminski's precise activities in Lodz but knew he remained there until a few years before the end of the War, when he was interned in several concentration camps, including Auschwitz and Gross-Rosen. His father, mother, two brothers, and one sister all reportedly died in concentration camps during the Nazis' wholesale liquidation of Polish Jewry.

After the War ended, most liberated Jewish refugees departed Germany within a few years. But Kozminski remained, settling in the Munich suburb of Schwandorf, where he soon initiated a prolonged course of duplicity, double-dealing, and fraud. Government documents reflect that in the immediate postwar period, he received a commendation from the Allied Expeditionary Force Military Government for "organizing . . . entertainment of the American troops and . . . civilian population," while simultaneously operating a local bar that reportedly served as a front for Eastern Bloc Communist spies.

Kozminski's entry in the West German federal penal register, recently provided to us, revealed much about the nature of his nefarious activities in the ensuing period. On January 24, 1963, Kozminski was convicted by a Munich court for dealing in "groceries" by using misleading labels "in connection with attempted fraud" and fined 1,000 Deutsche marks. Nine months later, on October 17, 1963, the same court convicted him of making a fraudulent statement under oath "by negligence" and fined him 100 Deutsche marks.

On June 22, 1966, Kozminski was convicted by an Erding court of two counts of trafficking violations "in coincidence with coercion" and fined 200 Deutsche marks. Just five months later, on November 20, 1966, the same court convicted him of theft and fined him 300 Deutsche marks. Two months afterward, on January 9, 1967, Kozminski suffered convictions for three offenses of treachery and was sentenced to a fine of 500 Deutsche marks and ten days' imprisonment with probation until June 28, 1970.

Barely six months later, on June 27, 1967, he was convicted of fraud and sentenced to two weeks' imprisonment with probation until July 14, 1971.

Although details were sketchy about these offenses, we learned that one conviction resulted from Kozminski's scheme to defraud Holocaust survivors in Germany by collecting fees to "refurbish" their relatives' Polish graves. Charges were brought when one victim traveled to Poland to visit a refurbished gravesite and found nothing but unadorned dirt.

While the West Germans had treated this "stateless" Holocaust survivor with extreme leniency, their apparent patience eventually wore thin with the marked escalation and frequency of his crimes, at last prompting a short term of imprisonment and subsequent probation on his most recent convictions. With the vise clearly tightening, Kozminski evidently decided the time had arrived to seek greener pastures.

In 1968, while still on probation for two offenses, Kozminski abruptly fled West Germany. Upon entering the United States, he lied on his application for a nonimmigrant visa by failing to disclose his prior convictions, prompting the INS to launch proceedings culminating in several unsuccessful orders of deportation. Meanwhile, almost immediately after arriving in this country, Kozminski established his restitution business and had operated it continuously ever since.

THE EVENING before seeking an indictment, Kinzler and I ruminated over these critical pieces of the puzzle, still trying to fill in our elusive suspect's sketchy portrait. Facing me across a square table in a dimly lit conference room, Kinzler remarked, "OK. We know he's engaged in illicit activity for, what, three decades? And he doesn't seem to have any remorse or fear of being caught. What did he say to a victim who threatened to turn him in, '*To who? The American clowns in black robes?*'"

"Yeah, well, maybe he was onto something," I replied. "I mean, the guy's always managed to escape, one way or the other. What did he get, six convictions in Germany?"

"Right," Kinzler remarked. "And he served, like, ten days in jail."

"Exactly," I replied. "Then he comes here illegally but he's never been deported. Meanwhile, he operates this scam for thirteen years and nobody does anything."

Kinzler's brow furrowed, and his eyes filled with introspection. Then he slowly he queried, "Are you trying to . . . suggest something else?"

"I don't know, Lou," I responded. "But a lot of strange things happened after the War. Look at it this way: Could there be another explanation for his commendation from the Allied Expeditionary Force Military Government? Is it possible that he could have acted as a . . . double agent when supposedly operating a bar for Communist spies?"

"Yeah," Kinzler replied, now irritated. "And why the hell haven't we gotten his complete CIA file?"

"I don't know," I responded. "But remember, even the Vatican had an escape route for former Nazi criminals. Maybe Kozminski had his own guardian angel."

"Well," Kinzler ruminated. "We may never find out *those* answers. Hell, it's tough enough trying to figure *him* out. I mean, the pieces just don't seem to fit."

KINZLER WAS RIGHT, for the more I learned and the more I ruminated, the more a portrait emerged of a person whose persona bore a huge fissure, like a cracked foundation, with opposite traits stitched together into one unseemly whole.

Kozminski was a Jew who cheated other Jews and even sympathized with the SS. He was unusually boastful while undoubtedly harboring traumatizing fears. He was distinctly sociable, even charming, and yet probably fundamentally alone and depressed. He was persuasive and convincing (just ask his victims or Postal Inspector Bookie Almond) yet also was uneducated and spoke in broken English. He reportedly abused alcohol and, at the same time, abused his victims with oral taunts and even physical assaults. He seemed to be a pair of mirror images blending into one person, simultaneously sharing diverse and even opposite traits and behavior.

The farther back we explored Kozminski's background, the more I wondered whether he entered the concentration camps with a flawed character and there engaged in treacherous conduct or, rather, *emerged* from the Holocaust with his humanity skewed and his sanity shattered. While all of us are capable of bad acts as well as bad thoughts, something appeared to have gone seriously remiss with Kozminski. The troubling questions were when and why, assuming either could even be pinpointed, much less fathomed.

Even aside from our persistent curiosity, we were obliged to seek the truth about Kozminski to anticipate his likely defenses. While we would continue to dig deeper into his murky past, for the moment our preliminary expedition at last was complete. The time had come to present a criminal indictment to a federal grand jury, and we were on the verge of a virtual maelstrom.

Charges and Cuffs

Composed of twenty-three ordinary citizens, a federal grand jury's primary mission is to investigate "targets" suspected of committing violations of federal law by, among other things, authorizing the issuance of subpoenas for records or witnesses and hearing testimony. When an assistant U.S. attorney proposes charges, an indictment is issued if a majority of the grand jury finds that more probably than not a crime has been committed, otherwise known as "probable cause."

Grand jury evidence remains strictly sealed until shortly before trial, when the government ordinarily provides the defense with complete transcripts of scheduled trial witnesses' grand jury testimony.

Aware that prosecutors are afforded wide latitude in deciding how evidence should be presented to a grand jury, we chose to present our proof in the simplest and clearest fashion possible: through one witness, the investigating case agent. As a result, on June 28, 1982, Kinzler and I stepped alone into the grand jury room for the purpose of presenting our proposed charges and evidence and securing an indictment.

After exchanging casual greetings with several of the grand jurors, I sat facing the grand jury behind a small elevated table, with Kinzler sitting in a chair to my right next to flags of the United States and the State of California. The room fell silent.

Moments later, I began by reciting our twelve-page mail fraud indictment, which broadly summarized how Kozminski cheated Holocaust survivors, specifically cited fifteen instances (or counts) of Kozminski's use of the mails to execute his scheme, and graphically detailed the claims of ten victims: Hela Suchecki, Mordka Wolman,

Ella Mandel, Fela Fuchs, Zesa Starr, Theodore Seidman, Jacob Weingarten, Edith Teitman, Louis Konitz, and Arthur Reich.

As I finished reading the proposed indictment, for a moment there was utter silence in the room. I glanced at the grand jurors who were raptly attentive, several of them with furrowed brows and expressions of both concern and interest. One rotund woman in the first row stopped her incessant knitting and looked up with a frozen expression. Tears welled in the eyes of a middle-aged black man in the second row.

Then I turned to Kinzler and asked him to recite the evidence of our investigation. In a composed and professional manner, he carefully recounted the story. Beginning with our extensive collection and corroboration of evidence, he went on to describe the many and varied ways that Kozminski cheated his victims, including his use of the mails to accomplish his swindle. And then Kinzler was done.

Before this session, the grand jury had issued just a handful of subpoenas during our investigation and was less than familiar with Kozminski's scheme.

Now, after hearing Kinzler's detailed testimony, the grand jurors appeared even more stunned than after my reading of the indictment. Many had pained and disturbed expressions while others shook their heads in disbelief, and the entire room was oddly silent.

Finally, a few slowly raised their hands and posed routine questions to Kinzler.

Others, however, were not so routine, such as "How could he do this to those people?" And "How could he get away with this for so long?" And "Do you think any of the Germans collaborated with him on this?"

After Kinzler did his best to respond to the grand jurors' often pointed inquiries, we promptly excused ourselves and stepped outside. Less than a minute later, the foreperson emerged and somberly said, "We've voted an indictment. It was unanimous."

For a brief moment, Kinzler and I looked at each other and then slowly shook hands and smiled. We knew we had come a very long way and ever so briefly savored the moment.

So, AT LAST, after Kozminski had eluded American authorities for more than a decade, he was finally called to task. If convicted, he would face five years' imprisonment on each count for a total of seventy-five years in prison. The road to conviction, however, still appeared long and winding, and none of us knew what stood at the end.

That afternoon, Kinzler and Postal Inspectors Jim Vach and Bill Watson arrived at Kozminski's Beverly Hills apartment. Kinzler had not only figured out Kozminski's files, he was there to arrest him.

Moments after Kinzler knocked, Kozminski opened the front door.

Wearing a short-sleeve shirt and slacks, the bespectacled Kozminski peered at the three postal inspectors without expression. He opened his mouth as if to speak, but his attention was diverted to Kinzler's right hand, where handcuffs dangled with a soft chiming sound as Kinzler slowly raised them from his side.

Then all three postal inspectors abruptly stepped toward Kozminski.

A somber Kozminski remained composed and silent as the postal inspectors briskly handcuffed him, advised him of his rights, and carted him away.

3

EXPOSÉS AND CHALLENGES

Tracking the Trail

Usually after an indictment is issued, the grand jury's role ends and it then remains the government's job to prosecute. But this was no ordinary case. Convinced that Kozminski was fraudulently concealing his assets, an entirely separate crime, we would continue investigating him as long as any chance existed of locating and delivering purloined monies to a single victim.

Sure enough, during our ongoing probe we learned that Kozminski filed a bankruptcy petition on April 6, 1982, a tactic clearly designed to position him outside the reach of our ever tightening grasp.

Upon reviewing a copy of Kozminski's petition, we immediately noticed one glaring omission: The document made no reference to the $22,543.91 balance from Theodore Seidman's restitution payment forwarded to Kozminski's bank account on March 1, 1982, one month before he filed his bankruptcy petition, evidence we had recently confirmed in West Germany.

By contacting the Stuttgart Restitution Agency directly, Theodore Seidman had learned of the same payment and, thoroughly incensed, called Kozminski in early April. Blasting him as a "liar and thief" while demanding his money, Seidman threatened to report him to the authorities. The usually cocky Kozminski, fully aware that the government was on his heels after seizing his files, replied in a subdued tone that payment would be forthcoming "within two weeks." Nearly three months later, however, Seidman had received nothing.

When I met with Seidman for a second time and he recounted this story, it was evident that something had changed dramatically. His meek, mild-mannered expression was gone, replaced with a tone of unbridled indignation.

As Seidman remarked in a rising voice, "I had hoped that maybe it was all a mistake and Kozminski was not a crook. But now I know the *real* truth. He's a good-for-nothing."

Faced with Kozminski's unceasing and spiraling fraud, we quickly issued a grand jury subpoena for his bank account and soon traced Seidman's money to two certificates of deposit, both in Kozminski's name. Regardless of the pending indictment, we vowed to follow this trail relentlessly, wherever and to whomever it led.

Face to Face

The purpose of bail is to secure a defendant's appearance at trial. After considering several objective factors designed to quantify the risk of a defendant's flight, a judge may release the defendant outright on his or her "own recognizance" or set a bail which can range from the minimal to the very substantial.

In proposing a cash bail of $40,000 for Kozminski, we were keenly aware of our right to examine the source of any posted funds to ensure they were free from taint. This recommendation consequently placed Kozminski in a self-made pincers. How could he, on the one hand, legitimately claim *bankruptcy* and, on the other, produce $40,000 in cash *not* derived from his scam?

The afternoon of Kozminski's arrest, he was brought before the same judicial officer who issued our search warrant six months earlier: Magistrate Joseph Reichmann, a thin, gray-haired, bearded man in his forties, coincidentally of German-Jewish lineage. Pending arraignment the following day, Reichmann promptly set Kozminski's bail at the recommended $40,000, posing the imminent specter of an evening in jail for the newly charged defendant.

Ignoring his court-appointed counsel and the German interpreter standing next to him, Kozminski addressed Magistrate Reichmann directly. "I can't believe it, your honor," a shaken Kozminski pleaded. "I have nothing. You have my passport. Where could I go?" But there was no action Reichmann could or would take, at least until arraignment the following day.

We woke to feature articles on the case in both major Los Angeles newspapers. A headline in the *Los Angeles Herald Examiner* proclaimed, GERMAN IMMIGRANT ACCUSED OF DEFRAUDING HOLOCAUST SURVIVORS. Likewise, a *Los Angeles Times* headline announced, SURVIVOR OF NAZIS ACCUSED OF FRAUD and ran a lengthy article in which Anny Maass, the head of the Los Angeles office of the Restitution Organization, labeled Kozminski "a dark spot on the Jewish people." Since these reports were already generating wider media interest, we knew this case never would be the same. The courtroom would be full, and the bright lights of public scrutiny would glare down on all of us.

As KINZLER and I stepped into Magistrate Reichmann's courtroom, we observed that every seat was taken either by the media or Holocaust survivors (many of whom I recognized) eagerly looking on. Kinzler and I slowly walked to the table at the left front of the courtroom and took our seats.

A sense of electricity and palpable tension flooded the room. Churning with emotion, I felt a jangled sense of anticipation and excitement, trepidation about my impending argument, inspiration from the victims, and anger toward Kozminski. But I strained to retain my composure, aware that I needed to stay focused on the matter at hand. Kinzler, meanwhile, sat expressionless next to me, a silent but welcome fount of support and encouragement.

Moments after our arrival, Kozminski was swiftly escorted into the courtroom in handcuffs and brought to the defense table, where he sat next to his dark-haired wife, Esther, also a Holocaust survivor who had lost an eye and a finger at Auschwitz.

Dressed in standard blue prison garb, Kozminski looked just like the photos in our files: a diminutive, bald mustached man, thick glasses resting on his long thin nose. Still, I had an odd, almost surreal feeling as I finally encountered the target of our lengthy investigation face-to-face.

I am now aware that my "surreal" feeling was more a product of my imagination than anything, representing none other than the timeworn comeuppance of prosecutors in cases featuring unusually serious, if not heinous, crimes. For here stood Kozminski, by all appearances neither a monster nor evil incarnate. He was simply a man, and a Holocaust survivor married to another one at that. Neither physically imposing nor physically impressive, he did not even look untrustworthy. In an odd sort of way, it was almost disappointing.

Glancing in Kozminski's direction as he sat between his counsel and his wife, I tried to get a sense of his demeanor, even his thoughts. But Kozminski seemed unruffled on the surface and merely fixed his gaze straight ahead.

Shortly afterward, the spectators stirred audibly as Magistrate Reichmann took the bench and promptly announced our case.

Moments later the bail hearing commenced.

Rising behind the prosecution table, I renewed our recommendation of a $40,000 cash bond, duly advising the court that the indictment was "merely symbolic" of a broad pattern of fraudulent activity reflecting three thousand victims "in the United States and throughout the world" and receipts of more than $250,000 from victims since 1974 alone, *excluding* virtually thousands in untraceable cash payments. Citing Kozminski's record of six convictions in Germany, his flight to the United States, his resistance to two orders of deportation, and his receipt of a $22,543 restitution payment shortly before filing for bankruptcy, I concluded that the government suspected he retained "substantial resources" overseas and was a "substantial flight risk."

Directing his attention toward Ivan Klein, Kozminski's court-appointed counsel, Magistrate Reichmann pointedly said, "So tell me about this recent restitution payment for $22,000."

After Kozminski hastily pulled Klein aside and whispered into his ear, Klein turned back to the court and explained that the "money had been spent on debts."

Believing that Theodore Seidman's payment was actually in two certificates of deposit in Kozminski's name, I quickly retorted, "What Mr. Kozminski has just stated to the court is a lie."

But I could not elaborate. Laws protecting grand jury secrecy precluded disclosure of our bankruptcy-fraud evidence without court order.

Now launching into his argument, Klein first expressed his hope that "we can step back from the inherent emotional content of the charges and speak to the financial circumstances." Claiming that Kozminski possessed no assets, was legally bankrupt, and enjoyed substantial ties to the community, Klein then contended that he should be released on an "appearance" bond of $15,000, effectively an unsecured promise to return for trial.

Largely persuaded by Klein's argument, Reichmann replied, "Well, the court will accept a $25,000 appearance bond if Mr. Kozminski's wife is willing to sign it."

As if on cue, Esther quickly stepped to the podium and stood next to her husband, but her mind was clearly on matters other than the proposed bond.

Blithely ignoring the Magistrate's suggestion, Esther directed her attention elsewhere, remarking, "You should know, your Honor, my husband had *nothing* to do with this. It's all his *son's* fault . . . from a former marriage."

Her evasive response drew several loud snickers from Holocaust survivors among the spectators. After the courtroom finally quieted, the Magistrate returned to his proposed appearance bond, but Esther would hear nothing of it, abruptly snapping, "I don't have that much money."

Glaring at his wife incredulously, Kozminski demanded, "*Sign it, sign it!*"

Yet Esther remained undeterred. Boldly returning his glare, she wagged her finger and barked, "We've been married fourteen years and *you* won't even buy me a pair of slippers."

Kozminski, nonplussed, simply stared at his wife silently.

Then, after several long moments, Esther's expression suddenly softened and she slowly added, "But I love you very much. I don't know why." Pausing for effect, she concluded, "So I'll take the chance."

With that simple vow, much to our chagrin, Reichmann announced that Kozminski would be released. Several of the victims groaned, and a few hissed as Reichmann called a recess and left the bench. Kinzler and I were left to lick our wounds as the spectators streamed out of the courtroom behind us. Standing in the empty courtroom minutes later, Kinzler and I discussed our options in hushed tones.

We both suspected that the next day Kozminski would be back in his office fleecing Holocaust victims, both old and new. Even worse, we feared that like his flight from Germany fifteen years before, Kozminski now might seek to escape the United States, by hook or by crook. As a result of these concerns, we immediately resolved to appeal Reichmann's order to the federal district court judge on emergency duty, earnestly hoping we would find a more receptive audience.

The bail hearing also left a more subtle impression. After months of hard work and countless hours detailing the travails of many Holocaust victims, this brief courtroom scene seemed almost macabre, like a twisted black comedy. With a backdrop of hundreds of Holocaust survivors in the gallery, set in a powerful moment suffused with emotion, the hearing had largely been reduced to a rather unseemly and trivial squabble between Kozminski and his wife. Yet something about what had transpired gave me the distinct feeling that, in the end, this case would not be about Kozminski and surely would transcend him.

Off the Streets

While we suspected Kozminski lied in claiming he expended the Seidman payment on "debts," we could no longer locate the proceeds: Just one day after our hearing before Magistrate Reichmann, we discovered that Kozminski had cashed his two certificates of deposit and disbursed the money to unknown sources. Yet the disposition of these funds aside, we remained certain that his failure to

admit receipt of the Seidman payment constituted blatant bankruptcy fraud, and we decided we would prompt the duty judge to
reinstate our bail recommendation.

The assigned duty judge was A. Wallace Tashima, a dignified,
good-looking man in his midforties, who had been appointed to the
bench by President Jimmy Carter. Reputed to be a moderate who
imposed tough sentences under appropriate circumstances, Tashima
was a Japanese-American. Old enough to have been incarcerated
during the U.S. government's reprehensible detention of Japanese-
Americans during World War II, he undoubtedly knew something
about discrimination.

On July 1, 1982, Kinzler and I stepped into Judge Tashima's courtroom and headed to the prosecution table, while across the vast room
Lucian Kozminski sat impassively at the defense table next to his
bespectacled counsel, Ivan Klein.

At the appointed hour, Judge Tashima promptly took the bench
and, on cue, I approached the podium in the center of the courtroom.

After the judge granted an order permitting our disclosure of
grand jury evidence, I immediately launched into the government's
bail argument:

On March 1, 1982, by his own admission, one month before he filed that
bankruptcy petition, he received on behalf of a victim of Nazi Germany, one
Theodore Seidman, $22,543.
. . . Mr. Kozminski deposited [the funds] in the Union Bank in an account
in his name; he is the only signatory.
He created two accounts: One account was in his name, $2,000 [in] a
checking account . . . the other $20,000 [was placed] in certificates of deposit
in the name of Lucian Kozminski. . . .
On May 14, 1982, Mr. Kozminski wrote to the victim and said, "We will
settle this matter after bankruptcy proceedings." And only six days later, the
government found out yesterday, Mr. Kozminski cashed those certificates of
deposit, he withdrew them about one month ago. . . .
Well, your Honor, the government submits that Magistrate Reichmann
was not aware and could not be made aware that Mr. Kozminski has, in fact,
committed bankruptcy fraud.
He lied about his assets in the bankruptcy petition. He did not mention
the bank account, did not mention the $22,000, and then he turned around

when this prosecution was imminent, and he withdraws the $20,000, most of which was intended for Theodore Seidman.

I believe that this shows that the defendant is not trustworthy when he says he will return to court. . . . I think he's playing games with the Court. He could use the $20,000 to facilitate exit from this country.

After we had scrupulously refrained from citing evidence of Kozminski's bankruptcy fraud before Magistrate Reichmann, I winced upon hearing the response of Kozminski's lawyer, "Your Honor, there is *nothing new* here. This was presented in *great detail* the day before."

Judge Tashima, however, did not take the bait and grilled the evasive Klein until he finally relented.

Judge Tashima: The bankruptcy petition and schedule of assets were presented to Magistrate Reichmann?

Mr. Klein: I believe it was *discussed* before Magistrate Reichmann. The documentation was not delivered . . . but the $22,000 payment to Mr. Kozminski was discussed.

Judge Tashima: *No.* My question is, first of all, was Magistrate Reichmann actually aware . . .

First of all, do you contest the government's representation that in the petition for bankruptcy certain bank accounts were not listed as assets?

Mr. Klein: Well, I don't know enough now to even contest that, since I haven't had a chance to look through the package that was given to me.

Judge Tashima: Well, *I* will say it then. *I* will characterize it as a fraudulent petition. Was that disclosed to Magistrate Reichmann?

Mr. Klein: Yes.

Judge Tashima: So, in other words, he knew that a fraudulent petition had been filed?

Mr. Klein: Again, the facts presented to Magistrate Reichmann surrounded a bankruptcy petition. There was no . . .

The words *fraudulent petition* were not used, but that was the thrust of the argument.

But I think everything Mr. Kalmansohn has just said, including the convictions in Germany, including his belief—

Judge Tashima: *No.* All I am talking about is the bankruptcy petition.

Mr. Klein: That was talked about at the hearing.

Judge Tashima: Well, talked about is *not* my question. What was he *told?* Was he told that the defendant had bank accounts, substantial sums which were not listed on that schedule of assets?

Mr. Klein: I don't think he was told that.

Judge Tashima: That is the key, I think, to the whole thing.

Finally having secured counsel's reluctant admission, Judge Tashima swiftly concluded the arguments. Promptly granting our motion reinstating a $40,000 cash bond, he remanded Kozminski to the temporary custody of Lou Kinzler, who would produce him to the U.S. Marshals, pending trial.

Moments later, as Kinzler handcuffed to him outside the courtroom, Kozminski glanced at him with just a glint of fear in his eyes and spontaneously muttered, "I told my wife I'm in *real* trouble now."

While that definitely still remained to be seen, at least for now Lucian Ludwig Kozminski was off the streets.

Rounding Out the Cast

The assignment of our trial judge was imminent. Somberly administered by a magistrate, it would be a random selection pulled from a rotating tumbler, a virtual Russian roulette that assistant U.S. attorneys wryly termed "the Wheel." Like contestants in a game show, we anxiously awaited the result.

The evening before selection of our judge, Kinzler and I reviewed the prospective candidates over German beers at a downtown bar.

"You know," I began, "in this case I don't really favor any particular judge, and philosophical bent doesn't seem to matter."

"What do you mean?" Kinzler queried.

"Well," I responded, "a liberal or moderate judge may be a little more pissed at Kozminski for cheating Holocaust victims. On the other hand, conservative 'law and order' judges tend to be tougher sentencers, period."

"Yeah, that's true," Kinzler concurred. "And there are a few liberals *and* conservatives who just don't like to slam *nonviolent* offenders like Kozminski."

"To me," I confided, "what really matters are intelligence and temperament. And judging by that, my preferred list would include three Carter appointees, one Ford appointee, two Nixon appointees, one Johnson appointee, and one Kennedy appointee."

"That's a pretty good spread," Kinzler added.

"It is," I concurred. "And, frankly, I'm only hesitant about three judges. Two because of their testy courtroom manner, especially one who speaks in some sort of fifteenth-century English."

Kinzler remarked, "Oh, you must mean Kell—"

"No names, Lou," I interjected. "Someone may overhear us."

"Oh, you mean, like the bartender?" Kinzler queried playfully.

"No, actually, it's the waitress who's suspicious," I retorted, glancing at our server as she strolled past our booth grasping several bottles of beer. "Anyway, all kidding aside, the last judge . . . well, he's just plain unstable. And when *he* gets mad, he's liable to destroy your case or send counsel to lockup in handcuffs."

"Hmmm," Kinzler ruminated, clinking his bottle with mine, "well, here's to *not* getting one of those three."

The next day—one day before Kozminski's scheduled arraignment—we finally learned the results of the fateful spin of the Wheel. Residing neither at the top nor the bottom of our list, the assigned judge was David J. Kenyon, a recent Reagan appointee who had spent several years in the juvenile justice system.

We were intrigued by Kenyon's budding reputation. Though known to provide defense counsel great latitude in his courtroom, he also was reportedly a tough sentencing judge. Perhaps most important for our purposes, he was characterized as even-tempered, fair, and courteous. In the end, the more we heard about the qualities of this new judge, the more we considered ourselves extremely fortunate.

On July 6, 1982, Kozminski was arraigned before Judge Kenyon, a bespectacled, somewhat jowly, middle-aged man with a quiet demeanor. The judge directly set trial for August 31 and maintained bail as previously set by Judge Tashima.

While the arraignment was otherwise routine, we were surprised

that the "bankrupt" Kozminski was represented *not* by a federal public defender but, rather, by new *retained* counsel: J. Patrick Maginnis.

If there was ever reverse type-casting, Kozminski had achieved it
with his new lawyer. Maginnis was assuredly *not* an understated,
reflective Jewish attorney who could subtly elicit sympathy for the
"besieged" Kozminski. Not Pat Maginnis. Sporting bushy curled hair
and an almost Mephistophelean mustache and beard, with an
upturned bulbous nose and ruddy cheeks, Maginnis looked like the
quintessential Irishman.

At once feisty, formidable, entertaining, sometimes caustic, and
distinctly bombastic, Maginnis would assuredly make "shrill" the
prevailing tone for this defense. While he might prove irksome and
abrasive at times, we were relieved that for the duration of this most
sensitive case, the jury would see Pat Maginnis alongside Lucian
Ludwig Kozminski.

Our scheduled courtroom duel notwithstanding, Maginnis's path
would cross mine far sooner than could have been anticipated and
under circumstances unforeseen by either of us.

Two Birds With One Stone

Although the case was set for trial, our investigation continued. By
tracing Kozminski's cashed certificates of deposit, we hoped to sal-
vage funds for Theodore Seidman, as well as complete evidence-
gathering on proposed bankruptcy-fraud charges. We had already
confirmed that Kozminski's bankruptcy petition was virtually satu-
rated with falsehoods.

Hidden in a corner booth in a restaurant in downtown's Little
Tokyo district, Kinzler and I carefully reviewed the petition again
before making the final decision to seek a second indictment. Pointing to the document, Kinzler remarked, "Look, right after calling
himself a 'reparations counselor' from 1962 to the present, the Weasel
lists two 'personal' bank accounts but there's *no* mention of the Union
Bank account where he stashed Seidman's restitution payment."

"Yeah," I replied. "I remember that well. Plus he doesn't report any monies held in trust for Seidman or anyone else under 'Property Held for Another Person.'"

"And look here," Kinzler continued. "Remember this? The guy reports *no income* from his restitution business stating, 'None—lost money.' Incredible!"

"That's not all," I added. "He also lists just $50 'cash on hand,' $200 in 'deposits,' and total assets of just $8,700. What a shyster—"

"*Shyster's* the word," Kinzler interjected, pulling a document out of his pocket. "So get this. It turns out he just submitted a sworn affidavit to federal court. You know, after his arrest? Well, guess what *I've* got."

Glancing at the document in his hands, Kinzler continued: "And guess what it says. That he gets 'self-employment income' of *$2,000 monthly* and has '*total debts*' of only $440 a month!"

"Geez," I remarked. "So now, only *three months* after his bankruptcy petition, he's got steady income and minimal debts? Looks like we've *really* got him—"

"We've got him coming and going," Kinzler remarked, munching on a piece of sushi. "This Weasel's a dead duck."

In the end, these shenanigans were entirely predictable considering the gross fraud permeating Kozminski's recent federal tax returns. In 1978, for example, he claimed a business *loss* of $7,702, and requested a *refund* of $4,217. In 1979, he reported another business loss of $2,663 and also requested a refund. Again seeking a refund in 1980, he claimed a business loss of $2,277, based on purported "claim counseling" receipts of just $8,470 and expenses totaling $10,477.

As WE FINALLY prepared to present a bankruptcy-fraud indictment to the grand jury, one last startling piece of evidence materialized. Through our continuous tracing of the Seidman payment, we finally determined that $15,136.26 from a certificate of deposit cashed by Kozminski had ended up in the account of none other than J. Patrick Maginnis. Stunned by this development, I vowed to deal with Maginnis once we had secured the second indictment.

The presentation of the bankruptcy fraud indictment was relatively simple. After citing evidence of Kozminski's failure to disclose a $20,000 Union Bank certificate of deposit in his own name, we proposed that he be charged with one count of committing a false oath in bankruptcy and one count of concealment of assets in bankruptcy. After a brief session, a visibly incensed grand jury formally returned the indictment on July 25, 1982, about one month prior to the scheduled trial.

A few days before Judge Kenyon arraigned Kozminski on the second indictment, I placed a call to Pat Maginnis. Dispensing with formalities, I abruptly advised him that we had traced a Holocaust survivor's restitution payment through Kozminski's bank account and into his own.

Apparently stunned by this revelation and uncharacteristically silent, Maginnis finally stammered, "I . . . I'm holding those funds for Ludwig [Kozminski] in trust."

But I had no patience for this explanation and quickly responded, "I will provide you with positive proof that this money is Ted Seidman's. Then if you still don't want to hand it over, you can explain your story to the grand jury."

Maginnis was aware this was no idle threat. I meant it. I did not ordinarily target defense counsel and he knew it. Again there was a long pause. Finally, Maginnis slowly responded, "OK, OK. We don't have to go through all *that*. I'll have a check for you at Ludwig's arraignment."

True to his word, Maginnis brought a check to court, but in a classic demonstration of chutzpah had deducted an additional 15 percent for Kozminski's "counseling fee." While incensed at the defense team, we were not about to refuse a $12,866 payment to Theodore Seidman for his wartime injuries and incarceration and, as a result, took what we could and resolved to obtain the rest later.

The Snowball Effect

Until Kozminski's first indictment, Lou Kinzler and I slogged away in the trenches building our case in virtual anonymity, at times feeling like we were tilting at windmills. But all that had changed.

The case seemed to eclipse Kinzler and me, and it was developing such momentum we feared it might veer out of control. Headlines on our prosecution splashed across front pages of Los Angeles's three major daily newspapers, and articles appeared in the *New York Times*, the *Wall Street Journal*, the *Jerusalem Post*, and other publications in the United States, Germany, and elsewhere. The case was a lead or featured story on several local television broadcasts, and Kinzler and I both were interviewed extensively.

During this media blitz, we remained mindful of several restrictions, self-imposed and otherwise. Paying special heed to the Justice Department's guidelines on pre-trial public comments by prosecutors, we sought to avoid any claim that reference to matters outside the record influenced the potential jury pool. As a result, we carefully tailored our public statements by refraining from characterizing Kozminski beyond existing charges, while purposefully diverting attention toward the victims' suffering and courage. This was no time to jeopardize our long and difficult effort.

Nonetheless, the sheer volume of publicity spurred the case's rapid growth. Now that the cat was out of the bag, further evidence of Kozminski's fraud emerged daily. Complaints from around the world inundated us, as Kinzler alone handled seventy-five to one hundred calls from new victims in less than two months.

Several victims regularly took the bus to the U.S. Attorney's Office and, upon arriving, sat patiently in the lobby waiting to meet with me. Some just wanted to offer heartfelt thanks or deliver homemade strudel and other sweets, while others presented fresh stories of woe perpetrated by Kozminski. I tried to meet with all of them and eventually enlisted several new witnesses to Kozminski's fraudulent scheme.

Among the most memorable were Molly and Henry Schimel, a diminutive, amiable couple in their late fifties. Upon entering my office with her husband, Molly smiled broadly as she presented me with a tin of freshly baked cookies. Graciously accepting her gift, I sat behind my desk facing Molly and Henry, with Kinzler sitting to the side. A gray-haired woman with a partially disfigured face, Molly was a virtual ball of energy. Thrilled that someone was finally interested in her story, she chuckled almost giddily and bantered with us for several minutes before finally calming down and launching into her story.

IN EARLY September 1939, shortly after Molly's fourteenth birthday, she and her family vacationed at a resort in Plosk, Poland, twenty-five miles from their home in Zamosc. One day, while sunning herself outside, Molly heard the ominous roar of engines overhead and glanced up as several *Luftwaffe* planes swooped down upon her.

Bombs soon exploded everywhere, blowing up an adjacent school and train station, and searing shrapnel flew through the air "like leaves from a tree." Trapped in this hellish vision, Molly suddenly felt intense pain as shrapnel sliced deeply into her body, breaking three bones in her jaw and six of her ribs.

Molly collapsed to the ground and writhed in agony, as her family rushed to her side. Unable to speak, still dripping blood and in shock, hours later she was brought to a nearby tent hospital. There she was treated not with emergency surgery or painkillers, but with primitive bandages barely covering her wounds.

Yet Molly's wartime ordeal had just begun, for another party to the infamous Nazi-Soviet Pact of August 1939 was poised to rear its own ravenous head.

Only sixteen days after Germany's pulverizing onslaught of western Poland, hordes of Soviet forces launched their coordinated attack on the east, seizing a 120,000-square-mile area and completing the wholesale dismemberment of the Polish nation. Soon engulfing Zamosc and its environs, occupying Soviet troops promptly rounded up Molly, her parents, her younger sister, and other residents and shipped them on an old freight train to Siberia.

For the next thirty-five days, the train slowly made the exhausting eighteen-hundred mile trek. After five more days on a boat, Molly and her family finally arrived in the forests of Siberia, where they lived in log cabins for almost five years, amid a diverse group of former Polish residents including Ukrainians, Polish gentry, Swedes, Koreans, and Japanese.

While most Polish Jews and foreigners warmly welcomed the Soviets' smothering embrace and would be shielded from the Nazis' unexpected assault on the Soviet Union two years later, the Russians had forcibly resettled them for a less than altruistic purpose: to protect *themselves* from "bourgeoisie" elements undermining their war effort.

Though most of the resettled populus would manage to survive on a subsistence diet, with no medical attention or amenities, some would not. Uprooted from his home, community, and occupation, Molly's father died as a captive in those far-flung Siberian forests during 1942, a victim of an otherwise treatable illness. Even worse than the shrapnel from the *Luftwaffe*'s bombs, the premature death of Molly's father caused searing pain and a wound that would never quite heal.

Later transported to Tashkent in Middle Asia, Molly, her mother, and her sister resided there until one year after the War ended, when they were belatedly shipped on a freight train back to Poland. However, rather than return to their native Zamosc, where "fellow" Poles had confiscated their family's property and dreaded return of any Jews, Molly and her sister chose to reside in several communal Jewish *kibbutzim,* barely eking out a precarious daily existence.

After their mother finally returned from a lengthy trip to settle the family's outstanding affairs, the girls moved with her to a town near Munich and, later, Stuttgart. Two years afterward, Molly emigrated to Vancouver and resided there until ultimately settling in Los Angeles.

While Molly, her younger sister, and her parents suffered during the War, the rest of their family fared no better. Sarah, Molly's elder sister and a licensed medical doctor, fled to the Ukraine with her husband, their small child, her husband's parents, and several neighbors and friends. They there lived a fearful existence ensconced in a bunker for several years, even as the sea of blood unleashed by Germany's savage invasion of the Soviet Union engulfed the terrain surrounding them.

But sometime in 1942, apparently after hearing that Jews were hiding in the vicinity, a Nazi motorcycle unit approached the bunker and tossed several grenades inside. The ensuing explosions rocked the area and instantly extinguished the lives and dreams of all the bunker's occupants. The remainder of Molly's family met a similar fate, as her many uncles, aunts, cousins, nephews, and nieces were all incarcerated and then systematically murdered at the Auschwitz and Treblinka extermination camps.

AFTER RECOUNTING this poignant saga, Molly exhaled as if her
lungs were still seared with grief. Smiling nervously, she asked
almost playfully, "And *now* do you want to hear about Mr. Kozminski?"

For a moment there was only silence, as Kinzler and I both tried
to absorb the long trail of pain and death she had recited. Though
still at a loss for words, I slowly nodded my assent, and she began
again, "Well, I first met Kozminski at his office, I think it was 1969.
After listening to my story, he said he would file several claims for
me. But he said I had to pay him $150 for 'registration and handling.'
I just didn't have the money, so I gave him $50 cash I borrowed from
a friend. He wasn't very happy but he took it.

"Believe it or not," Molly continued, "for *twelve years* I got nothing. Absolutely nothing. When I called him or went to his office, he
usually yelled at me, saying things like, 'Stop bothering me!' Or
'You're interfering with my business!'"

Molly paused in reflection and then went on, "Well, everything
changed in, I think it was December 1981. He called me up and said,
'Come over to my office right away. I've got a surprise for you.' So I
went there quickly, in about a half hour.

"When I got there, Kozminski said, 'In just one month you're
going to get a bundle of money, $25,000, and a monthly pension of
$250 to $500. All I need is $50 cash for forwarding by registered
mail.' Well, I just didn't have it, but I offered him $25. And he got
mad. He said, 'I work so hard for you and you can't pay me?' He
screamed at me for several minutes, but, finally, he took the money
and stuffed it into his pocket. But when I asked for a receipt, he said,
'No. I'm sorry. I don't want to pay income tax.'"

Molly's expression dropped as she slowly added, "Each time I
would call him after that he told me he's in a hurry and said the
money would come soon. But I never got anything. Not a penny."

As Molly finished her story, she looked at me with earnest, almost
pleading eyes. Then, after a long pause, she added, "Even if you can't
get me my money, I hope you can get *him*."

I responded that we would, knowing that I was personally committed to this objective, far beyond my professional duties.

Then there was George Chybinski, a survivor of Auschwitz and other camps who sought restitution for his confinement and permanent damage to his health and body. A thick-haired, heavyset man in his fifties with a large round face, Chybinski recited his harrowing story with beaming eyes and exuding a sense of vindication.

Toward the end, he remarked, "I'm afraid to say that I paid Kozminski over $2,500 in cash. For all sorts of expenses like court fees, medical exams, secretaries, translators, postage, telephones, you name it. Each time he promised me that my restitution was about to arrive. Of course, it never came."

A few days after these meetings, I arrived home and turned on the evening news. Much to my surprise, there were the vibrant Molly Schimel and amiable George Chybinski, both being interviewed in a feature story about Kozminski. For some reason, this singular moment, perhaps more than any other, seemed to crystallize the new public magnitude reached by our case.

All the while, the victims who had worked with us for months evolved before our very eyes. As we continued our second, third, and fourth round of pre-trial interviews, many seemed to possess a new confidence and renewed faith, keenly aware that society was interested in their plight and that the system was actually fighting *for* their rights, rather than trying to suppress them.

Threat of Suppression

Just two weeks before trial, the defense belatedly filed a motion that directly challenged our search of Kozminski's offices, jeopardized nearly all our evidence, and threatened to shrink our case like the head of a witch doctor's victim, leaving us to reassemble and recompose the truncated remains on the very eve of battle.

As we anticipated when we prepared the search warrant, Maginnis did not claim we lacked probable cause to search Kozminski's offices or attack the scope of the actual search. Applying a scalpel rather than a sledgehammer, he instead argued that the search warrant *itself* "was not particularized . . . enough" and should have been restricted to records relating to complainants then known to the government.

"What does this mean?" Kinzler anxiously queried in a meeting in my office.

"Well," I responded, "it's the old good news and bad news. The good news is that since Maginnis doesn't challenge their affidavits directly, Stefan Mandel and Hans Wittner won't have to testify at the hearing."

"All right," Kinzler muttered, only slightly mollified. "What's the bad news?"

"Yeah, I was afraid you'd ask me that. The bad news is that if the motion's granted, all evidence gathered in our search is deemed inadmissible. That means we lose all our victim files and any tainted evidence derived from seized materials, like the testimony and documents we secured in Germany."

"Christ!" Kinzler exclaimed. "We'd be left with practically nothing."

"You said it," I soberly remarked.

Maginnis was presumably aware that using a small but firm wedge, we had gotten our foot in the door to expose Kozminski's much wider fraudulent scheme. In seeking to slam this door tightly shut, he threatened to throw our case into complete and irreversible disarray. As Maginnis blithely remarked on the phone to me shortly after filing his motion, "This is the beginning of the *end* of your case."

I knew full well that his threat was very real and ominous. For the simple fact remained that most of our hard work could be ruined in the single stroke of a pen.

Cause in the Balance

While some people seem to carry the weight of the world upon their shoulders, I have always found life's ordinary stresses and traumas more than sufficient. But now the pressure clearly was on. We knew we could not let this defense challenge impale the heart of our case, raise the palpable prospect of Kozminski getting off, and crush the hopes of the victims.

With trial looming large, our opposition to the defense's motion to suppress was due in just one week. As my days were consumed preparing witnesses, organizing exhibits, and coordinating trial logistics, by necessity I was relegated to burning the midnight oil trying to stave off Maginnis's challenge. Forged amid this crucible of evaporating time and mounting tension, our lengthy opposition to the defense motion cited forty-two legal opinions and incorporated a detailed affidavit from Lou Kinzler as well as a host of exhibits.

Maginnis had primarily claimed that the *scope* of the warrant was impermissibly "overbroad" and should have been restricted to the files of our two named complainants, or at most the hundred complainants then known to the government. We vigorously disagreed, asserting that the breadth of the warrant was perfectly consistent with the magistrate's finding that Kozminski's entire business was permeated with fraud.

Accordingly, we directed the Court to *United States v. Brien*, in which the defendant claimed a search warrant for his offices should have been restricted to files of 250 known, pre-existing complainants. In categorically rejecting the defense argument and upholding the warrant, the *Brien* court pointedly noted that:

> [The] mail fraud . . . statute focuse[s] on the scheme, *not* the implementation of it. The 250 complaints were relevant to the probability that *other* [of the defendants'] customers were treated similarly, *as well as* to whether actual fraud was committed upon the complainants. [emphasis added]

Based on this compelling authority, we asserted that Maginnis's virtually identical challenge should be rejected.

On August 26, just five days before the scheduled trial date, the hearing on the defense motion commenced.

Judge Kenyon sat sphinxlike on the bench, facing Kozminski and his interpreter at the defense table and Lou Kinzler and me at the prosecution table. Pat Maginnis, meanwhile, stood at the podium in the center of the cavernous courtroom.

For several minutes Maginnis railed against the government's motives in the case, minimized the significance of our prosecution, challenged the breadth of the search warrant, and argued vociferously in favor of the motion to suppress. All the while, a silent Judge Kenyon listened patiently, waiting for Maginnis to finish.

As Maginnis argued, I anxiously fixed my gaze upon Judge Kenyon, searching for any sign of reassurance that our case would not be destroyed. But I could glean nothing from his stone-faced expression, not a raised eyebrow, a furrowed brow, or even a darting glance of disapproval.

When Maginnis finally completed his blustery argument, I stood to reply but uttered nothing as Judge Kenyon slowly nodded at me, remarking, "Mr. Kalmansohn, I don't believe I need to hear your argument."

For a moment I stood stunned and had a fleeting, nightmarish vision that the judge believed our papers were so defective no amount of argument could save us. But as I slowly sat, reality firmly took hold: We were about to prevail, for if the judge retained even the slightest doubt he would have been required to hear my argument.

And then Judge Kenyon began. Remarking that the government's opposition was thorough and persuasive, he announced that based on the authorities and evidence we cited, he had concluded the search warrant was clearly *not* overbroad.

Peering at a stack of papers before him, the Judge then read directly from portions of our opposition and, pausing slightly, quietly stated, "The defense motion is denied."

Judge Kenyon's eyes briefly locked with mine, and then he stood at the bench, turned, and was gone. Sitting alone at the prosecution table, Kinzler and I looked at each other silently. We did not have to say a word, for undisguised relief was etched into both of our faces. The good news could not be minimized: Maginnis had shot a major wad of ammunition and lost. *All* our hard-earned evidence would be preserved for trial.

The Avenging Angel

In the throes of trial preparation, one evening we turned to an all-too-familiar topic: Kozminski's likely defense. As Kinzler remarked,

"You know, I still think 'Koz's' *best* chance would have been to plead insanity. But Maginnis didn't give you notice of that defense, huh?"

"No," I replied. "So he *can't* raise it. Looks like Koz may have been a little too stubborn . . . or prideful to claim he's crazy."

"All right," Kinzler remarked. "So you know what's left? The little Weasel's gonna get tears in his beady little eyes and say, 'I'm a devout Jew. You know, I used to be president of some such Jewish federation in Germany—'"

"'And, don't forget, I'm a Holocaust survivor, too,'" I added.

"Yeah," Kinzler concurred. "So then he says, 'My files, they're such a mess. You know, it's what the Nazis did to me. And sometimes I get a little drunk and don't know what I'm doing. But, *mein Gott*, I would *never, ever*, take this blood money from *mein* own people. *Heaven forbid* I would do such a terrible thing!'"

Chuckling at Kinzler's humorous but eerie impression, I remarked, "I'm glad *he's* gonna testify and not you. You're too damn good."

Pausing briefly, I went on, "So here's what we're gonna do. If *anyone* can find something about his background that can refute this defense, it's the Israelis—"

"That's true," Kinzler interjected. "What do they have, 300,000 Holocaust survivors? *And* the best intelligence network in the world?"

"That's right," I replied. "Look, it's a real long shot . . . but what the hell?"

Responding to our request, the Justice Department promptly placed me into contact with Menahem Russek, a lieutenant colonel in Israel's National Unit of Criminal Investigations, charged with gathering evidence of war crimes committed by former Nazis and their collaborators. Russek and I spoke several times over the telephone, about Kozminski and other matters more personal and profound.

His voice often quivering, Russek finally recounted his own saga, which, curiously, intersected with Kozminski's experience at several notable junctures.

Like Kozminski, Russek hailed from Lodz, Poland. Swept up by the Nazis during the War, while barely twenty years of age, he was interned in the Auschwitz death camp, where both of his beloved parents perished, and was later transported to several other concentration camps, including Hirschberg, a subcamp of Gross-Rosen (where Kozminski was interned). Still too "painful and personal" to reveal, the horrid details of this experience remain the exclusive province of Russek's private memories.

Upon being liberated in the Silesia region of Poland, Russek headed away from the Russian occupation zone and, after a lengthy trek on foot, finally entered a refugee camp near Frankfurt. He soon dismissed the prospect of returning to his native Poland, where he heard that Holocaust survivors typically received the snide greeting, "What? *You're* still alive?" and remained instead for the next three years in Germany. There he met and became betrothed to Rose, a Holocaust survivor and fellow student at the University of Frankfurt.

At the end of 1948, both sensing that the time had come to seek the Promised Land, Russek and Rose departed on a circuitous "illegal" journey to the new nation of Israel, stopping long enough in France to be married. Once the couple arrived at their destination, Russek spent the next forty-one years on the trail of justice, relentlessly hunting down former Nazis and their accomplices.

Aside from Martin Bormann and other leading Nazis, one special target eluded Russek and the Israelis: Josef Mengele, the notorious "Angel of Death" of Auschwitz, the memory of whom was seared into the minds of Russek, many of the victims in our case, and presumably Kozminski himself.

A medical doctor until his license was revoked years after the War, Mengele, together with his cohorts in the German medical and scientific community, formed the soulless, sterile foundation for the Nazi plan of extermination.

Having devised and propagated charlatan theories of Aryan genetic superiority long before the War, they soon instituted a "euthanasia" program featuring the murder through gassing or lethal injection of more than 70,000 "handicapped" and "retarded" Germans, many of them infants with birth defects, and upon Himmler's order later extended the pool of prospective "patients" to include healthy Jews, Communists, and dissidents. This expanded "medical" application coincided with the invention of the death camp itself, where prominently placed Nazi doctors oversaw the haphazard "selection" process and later recorded inmates' "official" causes of death, thereby providing SS killers with "plausible deniability" for mass genocide.

Having renounced their Hippocratic oath to save and preserve human life, these wanton butchers armed with scalpels, forceps, and needles concocted a host of ghastly "medical and scientific experiments." The most conspicuous were conducted by Josef Mengele, who injected methylene blue into Jewish inmates' eyes in a futile and sadistic effort to make them appear more "Aryan," sterilized young Jewish girls with injections of liquid cement into the uterus, castrated males through incision or X-rays, injected "freezing" drugs into live subjects, drew massive quantities of blood along with other perverse procedures on Jewish twins and dwarfs, and killed inmates spontaneously with injections of phenol, benzene, hydrogen peroxide, chloroform, cyanide, and air. Through all this clinical savagery, torture, and mayhem, only Mengele's dark "dead eyes" belied his seemingly elegant, cultured, and handsome facade.

Over the years, from reports of Mengele's mysterious postwar release by the American army to his relocation in Paraguay, Argentina, and Brazil, Russek exhaustively followed every lead and rigorously scrutinized each scrap of evidence. Finally, despite belated claims of Mengele's family and subsequent scientific "confirmation," he wrote a definitive report questioning whether Mengele actually drowned in Brazil in 1979. The doubts raised by his own evidence continued to plague Russek, as the prospect that the reclusive Mengele still might be alive haunted him like a recurring nightmare.

TURNING FROM THE prolonged hunt for a war criminal to a man who had cheated victims out of restitution for their wartime losses, Russek confidently vowed, "I am sure we will find some very useful information about Kozminski."

Kinzler and I, however, remained less optimistic. While we placed great faith in the abilities of Russek and the Israelis, we seriously doubted they could penetrate the dusty and buried remains of the distant past. As a result, we returned to the challenge of trial preparation knowing that, at the least, we had left no stone unturned.

The Righteous and the Wicked

Shortly before trial, Menahem Russek unexpectedly called me from Israel and, much to our surprise, advised me that he had located a missing key to Kozminski's past within the memory of a Tel Aviv resident named Shlomo Blajman. When I implored him to divulge this new evidence, Russek responded, "OK, but you must hear the entire story." And then he began, in a deliberate and suspenseful tone.

A native of Lodz, Poland, Blajman reportedly lived with his parents before the War at 104 Limanovskego Street, near an ancient Jewish cemetery and just down the road from a barber shop owned by Kozminski's uncle. Lucian "Lutek" Kozminski was a familiar face in the neighborhood, and Blajman vividly recalled one incident where a teenage Lutek brazenly stole milk from a local shop for pocket change.

A teeming, bustling, and charming metropolis with ancient cobbled streets and cable cars, Lodz and its residents would soon have a cruel date with destiny. In August 1939, one month before the German invasion of Poland started World War II, Blajman was drafted into the Polish army. During their ensuing rout of Polish forces the Germans captured him as a prisoner of war and, unaware of his Jewish heritage, released him several years later. Blajman promptly returned to his hometown of Lodz, but upon arriving discovered that everything had changed.

On October 18, 1939, just two months after Blajman was inducted into the Polish army, the Nazis had committed their first act of mass murder in Lodz, as SS men drove over and crushed one hundred Jews at the Astoria Cafe. One month later, on November 11, 1939, they celebrated the first anniversary of Germany's anti-Jewish *Kristallnacht* riot (literally "Night of Glass") by burning down all of Lodz's synagogues.

By this time, all Jews were ordered to wear a Star of David armband, prohibited from using public transport or attending religious services, compelled to relinquish their bank accounts and businesses, and stripped of their professions and employment. Yet this was merely an interim stage in a developing blueprint for genocide.

In April 1940, the Nazis methodically engineered their next fateful step, forcing all of Lodz's Jews into a one-and-one-half-square-mile ghetto surrounded by barbed-wire fences and guarded by heavily armed SS patrols.

With food and fuel supplies purposefully constricted by its Nazi overlords, and virtually bereft of running water or a sewer system, the ghetto was soon plagued by starvation, disease, and a burgeoning death rate that would quadruple within three years. By 1942, the Nazis had confined 200,000 Jews into the cramped, sealed-off ghetto area and deported another 75,000 to nearby Chelmno, where they were asphyxiated in specially designed mobile gas vans.

For the next two years, the Germans let the ghetto languish while 20 percent of its residents died just from harsh living conditions. As Zelig Kalmanovich of the Vilna ghetto wrote, the worst prison could not compare to ghettos where Jews were "incarcerated though innocent of any crime."

During this period, the ghetto became a grueling forced-labor factory with 80,000 Jews accounting for 95 percent of armaments production and 67 percent of textile production in the entire region. Acknowledging its role as a major, lucrative war producer, the German army endeavored to maintain the ghetto's forced-labor status. But ultimately even that subhuman indignity would not suffice. In June 1944, the SS overrode the army's objection as Himmler ordered mass deportations of Jews to work camps in Germany and the extermination camps at Chelmno and Auschwitz-Birkenau. Two months later, the ghetto was entirely free of Jews.

Incarcerated in the ghetto upon his return, Blajman was caught up in its forced liquidation and shipped with his family 125 miles due south, directly to the gates of Auschwitz. Like the other notorious Nazi death camps, Auschwitz graphically embodied the new policy formulated by Nazi leaders at their Wansee Conference in January 1942. By that time, nearly one million Jews had already been savagely butchered by Nazi *Einsatzgruppen*, German Order Police Battalions, and their accomplices, largely coinciding with Germany's massive invasion of the Soviet Union in June 1941, code-named Operation Barbarossa. But concerned by reports that the killers themselves had become "neurotics or savages" and effectively were "finished for the rest of their lives," the Nazi High Command now instituted a more impersonal, sterile method for achieving mass murder: gas chambers and crematoriums housed in large, isolated death camps. Built with characteristic Nazi efficiency, virtually all of these killing centers would be operational within one year. The largest and most murderous was Auschwitz.

As many as 12,000 Jews were gassed daily at that infamous death mill, prompting even the camp commandant, SS lieutenant colonel Rudolf Franz Höss, to complain about undue strain upon the camp's forty-six crematorium ovens. Eventually forced to improvise, the ever inventive SS poured pails of scalding human fat into makeshift trenches to burn the surplus bodies.

In order to achieve this deadly capacity, the SS implemented several notable "improvements" over the Treblinka extermination camp. Faster-acting Zyklon B gas was substituted for carbon monoxide, gas chambers were expanded to accommodate more than two thousand people at a time, and crematorium ovens were conveniently situated in the same building.

The most treacherous innovation, however, was carefully designed to avert the frequent uprisings on death's threshold that plagued Treblinka's operation. Grafting a smarmy mask of deception onto the bony face of death itself, the SS cynically disguised Auschwitz's chambers of no return as pleasing and enticing facilities for sanitation. Outside the brick structures adorned with windows and curtains, signs reading *baths* were posted next to a green lawn, white picket fences, and flowers. Young girls in blue-and-white dresses played operatic music as prisoners were ushered inside for "delousing." Within the sterile concrete chambers, several rows of showerheads hung from the low ceiling.

But no drains existed and no water sprinkled down upon the huddled inmates. Rather, a blue poisonous gas wafted down from ceiling vents, prompting terrified prisoners to storm the locked metal door in sheer panic.

In fifteen minutes they all were dead, a bluish, blood-splattered mass.

A short while later, after sucking the deadly gas out of the chambers below, the SS sent in prisoners (*Sonderkommandos*) to extract gold, teeth, and hair and to remove the twisted corpses for incineration. This was the only means of departure, for as camp commandant Höss would boast, "In all the years, I know of not a single case where anyone came out of the chambers alive."

In addition to the death camp at Auschwitz II, or Auschwitz-Birkenau, two other related camps also existed. Though Auschwitz I was largely a penal camp, Nazi doctors there regularly performed sadistic pseudoscientific experiments on infants, pregnant women, twins, and dwarfs, and thousands were executed in gas chambers and at the infamous "Black Wall." Auschwitz III, on the other hand, was a grueling, "work to the death" labor camp subsidized by I. G. Farben, Erdöl Raffinerie, the German Armaments Works, and other complicit elements of German industry.

When Jews arrived at Auschwitz in cattle cars, the young Josef Mengele often greeted them by pointing in one direction or the other, thereby deciding their fate. The elderly, infirm, pregnant, and children were invariably designated for immediate extermination. For most of the others, death's embrace was slower. Though Nazi doctors uniformly falsified inmates' death certificates by citing "natural causes," Auschwitz was an undisguised killing enterprise featuring mass gassings, cremation, bullets, torture, electrified fences, rampant starvation, and deadly disease.

Unlike the rest of his family and nearly two million others, Blajman managed to survive. With the dismantling of Auschwitz and the end of the War nearing, he and other prisoners were marched to the Flossenbürg concentration camp and, shortly afterward, to the last stop on Blajman's perilous journey: Gross-Rosen, a system of sixty subcamps in eastern Germany, where a third of the 120,000 prisoners had been worked to death in a nearby granite quarry and armaments production.

It was spring of 1945. The air was thick with death though tinged with an odd, faint scent of rebirth. Disease was rampant. Prisoners were haggard and exhausted, and the camp had been without bread for several days. But signs of Germany's impending defeat also abounded.

One day during this peculiar period, Blajman saw a black car drive through the misty haze and park near the camp's kitchen. Out

stepped a well-dressed, apparently well-fed Lucian "Lutek" Kozminski, who directed several people carrying large quantities of
bread from the car to the kitchen.

Turning toward Blajman in recognition, Kozminski nonchalantly
approached and remarked in Polish, "Hey, don't you remember me?
It's Lutek."

But Blajman, taken aback, could only nod stiffly in response before
Kozminski quickly turned and walked toward the kitchen.

For Blajman had been instantly aware that Lutek Kozminski was
no common inmate. Unlike emaciated camp prisoners clad in striped
prison clothing who went barefoot or wore ragged shoes, Kozminski
had worn a thick wool sweater and black boots. Even more extraordinary, he had sported a black armband with bold white lettering
conspicuously reading OBERKAPO.

Soon after this brief but memorable encounter, the SS abandoned
the Gross-Rosen camp, leaving it to be liberated by Allied troops.
Blajman did not see Kozminski again during this tumultuous period,
but he would never forget the chilling vision of his OBERKAPO armband.

THE TERM *oberkapo* had a distinct and chilling meaning for camp
prisoners. Based on his direct observation at Auschwitz, Flossenbürg,
and Gross-Rosen, Blajman reported that at the SS's behest, *oberkapos*
supervised a cadre of *kapos* who administered frequent beatings,
guarded prisoners, sent youth to forced labor, and otherwise followed
SS orders. As evidence of their exalted status, Blajman advised that
during his incarceration at Gross-Rosen he observed just eight to ten
oberkapos. Other than Kozminski, only one was a Jew.

Historical accounts confirm Blajman's graphic portrayal of *oberkapos* and *kapos*. As Leni Jahil reported in *The Holocaust:*

[K]apos . . . and . . . other figures of authority—such as the people
responsible for the *kitchens* . . . wielded great power. . . . They were
present 24 hours a day and unabashedly exploited the authority placed
in their hands. . . . In the course of time, the number of these petty
despots grew in all the camps, reaching into the thousands—including
also Jews. . . . The relish with which these supervisor-prisoners persecuted, harassed, and tormented their comrades was incredible.

In the end, there was no doubt: Russek's evidence was a bombshell. Although Blajman had not witnessed any specific "bad acts" by Kozminski, the *oberkapo* role alone showed undeniable complicity with the SS, flatly contradicting Kozminski's likely claim that he never intentionally cheated his own people, particularly Holocaust victims. If used on Kozminski's cross-examination or in rebuttal (after presentation of the defense case), this evidence would undoubtedly have a profound impact.

Meanwhile, Russek's enthusiastic tone grew somber as he reported, "While I'm very glad we were able to discover something . . . useful, I must advise you that Mr. Blajman may not be able to come to your trial. Don't get me wrong. He is very eager to testify, but he suffers from a heart condition and may be unable to travel, at least without proper precautions."

Concerned about Blajman's condition and aware of his importance to our case, I responded, "I can assure you, Menahem, that we will spare no effort. We'll get a full-time paramedic, arrange for the most comfortable and convenient accommodations, and do everything possible to safeguard his health. But if that's not enough, you must tell me. Because I certainly don't want to jeopardize his life."

Russek quietly replied, "Well, that's very kind of you. I . . . I'll talk to Mr. Blajman and . . . we'll just have to see. I can't promise you anything."

And so the story nearly came full circle. Russek, a native of Lodz, tracked down Blajman, a native of Lodz, to testify against Kozminski, a native of Lodz. In several ways, all three had lived parallel lives. But one diverged drastically from the others. He had turned against his people, and done it again and again. Now his own past threatened to be his final undoing.

IN THE MEANTIME, I received a call from Rabbi Abraham Cooper of the Simon Wiesenthal Center in Los Angeles, who reported that a most unusual and distinguished person wanted to meet with me.

The next day, I was ushered into a hotel room where in the center sat a dignified, gray-haired older man. It was none other than Simon Wiesenthal, the venerated, world-famous Nazi hunter, who had heard about our case from Rabbi Cooper. I was awed to be in his presence.

Perhaps sensing my anxiety, Wiesenthal greeted me warmly, and we exchanged small pleasantries before he slowly steered our conversation to the past. Graphically describing his internment in several concentration camps, including Auschwitz, he told me about the loss of his entire family to the Holocaust and his later resolve to spend the rest of his life hunting Nazis and their collaborators.

Wiesenthal's bluish-green eyes suddenly shone with a transcendent quality, virtually beaming with the spirit of life.

Now referring to the boxcars on trains transporting Jews on the long journey to Auschwitz, he recounted, "I remember how I stood absolutely immobile, unable to move, in a huddle of frozen bodies under an open roof. I only survived by catching falling snowflakes on my tongue."

Pausing, he added, "It may not sound like much, but it was the difference between life and death."

For a moment his eyes grew distant, and then ever so slowly fixed on me. He then quietly remarked, "I naturally am very interested in your case and its . . . ramifications. So I would like to volunteer to testify, if you choose to use me, as an expert witness on activities of *oberkapos* in the camps. I think you'll find I know a great deal based on . . . personal experience."

Deeply flattered by this unexpected offer, I immediately accepted, knowing that in the unique Jewish universe of the Holocaust, Wiesenthal would represent a shining light in distinct contrast to the murky cloud now enveloping Lucian Ludwig Kozminski.

Eve of the Duel

As I drove to work one day listening to KCRW's *Morning Becomes Eclectic*, a potpourri of international music, the announcer suddenly ended my brief respite by declaring, "An odd and unusual case involving a Holocaust survivor accused of cheating thousands of other survivors begins in federal court next week."

This moment clearly signified that the walls were inexorably clos-

Sarah Wittner holding a photograph of the late Hans Wittner

Theodore Seidman

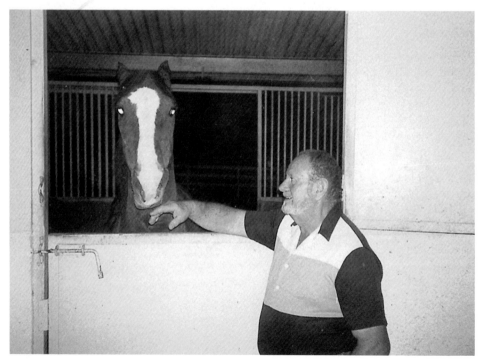

Mordka "Max" Wolman with his mare Cognac

Jacob "Jack" Weingarten

Stefan and Ella Mandel

Menahem Russek in 1983

Shlomo Blajman in 1983

Lucian Ludwig Kozminski in a 1982 mug shot

(Clockwise) Hans Warter, Walter Heeren, Wolfgang Momper, Otto Gnirs, Joseph Thalmayr, Lou Kinzler, Wolfgang Meineke, and the author

Lucian Kozminski's last reported residence

CERTIFICATE OF DEATH
STATE OF CALIFORNIA
USE BLACK INK ONLY

STATE FILE NUMBER

LOCAL REGISTRATION DISTRICT AND CERTIFICATE NUMBER

1A. NAME OF DECEDENT—First (Given)	1B. MIDDLE	1C. LAST (Family)	2A. DATE OF DEATH—MO. DAY. YR	2B. HOUR	3. SEX
Lucian	L.	Kozminski	Jan. 19, 1993	1505	Male

4. RACE	5. HISPANIC—SPECIFY	6. DATE OF BIRTH—MO. DAY. YR	7. AGE IN YEARS	IF UNDER 1 YEAR MONTHS / DAYS	IF UNDER 24 HOURS HOURS / MINUTE
Caucasian	YES ___ [X] NO	July 5, 1916	76		

DECEDENT PERSONAL DATA

8. STATE OF BIRTH COUNTRY	9. CITIZEN OF WHAT COUNTRY	10A. FULL NAME OF FATHER	10B. STATE OF BIRTH	11A. FULL MAIDEN NAME OF MOTHER	11B. STATE OF BIRTH
Poland	Stateless	Abraham Kozminski	Poland	Unknown Unknown	Poland

12. MILITARY SERVICE?	13. SOCIAL SECURITY NO.	14. MARITAL STATUS	15. NAME OF SURVIVING SPOUSE IF WIFE, ENTER MAIDEN NAME
19___ TO 19___ [X] NONE	242-46-3344	Divorced	None

16A. USUAL OCCUPATION	16B. USUAL KIND OF BUSINESS OR INDUSTRY	16C. USUAL EMPLOYER	16D. YEARS IN OCCUPATION	17. EDUCATION—YEARS COMPLETED
Banker	Financial	Self	45	0

USUAL RESIDENCE

18A. RESIDENCE—STREET AND NUMBER OR LOCATION	18B. CITY	18C. ZIP CODE
137 S. Crescent Dr.	Beverly Hills	90210

18D. COUNTY	18E. NUMBER OF YEARS IN THIS COUNTY	18F. STATE OR FOREIGN COUNTRY	20. NAME, RELATIONSHIP, MAILING ADDRESS AND ZIP CODE OF INFORMANT
Los Angeles	75	California	Adam A. Bigwood (Son)

PLACE OF DEATH

19A. PLACE OF DEATH	19B. IF HOSPITAL, SPECIFY ONE: IP, ER/OP, DOA	19C. COUNTY	8424-A Santa Monica Blvd.
Century City Hospital	IP	Los Angeles	West Hollywood, Ca. 90069

19D. STREET ADDRESS—STREET AND NUMBER OR LOCATION	19E. CITY	TIME INTERVAL BETWEEN ONSET AND DEATH	22. WAS DEATH REPORTED TO CORONER? REFERRAL NUMBER
2070 Century Park East	Los Angeles		YES / [X] NO

CAUSE OF DEATH

21. DEATH WAS CAUSED BY: (ENTER ONLY ONE CAUSE PER LINE FOR A, B, AND C)

IMMEDIATE CAUSE	(A) Cardiopulmonary Arrest	▶ 10 Min.	23. WAS BIOPSY PERFORMED? YES / [X] NO
DUE TO (B)	Adult Respiratory Distress Syndrome	▶ 2 Days	24A. WAS AUTOPSY PERFORMED? YES / [X] NO
DUE TO (C)	Pneumonia	▶ 7 Days	24B. WAS IT USED IN DETERMINING CAUSE OF DEATH? YES / NO

25. OTHER SIGNIFICANT CONDITIONS CONTRIBUTING TO DEATH BUT NOT RELATED TO CAUSE GIVEN IN 21	26. WAS OPERATION PERFORMED FOR ANY CONDITION IN ITEM 21 OR 25? IF YES, LIST TYPE OF OPERATION AND DATE.
None	No

PHYSICIAN'S CERTIFICATION

I CERTIFY THAT TO THE BEST OF MY KNOWLEDGE DEATH OCCURRED AT THE HOUR, DATE AND PLACE STATED FROM THE CAUSES STATED.	27B. SIGNATURE AND DEGREE OR TITLE OF CERTIFIER	27C. CERTIFIER'S LICENSE NUMBER	27D. DATE SIGNED
27A. DECEDENT ATTENDED SINCE / DECEDENT LAST BEEN ALIVE MONTH, DAY, YEAR / MONTH, DAY, YEAR	▶ Warren L. Roston MD	G 41613	1/20/93
1/10/93 / 1/18/93	27E. TYPE ATTENDING PHYSICIAN'S NAME AND ADDRESS Warren L. Roston MD 2080 Century Park East L.A.Ca.		

CORONER'S USE ONLY

I CERTIFY THAT IN MY OPINION DEATH OCCURRED AT THE HOUR, DATE AND PLACE STATED FROM THE CAUSES STATED.	28A. SIGNATURE AND TITLE OF CORONER OR DEPUTY CORONER	28B. DATE SIGNED
▶		

29. MANNER OF DEATH	30A. PLACE OF INJURY	30B. INJURY AT WORK	30C. DATE OF INJURY MONTH, DAY, YEAR	31. HOUR
		YES / NO		

32. LOCATION (STREET AND NUMBER OR LOCATION AND CITY)	33. DESCRIBE HOW INJURY OCCURRED (EVENTS WHICH RESULTED IN INJURY)

FUNERAL DIRECTOR AND LOCAL REGISTRAR

34A. DISPOSITION(S)	34B. PLACE OF FINAL DISPOSITION—NAME AND ADDRESS	34C. DATE MO. DAY. YEAR	35A. SIGNATURE OF EMBALMER	35B. LICENSE NUMBER
CR/RES	8424-A Santa Monica Blvd. West Hollywood, Ca.	1/21/93	Not Embalmed	

36A. NAME OF FUNERAL DIRECTOR (OR PERSON ACTING AS SUCH)	36B. LICENSE NO	37. SIGNATURE OF LOCAL REGISTRAR	38. REGISTRATION DATE
Gold Cross Mortuary	FD 1303	▶ Robert C. Katz	JAN 21 1993

STATE REGISTRAR

A.	B.	C.	D.	E.	F.	CENSUS TRACT

(REV. 3-91)   MAKE NO ERASURES, WHITEOUTS, OR OTHER ALTERATIONS

THIS IS A TRUE CERTIFIED COPY OF THE RECORD FILED IN THE COUNTY OF LOS ANGELES DEPARTMENT OF HEALTH SERVICES IF IT BEARS THIS SEAL IN PURPLE INK

JAN 21 1993

60

Director of Health Services and Registrar

A copy of Lucian Kozminski's death certificate. Note how the document appears to have been tampered with at the top of the Social Security number box.

ing in, as even our small places of refuge were disappearing. On the verge of trial and under the microscope, we simply would have no escape until the ordeal was done.

So we thrust ourselves with renewed dedication into the last lap of our long trek, working furiously day and night during the final week before the trial. As we delved into this pre-trial phase, our written materials appeared to be in order. While I had carefully prepared lengthy jury instructions and a trial memorandum for the Court, Kinzler and I together had meticulously assembled several hundred exhibits, most accompanied by English translations from various foreign languages. But amid all our voluminous materials, the very linchpin of our prosecution was embodied in a single emblematic chart conceived from recent formative experience.

Just one month before, Kinzler had entered my office while I knelt down scribbling on a piece of paper the size of a movie poster on the floor. Chuckling briefly, he had exclaimed: "And just what the hell are *you* doing?"

Turning toward him, I replied matter-of-factly, "It's our *chart*, Lou."

Now with a quizzical look, he asked, "What in the heck do we need a chart for?"

Slowly putting my pen down, I responded, "Yeah, I would have asked the same thing a while ago. But now I've learned from handling a bunch of white-collar fraud cases. As a prosecutor you, can get so close to the evidence, and it's usually pretty complex stuff, that you *think* you're leading the charge. But the next thing, you turn around and realize you've lost the troops—judge *and* jury."

Kinzler, now ruminating, remarked, "I see what you mean."

Having captured his attention, I continued, "Well, it's the same thing in our case. You know our proof is pretty damn strong. But, Jesus, we've got documents showing claims filed by Kozminski, letters between him and the victims, letters with West German attorneys and restitution agencies, restitution awards, and bank records. It's really quite a pile—"

Kinzler now playfully interjected, "A pile of *what*?"

But I went on, "You know. A pile of . . . you know. Anyway, *here's* something that captures it all. I'm talking about *ninety* critical pieces of evidence on *ten* victims, placed in chronological order in one spot. And I hope it'll be pretty damn impressive. Here, look."

Flattening the paper on the floor, I showed him the blueprint for the chart that would eventually be our cornerstone trial exhibit.

As Kinzler peered downward, his eyes widening in curiosity, I pointed at the last two columns, remarking, "See, look at these headings: 'Date and Amount *Paid* by Kozminski' and 'Percentage of Award *Received* by Victim.' And the entries under them for the first *seven victims* read 'none' and '0%.' All in bold print. That's what we want on display for the entire case."

Kinzler, nodding with a glint in his eye, responded, "Yeah, I think the jury's really going to *feel* these figures. And it sure makes the whole thing pretty damn simple. I mean . . . it's our *entire* case."

BUT THE CHART was only the half of it. For we also had to ensure that it reflected evidence actually admitted at trial. As the witnesses were the core of this proof, we planned to make them the focus of our efforts.

Concerned that Kinzler might be stretched to his limits as point man for all witness coordination, among other pressing duties, I cornered him in my office one afternoon and tactfully asked, "Lou, are you really going to be up to . . . doing all this?"

But Kinzler would hear nothing of my unease. Flashing a mischievous wink and smile, he parried my query by mimicking Kozminski's own stock phrase, asking in mock indignation, "*Vat's da* matter *mein* friend—don't you *trrrust* me or something?"

And with that playful reassurance, we launched into a flurry of final pre-trial interviews.

Beginning with our many out-of-town witnesses, whom Kinzler ceaselessly shuttled from hotel to pre-trial interview, we primed West German restitution agency officials and attorney-contacts, with Kinzler serving as able interpreter for many.

Then we quietly comforted and prepared Hela Suchecki, Kozminski's principal Israeli victim, as well as several other foreign victim-witnesses slated to testify on Kozminski's scheme to defraud. Caught in the swirl of pre-trial activity, disoriented by their surroundings, and often fearful of testifying, many of these witnesses needed inter-

A Victim	B Date and Amount of Award by Restitution Agency	C Attorney Contact in West Germany	D Date and Amount Sent to Kozminski	E Date and Amount Paid by Kozminski	F Percentage of Award Received by Victim
HELA SUCHECKI	September 19, 1974 **$12,754.00** *Munich*	OTTO KNOLL	May 7, 1975 **$9,363.63** *Bank Of America*	NONE	0%
MORDKA WOLMAN	March 28, 1978 **$3,738.16** *Dusseldorf*		May 31, 1978 **$3,738.16** *Bank Of America*	NONE	0%
ELLA MANDEL	August 6, 1976 **$1,076.00** *Berlin*	FELIX WETZEL	December 23, 1976 **$932.82** *Bank Of America*	NONE	0%
FELA FUCHS	May 26, 1978 **$1,029.00** *Berlin*	FELIX WETZEL	July 19, 1978 **$920.25** *Bank Of America*	NONE	0%
ZESA STARR	June 16, 1975 (2) **$931.00; $775.00** *Berlin*		July 22, 1975/August 4, 1975 **$931.00/ $775.00** *Bank Of America*	NONE	0%
THEODORE SEIDMAN	October 29, 1981 **$29,222.00** *Stuttgart*	HANS ROCK	March 1, 1982 **$22,543.91** *Union Bank*	NONE	0%
JACOB WEINGARTEN	September 15, 1975 **$3,747.62** *Stuttgart*	LUDOLF LERMAN	October 7, 1975 **$3,747.62** *Bank Of America*	NONE	0%
EDITH TEITMAN	July 18, 1977 **$32,690.00** *Neustadt Saarburg*	HANS ROCK	September 1, 1978/January 17, 1979 (2): **$29,110.76** *Bank Of America*	March 17, 1979 **$10,397.00**	32%
LOUIS KONITZ	November 11, 1977 **$1,202.31** *Berlin*		December 30, 1977 **$1,202.31** *Bank Of America*	February 10, 1978 **$473.00**	39%
ARTHUR REICH	February 3, 1975 **$1,008.40** *Berlin*		March 13, 1975 **$1,008.40** *Bank Of America*	February 20, 1978 **$403.50**	40%

mittent reassurance from Kinzler and me, even while we were privately plagued by our own intense anxieties and pressures.

We later returned to each of the local victims, concluding many months of patient preparation with one final pre-trial session. Though the time had at last come to gird them for cross-examination, the specter of Maginnis's interrogation concerned us little.

Placed squarely in an ineluctable bind, Maginnis undoubtedly knew that if he treated these victims of the Holocaust too gently on the stand, he would make no dent into their forceful testimony. Yet the alternative was even worse, for if he attacked them or even *appeared* facetious or disrespectful, he risked incurring the jury's wrath and watching his entire defense instantly self-destruct.

Considering Maginnis's predicament as well as the survivors' age, infirmities, and sensitivities, we prepared them for cross-examination in a deliberately cursory and casual manner. In the end, having witnessed the steady growth of their confidence and ability as prospective trial witnesses, regardless of how they fared on cross-examination, we remained convinced their testimony would prove lucid, captivating, and compelling.

During our final sessions, these survivors invariably expressed anxiety and even fear about testifying, but most concluded by stoically remarking, "I'm as ready as I'll ever be." Or "I promise you I will do my very best."

Perhaps, in this wistful parting of sorts, some of them were trying to reassure Kinzler and me, sensing that behind our composed facades we were wracked by our own anxieties. For we knew that our quiet, intensely personal sessions with these witnesses now were over. Instead, Kinzler and I would be responsible for ushering them into unchartered territory replete with a packed courtroom, a voracious public, the unrelenting glare of Lucian Kozminski, and the prospect of emotional and even physical strain and trauma.

OUR FINAL AND most memorable pre-trial meeting was with the irrepressible Shlomo Blajman, who had arrived from Israel just before trial eager to relate his story about Kozminski in the camps.

By the time Kinzler and Blajman arrived at the U.S. Attorney's Office from Blajman's local hotel, they already had established a rapport. I grasped hands tightly with Blajman, a man in his late sixties with large ears and a bulbous nose, whose remarkable blue eyes beamed with joy and exuded a glowing spirit.

The three of us launched into a lengthy and at times uproarious session, as we laughed, ranted about Kozminski, and conversed about the painful past. At the end, Blajman's voice suddenly softened, and with an earnest expression, he remarked, "Mr. Kalmansohn, I am extending you a personal invitation to make your first visit to the State of Israel after this is all over."

Somehow I knew that, no mere polite gesture, this heartfelt invitation from a virtual ambassador of the Jewish state simply could not be refused.

In the meantime, we sought to make every appropriate arrangement for the trial, including safeguarding against troublesome contingencies. While enlisting qualified interpreters in seven languages, engaging two full-time paramedics for infirm witnesses and spectators, and arranging for the federal courthouse lunchroom to provide kosher food, we also worked with the U.S. marshals to ensure *Kozminski's* safety, keenly aware of reports that his life had been threatened, possibly by a militant Jewish group, and that his first restitution office had been firebombed several years before.

Yet despite our efforts, a few things inevitably fell through the cracks. The most notable culprit was the redoubtable bureaucratic maze, through which we had earlier had slipped unscathed. For two months, we had sought to obtain certified copies of Kozminski's six West German convictions. Rather than simply obtaining them from West German courts, however, because of the ban on our "direct" contact with foreign governments we had to work with the minions of U.S. government bureaucracy. Again and again we tried to process our request through disinterested clerks in Washington, D.C., who took long lunches and "worked" from nine to five. The closer we got to the trial, the more insistent we became, but it was all to no avail. Certified copies of Kozminski's convictions never arrived. As a result, we voluntarily acceded to the defense motion seeking to exclude them from evidence.

In the end, though frustrated by this inexcusable bureaucratic foul-

up, we remained grateful that nothing more serious had impeded our
progress toward confronting Lucian Kozminski in court.

Pinning the Tail

In the midst of this swirl of activity, I continued to prepare my most
important series of questions—for the cross-examination of Lucian
Ludwig Kozminski. This was no idle exercise. Although a defendant
may not be compelled to take the stand, we were certain Kozminski
would testify to have *any* hope of gaining acquittal.

Aware that a person's past conduct often augurs his future behavior, I pored over Kozminski's prior sworn testimony, devoting special
attention to his deposition in Edith Teitman's civil suit. It was not
encouraging. In his broken English, which we suspected he feigned
at times, Kozminski deliberately shrouded the truth and boldly challenged the victim's version of events.

For example, when queried about the exorbitant fees deducted
from Teitman's $32,690 restitution award, resulting in payment
nearly two years later of just $10,397, Kozminski responded:

> No people can talk—can no [*sic*] take care of this case. I take care of
> this, and I look [*sic*] this is special case. I'm on many cases, I take 40
> percent, 50 percent. I tell the people, 'You like [*sic*] sign this, okay. If
> no, forget it.' They come back and they sign me.

After Teitman's counsel pressed the issue, Kozminski dodged and
weaved until the record became a prolonged, muddled mess. Questioning Kozminski was like trying to pin the tail on a donkey while
blindfolded and with a moving target:

> Q. Well, in other words, you were entitled to retain, you say, 40 percent of that
> $26,717.73, right?
> A. Yes.
> Q. But yet you paid her only—16—I'm sorry. You only paid $10,397.70?
> A. There [*sic*] one sum here, 977.40. This is marks. And the balance is
> $10,397.70.

Q. Well, Mr. Kozminski, do you follow my questions? Let me backtrack just so we understand each other. You received 26,717.73—

A. Right.

Q. —in United States dollars?

A. Right.

Q. You paid Mrs. Teitman $10,397,70.

A. Right.

Q. Okay. You say you were entitled to a fee of 40 percent of the $26,000, right?

A. Right.

Q. Okay. That would be a little over $10,000, correct?

A. This time the balance, 22,000 mark [sic], 465.86. That's why the balance [sic] from the 55,000 mark.

Q. I don't understand. How? What balance? You received $26,000?

A. Yes, right. Here. Everything [sic] in letter here.

Q. Everything is in this letter of March 17?

A. Yes. Up here [sic] everything.

Q. All of that is in German, and I don't read German.

A. Okay. I give [sic] that translation.

Q. Why don't you tell me how you calculated what you were entitled to keep?

A. I keep [sic] 40 percent for this contract, one—

Q. I understand that.

A. I keep [sic] approximately 977.40 marks; this is approximately 1,000 for the three months security check, was the life security check for the three years.

Q. That's for this annuity payment?

A. Yes. This is the contract here, 50–50.

Q. I just want you to tell me what you did and why.

A. Yes. And is the lump sum stay [sic] for Mrs. Teitman 22,000 mark [sic], 465.86.

Q. Mr. Kozminski, let me go back to my question. My question had to do with this: You received 26,000 for Mrs. Teitman, but yet you paid her only 10,000 plus. Now, why is it that you—

A. We take—

Q. —16,000—

A. We talk [sic] from German marks, okay?

Q. No, this was converted.

A. But is [sic] German marks here. The German letter [sic] from me here, and this is exactly right here. 40 percent for my fees, 21,643 marks. I show you, you can spell [sic] later. This 21, this is my fee, okay? The balance is for Mrs. Teitman, 32,465. 977.40 is for three years security check.

Q. Now, I'm first referring to this Paragraph 3 of your letter where it says, of the remaining 32,000 plus German marks, an amount of 10,000 German marks is to be deducted for your former attorney, Mr. Traum. Tell me by what authority, by what right, did you have the right to deduct 10,000 German marks?

A. No, not me. The court in Germany. Not me.

Q. I see.

A. Not me.

Q. Not you?

A. No.

Q. The court in Germany?

A. Right.

Q. Tell me by what right or authority did you have the right to withhold from Mrs. Teitman 10,000 German marks from her money?

A. No, the money no come [sic] to me. They stop [sic] the money.

Q. Apparently you don't understand me. Now, follow me.

A. *You confuse me, anyway.*

Q. Then you claim that you are withholding 10,000 German marks from the 32,000.

A. This is the court was they stop [sic] the money in Germany. I found out maybe the money—the money's no [sic] in Germany; by [Hans] Rock's is [sic] those marks. This is possible.

Q. What do you mean, you don't know. You kept it.

A. I no [sic] kept it. I no [sic] kept it.

Q. You didn't?

A. No, no way, no way.

Q. No way?

A. No way.

Q. Well, you did receive the 26,000, didn't you?

A. Yes. I pay [sic], and I take [sic] my fee. Every [sic] people must pay. That is legal. *You cannot do nothing [sic] to me, I tell you.*

Q. Did you keep the 16,320.03?

A. You know *das* [sic].

Q. Just answer my question. Did you keep it?

A. What?

Thus, we had clear forewarning. We knew we must avoid Kozminski's strategy of evasion and not permit him to slither and slide into thorough confusion. Just one day of meandering, chaotic testimony on cross-examination could drag the entire trial down into Kozminski's bog.

Mindful of this concern, I fashioned Kozminski's cross-examination by forming short, direct questions designed to pin him down step by step. If he was unresponsive, I would turn to the judge to intercede, and if that proved ineffective I would pointedly ask if he was deliberately trying to avoid my questions.

In the end, Kozminski would answer—and incriminate himself—or evade and slide down his own slippery slope before the jury's watchful gaze.

So at last we were ready, poised on the precipice of a monthlong trial. The beginning of the end had finally arrived.

4

BATTLES NEAR
AND FAR

The White Flag?

Shortly after Kozminski's second indictment, Kinzler and I ducked
out of the office for a quick Mexican lunch on nearby Olvera Street.
Strolling on a red cobblestone road packed with novelties ranging
from sombreros to serapes, we eventually turned to the case at hand.

Reaching over to a examine a shiny sword hanging outside a small
tourist shop, Kinzler remarked, "Well, I guess we have to make the
Weasel a plea offer."

"Of course, Lou," I responded. "Like it or not. Because as much
as we want to go to trial, there's always a *chance* Kozminski could be
acquitted or his conviction could get reversed on appeal."

"I know, I know," Kinzler muttered, moving on to examine some
brightly colored maracas. "But I still hate to let him plead to less than
on all counts."

"Yeah, me too," I responded. "But look at it this way. If he pleads
to just, let's say, five counts, then he's still exposed to *twenty-five years*
in prison. And what's the chance he'd ever get that type of sentence?
I'd say zero."

"OK," Kinzler remarked, strolling at my side. "But the more
counts he pleads to, the more restitution to the victims the court can
order."

"I agree," I replied. "So let's see. If he pleads to seven out of fifteen mail counts, that'll still cover some 95 percent of the money in the indictment."

"And one bankruptcy count," Kinzler insisted. "He's got to plead to one of those, too. That's eight counts."

"Then eight counts it is," I concurred. "And potentially forty years in jail."

"Not enough, but it'll do," Kinzler muttered, now approaching a light blue piñata hanging from the ceiling of a shop. Jabbing the piñata with his finger, he added, "But I still want to get him in court and . . . bust him open like one of these things."

THE NEXT DAY I submitted a routine plea offer to Maginnis, proposing that if Kozminski pled guilty to seven mail-fraud counts and one bankruptcy-fraud count, the government would move to dismiss the remaining counts in the two indictments. We also advised Maginnis that our offer expired two court days before trial: Unless Kozminski accepted by that deadline, we would require him to plead guilty to all counts in both indictments or face trial.

This initiated a high-stakes waiting game between prosecution and defense, made even more complex by a prospective rift between Kozminski and his counsel.

I knew that a defiant and unrepentant Kozminski may well have insisted on going to trial to prove his innocence. Maginnis, on the other hand, though usually happy to oblige a client seeking a jury trial, may have had misgivings about defending an accused Holocaust swindler. To compound his reluctance, Maginnis undoubtedly remained aware that exposing the court to live testimony by Kozminski's victims could increase Kozminski's sentence.

Yet even with the crush of evidence, publicity, and perhaps his own counsel bearing down upon him, we never suspected Kozminski would agree to plead guilty. The propensity to rebut truth and deny guilt appeared to be too deeply ingrained in his character. Faced with such defiance, and drawn to the trial limelight, even a reluctant Pat Maginnis seemed likely to eventually relent. As a result, we proceeded unabated to trial without giving the prospect of a guilty plea a second thought.

Shortly before our plea offer deadline expired, however, Pat Maginnis called me in my office. In an understated tone he succinctly remarked, "We're throwing in the towel. You may not believe this, but Ludwig's agreed to plead guilty to your eight counts."

Having raised the proverbial white flag, he quickly rang off, leaving us to ponder the ramifications.

Our initial shock soon faded into skepticism. We speculated about whether the defense intended to booby-trap a guilty plea, precipitating its collapse and leaving our prosecution in disarray with key trial witnesses already en route home to Germany, Israel, and elsewhere. Even if not a deliberate defense tactic, the prospect existed that Maginnis would lose control over his elusive and unpredictable client, who might change his mind or prove incapable of admitting his guilt.

Determining that discretion was the better part of valor, we decided to move forward unabated with trial preparation. All witnesses would remain, and we would be ready to proceed.

Onto the Tightrope

Lou Kinzler and I shared intensely mixed feelings as we entered Judge Kenyon's courtroom on August 30, 1982. Aware of all the logical benefits of a guilty plea, we had long before crossed an invisible barrier committing us to another path. Having exhaustively primed our witnesses, our case, and ourselves, we wanted a trial in which Kozminski's victims would see justice work and feel vindicated and the fruits of our labor would be reaped before a judge, a jury, and even society at large.

For the next several hours, however, we were tasked with dispelling this visceral notion while ensuring the successful entry of a guilty plea that would effectively conclude our prosecution. Virtually bursting with anticipation, the courtroom was filled with dozens of Holocaust survivors, witnesses, members of the media, and other interested observers. As all eyes fixed upon us, Kinzler and I briskly stepped past one row of seats filled with witnesses from West Germany and, crossing several more lined with our victim-witnesses, headed for the prosecution table.

Yet with the proceedings scheduled to begin and Kozminski seated impassively at the defense table next to a U.S. Marshal, Maginnis was nowhere to be seen. We waited and we continued to wait, beginning to wonder whether Kozminski had fired his third defense counsel unbeknownst to us or the court.

Finally, in a highly unusual move with Maginnis still absent, Judge Kenyon suddenly entered the courtroom, methodically climbed the stairs next to the bench, and sat at his elevated perch. Proceeding to leaf silently through a bulky file, he appeared almost oblivious to the tense and crowded courtroom directly before him.

Several minutes later, the rear doors suddenly swung open, and Pat Maginnis stepped into the courtroom. Clearly surprised to see Judge Kenyon already on the bench, he rushed to the defense table and quickly explained that he was detained in another courtroom proceeding.

Almost apologetically, the Judge quietly responded, "Well, we have been waiting since 11:30, and I figured we just simply had to come out here now. It's nine after 12:00."

But Maginnis needed even more time and swiftly requested a further delay until 1:30 P.M. Now studying him quizzically with a slight look of impatience, Judge Kenyon tersely replied, "I thought we were all ready."

Maginnis, however, would not relent, and Judge Kenyon, faced with little choice, finally agreed to recess the matter to 2:00 P.M.

This represented an odd and unusual development. Without providing customary notice to the Court's clerk, Maginnis had arrived forty minutes late. Now he required a lengthy recess. Prompted by these events, for the next two hours we soberly speculated about whether Maginnis had lost control over Kozminski and whether this guilty plea would *ever* occur.

AT 2:00 P.M., the proceedings finally resumed. As Kozminski stood at the podium flanked by Maginnis and a German interpreter, Judge Kenyon began by asking whether Kozminski "desire[d] to change [his] plea on some of these counts and to enter a plea of guilty?"

Kozminski answered in English, "Yes."

I rose to my feet and interjected, "Your Honor, I think it might be preferable if the defendant would answer in German, since there is an interpreter, so that the record will be clear."

I was aware, of course, that Kozminski spoke through a German interpreter at the bail hearing before Magistrate Reichmann and delivered hundreds of pages of testimony in other proceedings in a choppy, bastardized English. Now permitting him to respond in English would facilitate a subsequent claim that the plea was uninformed and "involuntary."

Evidently not appreciating my attempt to protect the record for all parties, Maginnis sarcastically snapped, "I think the defendant understands *enough* English to answer in English."

But Judge Kenyon understood the ramifications completely:

Judge Kenyon: Well, now, Mr. Maginnis, I don't think that was called for. I think it's very clear, and it's an important point, that we have at least got to set the ground rules, because if we have an interpreter, we usually use the interpreter. I certainly don't want any claims that there was a misunderstanding or anything like that.

Now, Mr. Kozminski, if you want to speak in English, you certainly may. Is that your desire?

Kozminski: Yes.

Judge Kenyon: All right. And do you think you understand English well enough to speak English?

Kozminski: I'll understand.

Judge Kenyon: I don't understand the answer.

Kozminski: I'll understand, your Honor.

Judge Kenyon: I'm not satisfied. I would just as soon have Mr. Kozminski speak in German. Would you mind doing that, sir? Which tongue do you speak better?

Kozminski: German.

Judge Kenyon: Would you rather, then, please speak in German so that we have less misunderstanding, or we have no misunderstanding?

Kozminski: Yes.

With this matter at last resolved, Kozminski would answer all questions in German, and we would hear his responses in English through the voice of a middle-aged Jewish man, Adam Rosenthal.

The formal plea now began. Peering toward Kozminski, Judge Kenyon matter-of-factly asked, "Do you understand that having been sworn, your answers to my questions will be subject to the penalties of perjury or making a false statement if you do not answer truthfully?"

Kozminski promptly replied, "Yes."

Kenyon briefly paused and then queried, "Mr. Kozminski, may I ask how old are you, sir?"

Without hesitation, Kozminski responded, "Fifty-six."

Seated at the prosecution table, Kinzler and I glanced at each other in surprise, fully aware that Kozminski had either just lied under oath or indirectly admitted to fraudulently obtaining U.S. Social Security payments for several years.

The Judge then posed the standard questions to a defendant entering a plea of guilty. Does he understand he is giving up his right to a jury trial? Does he understand what is happening today? Is he satisfied with his attorney's representation? And so on.

Each time, without exception, Kozminski tersely answered in the affirmative.

Now reading from our indictments, Judge Kenyon proceeded to summarize the pending charges. In response to the Court's pointed inquiries, Kozminski stated he understood the charges and desired to plead guilty.

Then we hit our next bump in the road. Judge Kenyon routinely asked whether any agreement existed other than the government's promise to move to dismiss the remaining counts in the two indictments.

Maginnis, to my surprise, replied that his "understanding . . . was that if the defendant made full restitution prior to sentencing, that would be a very heavy factor in weighing against jail time, and [the government] would consider the option of probation."

Directly contradicting his account, I advised the Court that my written plea offer said nothing of the sort and merely confirmed that "if the defendant before sentencing has made full restitution to the victims in the indictment, the government would factor this into any sentencing recommendation."

In no mood for Maginnis's games, Judge Kenyon curtly remarked, "Well, if there is a misunderstanding, then we simply should go forward with the trial."

After a long moment of tense silence, during which he undoubtedly sensed impending disaster, Maginnis quickly backpedaled and meekly responded, "The letter seems to speak for itself."

But even this concession failed to satisfy Judge Kenyon:

> Judge Kenyon: Well, I think that you had better stop and talk with your client, and if you don't agree with each other as far as the government's position and your understanding of it, then let's simply go to trial.

After a suspenseful five-minute break, Maginnis relented as he and Kozminski confirmed the plain meaning of my letter on the record.

THOUGH THE PLEA had commenced, this whole exercise was clearly extremely shaky and unstable. Either Kozminski or Maginnis could derail the proceedings at any moment, and the most difficult part was yet to come.

Crossing the Tightrope

We now would get down to brass tacks. Turning toward the prosecution table, Judge Kenyon asked me to provide the government's factual basis for Kozminski's plea, in effect walking through our evidence on each count. In order for the court to accept his plea, Kozminski would have to admit guilt on each claim without qualification or hesitation.

Stepping to our large chart, positioned to Judge Kenyon's left so that both he and courtroom onlookers could see it, I began by pointing to the entries at *Victim #1—Hela Suchecki*.

> Mr. Kalmansohn: [T]he government's evidence would show that Ms. Suchecki contacted Mr. Kozminski as early as 1971; that she signed pursuant to his request a power of attorney retainer agreement which provided for Mr. Kozminski's 15 percent of any restitution obtained from the West German gov-

ernment on her behalf, as well as a power of attorney or *vollmacht*, which provided that any payment would be sent directly to Kozminski.

He agreed to file a claim on behalf of her late husband Schapsa due to damage to his health and body as a result of injuries inflicted by the Nazis during World War II.

The government's evidence would further show that on September 19, 1974, an award for Ms. Suchecki on behalf of her late husband in the amount of $12,754 was forthcoming from the restitution agency in Munich, and an agency official would testify to that.

The government's evidence would further show that the agency informed Mr. Kozminski that it could not send the money directly to him because he was in another country. And therefore, for the purpose solely of receiving money and not doing any legal work on the claim, Mr. Kozminski retained Otto Knoll, an attorney in Munich, just to receive the money, deduct his percentage, and send it on to Mr. Kozminski.

Mr. Knoll received the $12,754 or 39,584 Deutsche marks, and he would testify that he then sent the money directly to Mr. Kozminski's bank account, pursuant to Mr. Kozminski's direction, at the Bank of America.

After Kozminski received the $9,363.63 in 1975, he continued to lull and deceive Ms. Suchecki in a number of letters, and the government has selected one, which would be Count One, as an example.

Over two years later, on October 19, 1977, based on the letter that he had received from Ms. Suchecki, who was then living in Jerusalem, Israel, he wrote to her at her address in Jerusalem, Israel, and said:

Re: Your restitution from Germany and your letter of August 21, 1977

Dear Ms. Suchecki:

Thank you for your above letter, and I inform you that soon I shall appear in person in Germany before the respective restitution authorities and of course I shall handle your matter there myself. As soon as I am back I shall let you know about it. Please be assured that I shall fight your case to a good end, as I have done countless other cases.

Mr. Kozminski never informed Ms. Suchecki that there had been a restitution award or any payment. She has not received a penny since the date of the indictment. . . . That zero percent [referring to the chart] would signify the percentage of the award received by the victim.

Judge Kenyon: Mr. Kozminski, do you agree with the prosecution's summary of what you did?

Kozminski: Yes.

Judge Kenyon: How do you plead to Count One of the indictment Number 540?

Kozminski: Guilty.

And so it went. Victim after victim. Count after count. With each recitation, I pointedly emphasized the letters Kozminski sent to his victims, not just because they embodied our mail fraud counts but also to graphically demonstrate his callousness and greed.

For example, I quoted from Kozminski's letter to Fela Fuchs, written six weeks after he deposited her restitution payment:

Dear Mrs. Fuchs:

I have received your last letter. In regard to your letter, I would like to inform you that your matter is being worked on. You must only have some patience since there have been summer vacations for the last two months in Germany, and therefore the delay.

Similarly, I read Kozminski's letter to Zesa Starr, written three and a half years after he deposited both of Starr's restitution payments:

Dear Mr. Starr:

Referring to our telephone conversation we had a few days ago, I am glad to return your file to you even to an earlier date as requested by you. I want to point out that the money you have paid me in the meantime does not cover even a part of my costs I have had in your case. Hoping that you find a better counselor.

I later quoted Kozminski's letter to Theodore Seidman, written two months after he received the victim's $22,543.91 restitution payment, converted it to certificates of deposit, and failed to disclose its existence in his bankruptcy petition:

Dear Mr. Seidman:

Honestly speaking, there would be no need for me to write to you, but I want to finish off this case. You have called me by telephone in April, 1982. Your behav-

ior on the telephone was shocking and impossible. During the call, I explained to you, in spite of your unjustified bad behavior, that you should come to see me. . . . Your threats and your impudent defamation and your threat with the District Attorney cannot move me. Here in Los Angeles and also in other cities I have handled hundreds of cases and every one of my clients received the payment to which he was entitled. . . . If we do reach an agreement . . . you will receive the money to which you are entitled after the termination of my bankruptcy proceeding and after a detailed accounting under the new contract.

The last mail fraud count to which Kozminski would plead guilty concerned Edith Teitman's claim. She was the victim whose frustrated attorney, in hour upon hour of civil deposition, could not elicit a straight answer from Kozminski. Now it was the government's turn.

Step by step, I recounted how Kozminski fleeced Teitman. He had directed his secretary, Ms. Schneider, to doctor Teitman's previously executed power of attorney by adding 25 percent to his existing fee. He had authorized his attorney-contact Hans Rock to deduct $6,000 for debts unrelated to Teitman's claim. He had retained another 10,000 Deutsche marks without her knowledge or approval. He had repeatedly lied to her in his letters. Finally, he had belatedly remitted just 32 percent of her restitution award. At the end of my summary, Judge Kenyon took over:

> Judge Kenyon: Mr. Kozminski, do you agree with the prosecutor's summary of what you did, sir?
>
> Kozminski: Yes.
>
> Judge Kenyon: Do you have anything you wish to add to the prosecutor's summary?
>
> Kozminski: No.
>
> Judge Kenyon: How do you plead to Count Thirteen of the indictment?
>
> Kozminski: Guilty.

We nearly had crossed the entire tightrope, with only the lone bankruptcy count remaining. But little could we know what would transpire next.

Collapse and Freefall?

Judge Kenyon turned to the charge that in failing to disclose his deposit of Theodore Seidman's payment, Kozminski lied under oath in his bankruptcy petition. Queried about the circumstances of the offense, Kozminski immediately began to wobble.

> Judge Kenyon: What happened?
> Kozminski: *I don't know.*
> Judge Kenyon: Don't know what?
> Kozminski: Why I did that. I thought at the time that I did it correctly.

Like an unexpected tremor, these two wavering responses endangered our entire plea. And this perilous situation would only worsen.

> Judge Kenyon: The question is—the charge is that you knowingly and fraudulently made a false oath and account before the bankruptcy—in the bankruptcy proceeding, and that you swore under penalty of perjury that you did not have certain funds, and that in fact, in truth and in fact, you failed to state in your bankruptcy petition that you did have a bank account at the Union Bank on Wilshire Boulevard and you had a certificate of deposit in your name. Now, do you recall that situation?
>
> Kozminski: No.

When Judge Kenyon diligently tried to retrieve the plea, Kozminski blatantly lied about when he received the Seidman payment, falsely characterized his assets, and still refused to acknowledge his guilt.

> Kozminski: I had been in bankruptcy two months before by [*sic*] attorney Kahn *before* the check for Seidman came. That was clearly and simply a mistake, and when I filed for bankruptcy I had *no money*.
> The Court: I thought we had an intention to plead guilty here.
> Mr. Maginnis: We do, your Honor. . . .

After I duly noted that Kozminski received Seidman's payment six weeks before signing his bankruptcy petition, Judge Kenyon turned to Kozminski one last time.

Judge Kenyon: Mr. Kozminski, the government is stating that you knew and you had this money six weeks prior to your filing bankruptcy. Is that not correct?

Kozminski: I understand the violation and I made a *mistake* here.

Judge Kenyon: Well, the Court at this juncture *cannot* accept the plea to this charge, and as I understand it . . . the *entire agreement* is predicated upon a plea to all counts. I am *not* going to accept the plea on this one at this point at any rate, because he is saying, in essence, that it was a mistake; so obviously, he is not pleading guilty to it.

I immediately grasped at our last straw. Presuming that Maginnis needed time to browbeat his client, I suggested that the remaining charge might be "clarified" during a short recess, and the court reluctantly agreed. Now all we could do was wait, poised on the verge of the trial the next day.

NONE OF THESE EVENTS was shocking to Kinzler and me, though we could not explain why they had occurred.

As Kozminski had already pled guilty to seven mail fraud counts, his hesitancy on the bankruptcy fraud did not seem tied to any rational strategy or litigation tactic. After all, if Kenyon refused to accept the guilty plea without Kozminski's plea on the bankruptcy count, then Kozminski would be forced to trial, which he could have opted for in the first place. On the other hand, if Kenyon pressured us to accept the plea on the mail fraud counts alone, the absence of a conviction on one bankruptcy fraud count surely would have minimal effect on the eventual sentence.

As the recess dragged on, Kinzler turned to me and queried in a hushed tone, "What in the *hell* is the Weasel up to? Is it *that* hard for him to tell the truth for *five minutes*, even if it may make things easier for him?"

Shaking my head, I slowly responded, "I really don't know, Lou. Maybe it's his survival instinct groping at a last chance to avoid conviction."

"Yeah," Kinzler replied, "well, it seems all too familiar to me. I'm just glad Kenyon didn't pressure us to accept Kozminski's plea on the mail fraud counts. He's supporting our complete plea agreement . . . it's all eight counts or trial."

After Kinzler and I paused silently, I added, "I can't help but wondering, Lou, whether deep down the judge *prefers* that we go to trial. I mean, he's got to feel it, too. It's like this whole process is too . . . routine without any . . . I guess you'd call it . . . any catharsis."

But now our ruminations abruptly ceased, as the back doors of the courtroom swung open and Maginnis and Kozminski stepped inside. For one of the few moments in this case, our fate now rested entirely in the hands of this approaching duo.

Moments later, as the recess ended, they both stood impassively at the podium facing Judge Kenyon.

Like an actor reverting to a role, Kozminski assumed the docile persona evident earlier in the hearing. Freely admitting that he had knowingly failed to complete several items in his bankruptcy petition, he acknowledged, "And . . . I did *not* list the Theodore Seidman account at that time."

But leaving nothing to doubt, the Judge induced one last concession:

> Judge Kenyon: And why didn't you list that account at that time?
> Kozminski: I did not want this to be part of the bankruptcy.
> Judge Kenyon: Did you realize that by not listing it that that would be dishonest?
> Kozminski: Yes.

With that brief response, Kozminski was finally finished. A factual basis for the plea now existed, and Judge Kenyon promptly found him guilty on all eight counts.

The trial of Lucian Ludwig Kozminski would not commence the following day.

Moments later, Judge Kenyon set Kozminski's sentencing date for September 20, 1982, formally adjourned the session, and swiftly departed the courtroom.

While two marshals grabbed the sullen Kozminski, handcuffed him, and escorted him away, Kinzler and I stood and shook each other's hands. Victims swarmed around us, some joyous and others weeping, and we both felt gratification and relief.

We were not the only ones. Outside the courtroom, in a fitting rejoinder to Maginnis's challenge to the gravity of our case, Edith Teitman's husband, Abraham, proclaimed in vindication, "A man that robs another man like that is *worse* than a murderer."

MINUTES LATER, I stood on the courthouse steps facing Furnell Chatman, a light-skinned African-American man in his early forties sporting a thick brown mustache.

Knowing him as an industrious, energetic, and trustworthy veteran reporter for a local television station, I had provided Furnell with scoops on several prior prosecutions, which led to feature on-the-air reports. More recently, amid a swirl of rumors raging through the local community of Holocaust survivors, I had privately confirmed reports he received regarding Kozminski's activities during the War.

Now, as Furnell stepped next to me, I quietly reminded him that "the *oberkapo* matter still was strictly off-limits."

Seconds later, we faced the camera, and after posing several routine questions, Furnell suddenly paused, a noticeable twinkle in his eye, and then mischievously asked, "Is there something else about Kozminski's past, as yet unrevealed, that may be . . . consistent with his recent criminal behavior?"

Straining to remain nonchalant, I looked directly into Furnell's eyes and quickly responded, "Well, Furnell, that really isn't something I can . . . address at this time."

But Furnell was not done. Boring in even more intently, he queried, "Might he have been an *oberkapo* or collaborator in the concentration camps?"

My jaw tensing, I stared at Furnell, surprised that he had decided to pose *the* question, especially when he knew I could not answer it. As his eyes danced playfully and studied me with anticipation, I politely smiled and concluded the interview with a terse "no comment."

THESE INCISIVE queries clearly signaled that despite Kozminski's conviction, our case was far from over. Besides revealing our untold story in the government's forthcoming sentencing recommendation, we would continue to search vigorously for victims' funds, this time in several far-flung places. But before we turned to these pressing matters, the moment had finally arrived to pause for celebration and gratitude.

The Bronze Snake

For two brief nights we reflected, celebrated, and bade fond farewell to several witnesses who would be returning to their homes.

The first night we took the West German restitution agency officials to a Japanese restaurant, which later prompted Kinzler and me to joke darkly about our Axis Powers dinner. But the contribution of these Germans was no laughing matter. These people, without exception, had been extremely cooperative, traveling thousands of miles to attend the trial, poring over voluminous files with us, and patiently participating in our pre-trial interviews. Now we were showing our deep appreciation for their efforts.

It emerged over dinner that the trip had created a lasting impression on the Germans. It may have been their firsthand exposure to several Holocaust victims, the odd vision of watching their own dusty files come to life, or the experience of witnessing Kozminski's guilty plea in an American courtroom. The reasons were unclear but the result was evident. The daily work of these people would never be the same.

Several enduring bonds were cemented that evening. Fourteen years later, Kinzler would remain friendly with Otto Gnirs of the Stuttgart Restitution Agency, among others. I would travel to West Germany shortly after the case and visit Wolfgang Meineke of the Berlin Restitution Agency, who would continue to correspond with me until his death a few years ago. In my short time with him, I would come to know Memeke as a good and gracious person with true depth and understanding.

THE NEXT NIGHT we dined with the survivors at a private banquet room in a local delicatessen. Almost all the victims named in our indictment attended, including Jacob Weingarten, Theodore Seidman, Arthur Reich, the Mandels, Hans Wittner, Mordka Wolman, Edith Teitman, Louis Konitz, and several others. I also was blessed with the attendance of another very special person: my mother.

These people appeared truly joyous. After years of contempt and disrespect from Kozminski, they had finally a sense of satisfaction and vindication, which they had assuredly earned. Summoning great courage to come forward, cooperate, and face public exposure as well as their tormentor, they had done so with dignity, pride, and a sense of justice. In the end, though bitten by proverbial snakes, like the ancient Israelites, these survivors looked on the curative bronze snake and ultimately lived as the heart of our case.

ALL ALONG, Lou Kinzler shined brightly amid this company of Holocaust survivors. Completely at ease, he traded quips in Yiddish with several while warmly hugging others and displaying a sense of true camaraderie.

These joyous evenings were not without ironies.

For one thing, we always scrupulously maintained separation between our two major groups of witnesses—the Holocaust survivors and the German restitution agency officials. Logistical considerations were certainly a factor, but we were primarily concerned about sensitivities: Many of the survivors would undoubtedly feel uncomfortable around the Germans, while some of the Germans would surely feel self-conscious in the company of the living embodiment of their own case files.

At the same time, we remained keenly aware that these poignant reunions and celebrations would not have been possible without one Lucian Kozminski. In his own strange way, he had made all of this possible and, in so doing, allowed at least one German and one Jew to form a kinship and bond that endure to this very day.

The Untold Story

In formulating a sentencing recommendation, we faced a difficult strategic choice. Throwing down the gauntlet, we could propose the specific *maximum* prison term we favored for Kozminski, or adopt-

ing an entirely different tack, we could urge the court to meet or
exceed a *minimum* term of incarceration. We eventually opted for the
second, less conventional approach based on several persuasive factors.

"Look," I explained to Kinzler in a decisive meeting in my office
one evening, "Judge Kenyon's got a reputation as a tough sentencer,
and he appears less than . . . enamored with Kozminski's conduct. I
trust his judgment."

"Yeah," Kinzler responded, "and in this type of high-profile case,
we *certainly* don't want to appear heavy-handed, like we're pressur-
ing the judge."

"Exactly," I replied, "and strange as it may seem, I'd like to give
Kozminski at least a small dose of that . . . I guess you'd call it . . .
quality of mercy. He may not have given it to *his* victims, but, after
all, he *is* a Holocaust survivor."

Kinzler nodded in agreement, remarking, "Well, in the end it's
the judge's decision, anyway. So let's go in with a minimum recommendation but lay out all the evidence. Pour it on. If the judge is
pissed off enough, he'll know what to do."

Accordingly, we submitted more than two hundred exhibits dram-
atizing Kozminski's fraudulent scheme, commission of tax fraud and
bankruptcy fraud, disdain toward his victims, and documented contempt for judges and the legal system itself. But that was not all, for
we also included Shlomo Blajman's sworn declaration attesting to
Kozminski's nefarious role as accused collaborator with the SS.

In our accompanying sentencing memorandum, I began by noting
that Kozminski had failed to make any restitution since his conviction, went on to summarize the government's evidence in detail, and
then characterized the nature of his fraudulent scheme:

> On July 15, 1944, shortly before her capture by the Nazis, Anne Frank
> wrote in her diary: "That's the difficulty in these times: ideals, dreams and
> cherished hopes all rise within us, only to meet the horrible truth and be
> shattered." Kozminski's victims already had lived this tragedy once. And
> then trying to build in a positive way on the dark past, these people have
> painfully seen more hope slip through their fingers and into the hands of
> Lucian Kozminski. This "blood money," kept and spent by Kozminski over

the past thirteen years, therefore symbolizes much more than a mere crime or illegal act: It also signifies the defendant's utter greed, ruthlessness, and moral depravity. How anyone in a civilized society could defraud this group of people of these particular payments is almost beyond belief.

Aware that Judge Kenyon was a decent person with a reputation for integrity, I again appealed to his sense of morality at the end of our memorandum. Before recommending a minimum of eight years' incarceration, as well as orders of restitution to the victims and the costs of prosecution to the United States, I implored:

> Kozminski's scheme was designed to defraud victims who have faced unspeakable suffering, tragedy, and unprecedented cruelty. These people have seen their rights stripped away, their homes destroyed, their families liquidated, and dreams vanquished. They have witnessed this mass extermination in a world where the prevailing attitude was one of indifference and the dominant reaction was silence. These people saw even free nations, including the United States and Great Britain, turn away ships of refugees back to Hitler's death mills in the name of immigration quotas. And now they turn to the American system of justice for vindication of their rights. The restitution monies, no more than symbolic payments for irreplaceable losses, are probably lost forever. But the painful memory persists.

Maginnis's sentencing memorandum was rather different. Attaching no sworn declarations or exhibits, he instead delivered a sharp response to our submission and a less-than-persuasive apology for Kozminski's conduct.

Maginnis began by placing a new spin on Kozminski's concentration camp activities, claiming that because Kozminski was "trained in speaking German," he was "chosen by camp personnel to serve as a trustee." Initially failing to clarify his reference to "camp personnel," Maginnis later, perhaps inadvertently, identified them as "Nazi Gestapo." Faring no better with "trustee," notably absent from historical accounts of the Holocaust, he neither defined the term nor distinguished it from *oberkapo*.

Next asserting that Kozminski in fact saved the lives of seven concentration camp inmates by giving them "bread and soup on a regular basis," Maginnis queried, "Why didn't Mr. Kalmansohn mention *that* in his sentencing memorandum?" Maginnis failed to note, however, that Kozminski's distinct ability to distribute "bread and soup" and his admitted "transportation" of "potatoes," "vegetables," and other "provisions" seemed to confirm his status as an *oberkapo*.

Maginnis also disregarded Kozminski's *own* restitution file, which rebutted the claim that the SS employed him because he was "trained in speaking German" and virtually conceded that he was an *oberkapo* at Auschwitz, in addition to Gross-Rosen. As Kozminski asserted in his 1949 restitution application, "I *accidentally* got a *good position* there [in the SS kitchen at Auschwitz]. I *tried* to take sides with the *Aryan side* because all the Jews were being taken away."

Ignoring Kozminski's West German conviction for defrauding fellow Jews, Maginnis then claimed that a Bavarian Jewish group elected him president five times between 1946 and 1950 and pointedly queried, "If Kozminski had actually collaborated with the Germans as the government contends in their sentencing memorandum, how could he have been elected president five times of an organization composed of concentration camp survivors?"

Later inveighing against the government's claim that Kozminski held "bank accounts in Switzerland or in Israel" as "merely more puffing," Maginnis simply neglected our lengthy attachment of exhibits, which included a statement from Kozminski's Israeli bank account, his written complaint about the bank's refusal to accept "advance fees" from Israeli victims, and extensive correspondence between Kozminski and the president of Handelsbank in Switzerland regarding a multimillion-dollar gold ingot transaction.

Finally admitting that Kozminski "took the money," Maginnis contended, "[i]t merely appears he used the money for living expenses on a day-to-day basis and to allow his sons to use the funds for living expenses."

Citing Kozminski's "advanced" age of 66 (apparently having matured ten years since his guilty plea), Maginnis lamented that his client's "sole source of income at the present time is his business involving restitutions" and then warned that incarceration would "effectively foreclose repayment to any of the victims." In other words, Maginnis's reasoning went, the Court should release this convicted felon to secure restitution payments for his victims!

In the final analysis, while Maginnis admittedly had little to rely on other than a pillar of smoke, Kinzler and I believed that the tone and substance of his memorandum would not appeal to this particular sentencing judge.

THE HEAT OF THE public glare again intensified. After we filed our sentencing memorandum, a *Los Angeles Times* headline proclaimed, BILKER OF HOLOCAUST VICTIMS LABELED NAZI COLLABORATOR. Similarly, the front page of the *Los Angeles Daily News* featured a sinister photo of Kozminski and the headline PROSECUTOR: SWINDLER WAS NAZI COLLABORATOR, with a smaller headline underneath reading, L.A. MAN LABELED "OBERKAPO."

Meanwhile, the defense requested and received a three-week continuance of Kozminski's sentencing, purportedly to collect funds for delivery to victims. Although Kozminski knew restitution would directly affect our recommendation, during the intervening period, he belatedly remitted just $875 to a single victim, Fela Fuchs.

Opening Salvo

Filled with Holocaust victims emboldened by Kozminski's conviction and eagerly awaiting his fate, the courtroom bristled with electricity as Kinzler and I entered and headed for the prosecution table. But despite the palpable sense of anticipation in the vast room, we harbored no false illusions. At least before the Judge imposed a sentence, we knew this session could prove both contentious and difficult.

Now facing a substantial term of imprisonment removed from his comfortable existence, Kozminski would likely be less acquiescent than in his last appearance. And after his client had pled guilty and he had forfeited the chance to cross-examine our witnesses at trial, J. Patrick Maginnis would undoubtedly take off the gloves in this singular moment to attack the government and offer plaintive excuses for Kozminski's conduct. While Maginnis certainly did not disappoint, he first directed his wrath toward a special and unusual target: the pre-sentence report prepared by Larry Teachout.

Before a judge imposes sentence in a federal criminal case, the U.S. Probation Office ordinarily prepares a pre-sentence report comprising interviews with the defendant and key witnesses, a characterization of the defendant's background and criminal behavior, and a sentencing recommendation to the Court. The typical pre-sentence report recommends a *lesser* punishment than requested by the government, and occasionally a greater one than that recommended by the defense. Indeed, in my entire career I had never reviewed a pre-sentence report containing a harsher formal sentencing recommendation than my own.

But this was no ordinary case. Presuming the Judge would be more likely to match or exceed a recommendation of the "neutral" probation office, we had confidentially suggested a ten-year term to the pre-sentence officer, Larry Teachout, two years more than our minimum formal proposal. Shortly before the sentencing, we were pleasantly surprised to see Teachout adopt our private advice at the conclusion of his detailed report.

As the hearing commenced, Maginnis and Kozminski were incensed at the pre-sentence officer's recommendation. After a fuming Maginnis cited several "discrepancies" in the report, Judge Kenyon looked toward Kozminski, who stood between his German interpreter and Maginnis at the podium.

Judge Kenyon: Mr. Kozminski, is there anything else in the report that you feel is inaccurate other than what Mr. Maginnis has stated?
Kozminski: I believe it's all false.
Judge Kenyon: All right. Thank you. If you wish to point out any specific things that you believe are false, then the Court certainly will want to hear it.
Kozminski: I would like to make a statement.
Judge Kenyon: Well, fine. Mr. Kozminski, certainly we want to hear from you if you would like to make a statement, but now I'm simply asking about the pre-sentence report. . . . if there is something in there that should be corrected . . . please feel free to do so at this time.
Kozminski: Not at this time.

It then emerged that, for some unknown reason, Maginnis had never reviewed the pre-sentence report with Kozminski assisted by an interpreter. Startled and disturbed by this revelation, Judge Kenyon granted the defense a lengthy recess to conduct that indispensable joint examination.

When the hearing recommenced nearly three hours later, Maginnis cited several of Kozminski's objections to the pre-sentence report, zeroing in on statements by Marguerite Schneider, Kozminski's former secretary:

> Maginnis: Now, with regard . . . to Miss Schneider, his previous secretary, he denies the remarks that he made statements to clients of his that they are senile and stupid, and offers to the Court the statement that he fired her for two reasons: Number one, in his mind *she* acted like a *Nazi*; and second, she was not Jewish and made a considerable amount of *disparaging remarks against Jewish survivors of the camps,* and that [any anti-Semitic] remarks basically *should be attributed to her* and *not* Mr. Kozminski.
>
> Judge Kenyon: All right.
>
> Maginnis: Is that correct, Mr. Kozminski?
>
> Kozminski: Yes.
>
> Judge Kenyon: All right.
>
> Maginnis: He also denies . . . the statement that 'I'm smarter than the police.' He denies that statement was made.

This brazen counterattack upon Ms. Schneider's integrity was especially ironic. The same person who cheated and mocked his Jewish victims, and apparently collaborated with the Nazis, now had the *chutzpah* to smear his former secretary with allegations that *she* disparaged Holocaust victims. Even if Schneider had harbored such sentiments (which I had admittedly considered in my private thoughts), this undoubtedly was just a glimpse of the tactics Kozminski would have employed at a trial.

As Maginnis next began challenging the report's reference to Kozminski's prior convictions, I attempted to intervene to expedite matters. After all, six weeks after Kozminski's conviction, we *still* had not received certified copies of his convictions from West Germany:

> Kalmansohn: Your Honor, I didn't want to interrupt, but I thought perhaps we could dispense with that. Perhaps the Court could indicate that it will disregard, in light of the government's sentencing memorandum, the German

convictions of Mr. Kozminski and indicate that any sentence is not enhanced because of them.

Judge Kenyon: That's correct.

Maginnis then swiftly moved to his next target: Shlomo Blajman's sworn declaration on Kozminski's activities at Gross-Rosen. Though Blajman had flown to the United States to testify, Kozminski's unexpected guilty plea had removed that opportunity. Now Maginnis sought to turn Blajman's "failure to testify" Kozminski's advantage:

Maginnis: [W]e have the statement by Mr. Blajman, who has never been in this court and has never been subject to cross-examination, and has never been produced by the government. . . . In our . . . sentencing memorandum, which was submitted to the Court, your honor—

Judge Kenyon: Let me just interrupt here. I do not believe this information, which is not subject to any cross-examination, should be considered in the sentencing; whether he was an *oberkapo*—certainly there is some indication by the type of conduct that he has engaged in recent years that it could well be true; it certainly is not inconsistent with the attitudes he has shown to people . . . but I think—and the Court has, in considering the sentence, felt it necessary to eliminate those things from its consideration as being just not proven sufficiently . . . very emotional allegations, and it just doesn't seem to be judicious or fair . . . to take those things as absolutely true.

The victims and courtroom observers may not have realized it, but this probably represented the best of both worlds. While Judge Kenyon noted that Blajman's declaration was consistent with Kozminski's past conduct, he specifically disavowed reliance upon it, thereby wisely eliminating the matter as an issue on appeal.

Moments later, Maginnis finally launched into his primary sentencing argument:

Maginnis: It appears to me, your Honor, that what we have here basically is, we have a person who has basically pled guilty of [*sic*] embezzling funds from some of his clients. Now, it's very hard for anyone to come before a court who has been in a position of trust and admit that to the Court.

Now, the government has done an excellent job in this case in trying to wield public opinion . . . and make allegations which they have not been able to prove about Mr. Kozminski. Now, with regard to the concentration camps, I'd like to discuss that issue because I think it's central to the whole case here.

Judge Kenyon: I don't believe it is. I already told you the Court's position on it.

Maginnis: Well, I'd like to bring up another point, your Honor. Mr. Kozminski's father, mother, his two brothers, and one sister were all killed in Nazi concentration camps in World War II. After World War II, after Kozminski was—(*Courtroom disturbance*)

This proved too much. Maginnis's biting, sardonic tone coupled with his whitewash of Kozminski was unbearable for some victims. After the volume rose in the hushed voices behind me, one victim simply snapped and heatedly yelled at Kozminski, "*He's a thief. He should burn in hell.*"

The judge responded quickly in a polite but firm tone:

Judge Kenyon: Just a minute. Nobody is specially privileged in this court. Nobody. If the President of the United States came in here, he would sit quietly or I would not tolerate it. Is that clear to everybody? And I don't mean to be impolite. I appreciate that there may be, obviously, some emotions here. But I can't do it. I don't have a bailiff, and I just have to run the court this way, because, quite frankly, I need to concentrate. And thank you. And I apologize for sounding a little disturbed.

Now continuing undeterred by the disturbance, Maginnis referred to Kozminski's purported role as president of a Bavarian Jewish group and opined, "This tells you a little bit about how the concentration camp survivors thought of Mr. Kozminski."

Briskly moving on to new terrain, he characterized Kozminski's motive for committing these crimes before launching into a wider attack:

Maginnis: Mr. Kozminski is before this Court. He is 66 years old. He is a survivor of concentration camps himself, and I submit to this Court that the number one reason why he is here . . . today is that he is unable to say to his two sons, 'Enough is enough.'

The government has provided me—and I have also seen the checks—check after check after check made out to Adam Bigwood. . . . Mr. Kozminski was actually supporting his son who was not working at all throughout this period. . . . He also sent money to his son in Germany, named Janosch [*sic*].

The government has not found any bank accounts, with the exception of the Israeli bank account, which they presented to the Court, which has less than $200 in it. There is no Swiss bank account that the government alleges.

The government of the United States of America has enormous power, diplomatically and worldwide, even in Switzerland. If Mr. Kalmansohn could really prove that Mr. Kozminski had a bank account in this case in Switzerland, I guarantee you he would have brought it before this Court. To me it's another example of his *puffing* and trying to blow this case up into something that it is not.

Now, basically, what Mr. Kozminski did is, he took the money out of his account and he used it for living expenses and what have you. Maybe he went to the Playboy Club; maybe he went to Harry's Bar in Century City; maybe he was picked up for a drunk-driving conviction, fine; he drinks, but there is no indication that Mr. Kozminski used the money to buy a fur coat for his wife, to take a trip overseas anywhere, to buy an apartment house, or to be involved in any greedy-type lifestyle.

The government has spent over $35,000 to recover $41,000. To me that's a *travesty of justice*. It seems to me that the amount of money that the government has spent on this case is *just a sin*. . . .

The government is making a big point out of the fact that they want to be compensated for their time and all of the witness fees they have paid in this case and what have you. Mr. Kalmansohn orchestrated this case from stem to stern. He investigated it; he brought it before the grand jury; he has prosecuted it. The pocketbook issue has been in Mr. Kalmansohn's vest pocket all along throughout this case, and I submit to the Court that Mr. Kozminski is not a very—shall we say—lovable individual as he appears before this Court for what he has done to the people. The fact that they may have been survivors of Nazi concentration camps should make no difference whatsoever. . . .

Now, I submit to the Court that putting Mr. Kozminski in jail in this case is not going to accomplish anything. He is 66 years old. . . . His son has consented to come in and run the business. . . . Mr. Kozminski from here on will not be allowed to handle money of clients. . . .

These people here in court today are here in court today—I don't know who they are; basically, I have never been introduced to anyone except for Mr. Seidman, and I don't know if he's here right now or not. Yes, there he is (*indicating*). To use the *vernacular* —(*Court disturbance*)

Maginnis's prospective use of the vernacular was interrupted by none other than Ted Seidman, whom he had just fingered in open court. This encounter was especially ironic: Maginnis, after all, had received fees from Kozminski consisting of most of Seidman's restitution payment, eventually relinquishing them when so advised.

Now no longer able to contain himself, the white-haired Seidman stood up on his gimpy leg, shook his fist, and yelled back at Maginnis. The Court quickly intervened, struggling to maintain control over the proceedings:

> Judge Kenyon: Sir, you are not special any more than I am. I would really not dream of speaking out in court, in anyone's court—
> A Voice: I'm sorry, your Honor.
> Judge Kenyon: So don't you do it, sir.
> The Voice: I'm sorry.
> Judge Kenyon: And be quiet, please. You put me in a most embarrassing position.

While this outburst was clearly improper, I was nonetheless emotionally stirred and felt a quiet admiration. For here in this setting, Ted Seidman had come full circle, from a meek and passive posture toward Kozminski's conduct, slowly evolving to indignation, and finally to a fulsome public outburst. The power and authority of the Nazi state may have crushed the lives of his loved ones, but now, even in open court, Ted Seidman would not let Maginnis's biting tone go unchallenged.

After the courtroom finally quieted, Maginnis casually sloughed off this further disturbance and proceeded apace to his conclusion:

> Maginnis: Now, your Honor, to continue with my train of thought, I don't know who these people are here in court. . . . The bottom line is, these people are here because they believe they were not given funds that were due them . . . and I submit to the court that what we should do in this case is to see to it that the victims are taken care of. . . .
>
> Mr. Kozminski is not the most lovable defendant that will appear in the Central District of California, but what is going to be done for justice? Is

putting Mr. Kozminski behind bars . . . going to give any of these people any further money? No.

And with that, he was done. I must admit, with the benefit of hindsight, that Maginnis had little to go on. Faced with the daunting task of representing Kozminski at sentencing, he possessed few favorable facts or compelling arguments. Those mitigating factors that did exist, such as Kozminski's own traumatic experience as a Holocaust victim and apparently unstable mental state, were likely to be discounted in the highly charged atmosphere of this case.

Mired in this difficult predicament, Maginnis was reduced to grasping at straws, citing virtually anything that might create sympathy for his client while occasionally lapsing into Pavlovian attack mode. It may not have been the best strategy, but under the circumstances none better may have existed.

And now it was Kozminski's turn:

Judge Kenyon: Mr. Kozminski, is there anything you would like to say?
Kozminski: No, judge; no.

And so we would never hear Kozminski's statement. After all these years—the orders of deportation, criminal convictions, overwhelming evidence of guilt, and other accusations of sordid conduct swirling about him—Kozminski would utter nothing. There would be no explanation, no apology, and no moment of atonement. As a prosecutor, I did not believe that any of these things were necessary, even perhaps desirable. But as a person who had lived and breathed this case for so long, and who consequently blurred the distinction between prosecutor and person, I wanted to hear all three.

Response and Rejoinder

Knowing that Judge Kenyon had already deliberated over Kozminski's sentence, I stood to present my argument with two discrete objectives. One was to challenge some of Maginnis's statements for the record. The other was to speak for the some of the victims.

After refuting Maginnis's claim that Kozminski (rather than Maginnis himself) paid partial restitution to Theodore Seidman, I turned to Kozminski's motive for his crimes and the existence of his foreign accounts:

> Kalmansohn: To say that this crime was not motivated out of greed, regardless of whether 10 percent of the [documented] funds go to his sons or not, your Honor, the government thinks is entirely inappropriate and not consistent with the facts. The *only* motivating factor for this crime, the government submits, was greed, and it must have been quite a greed to commit this crime and to do it to these victims.
>
> The Israeli bank account, it was in existence . . . based on the documents, as recently as April of '82. It was in existence at the time that Mr. Kozminski filed his bankruptcy petition. Did he mention it on the petition? No.
>
> Kozminski was soliciting concentration camp victims in Israel to send their advance fees to this very same bank, the Bank of Leumi, the very same bank account. . . . The account exists; it's not mere rhetoric; we have the proof.
>
> We have Kozminski's *own* words . . . in writing, indicat[ing] that he has an account in Switzerland and Germany where he is apparently contemplating the purchase of a restaurant. We have further indication, as a result of Kozminski's own writing, of his possible access to substantial funds. . . . And also he is apparently quite familiar with a Peter Gautschi, manager of Handelsbank, Geneva, Switzerland; so at least in the earlier stages of this . . . negotiation he received correspondence from Kozminski and sent it to Kozminski.

I next addressed Maginnis's proposal that Kozminski be granted probation in order to collect more restitution payments for his former clients.

> Kalmansohn: Your Honor, the defense counsel says forget about the crime; forget about the type of crime that it is; forget about the fact that Kozminski isn't even a United States citizen, that he stayed here fourteen years beyond his ninety-day nonimmigrant visa; and put him back on the street. Why? So that the victims can receive restitution.
>
> Kozminski has pled guilty to perpetrating a scheme to defraud over the last thirteen years. This Court has found that that business was permeated

with fraud. The government submits that it is the height of irony for defense counsel to now suggest that Kozminski step back into this business, either alone or through his son, and operate a business permeated with fraud.

Finally, I attempted to blunt Maginnis's attack on the government while building to the conclusion of our presentation.

Kalmansohn: [Defense counsel] indicates it's a travesty of justice for the taxpayers in this country to spend approximately $34,000 to prosecute this case. Your Honor, at least speaking personally, and I know on behalf of the United States Attorney's office, I am *proud* that the government has spent that money. The sky really was the limit, and that is because of the type of deed that was perpetrated. . . . It *is* a travesty of justice—it's a travesty of justice to see what Kozminski has done for the last thirteen years and to see him get away with it unscathed, and to see him make these dreams turn sour.

Your Honor, Kozminski has committed this heinous crime, one that still is almost too cruel to fathom. He has taken advantage of the hospitality of this country. He has taken advantage of the government of West Germany's attempt to atone in part for what may be the most horrible deed in this century. And he has taken advantage of victims, true victims. . . . And the defense counsel has said, your Honor, to look at it as any other crime. The government says we cannot.

Your Honor, the government submits that this was a terrible deed, that this was a shameless crime. Finally, we are at the end of the road. The government does ask for a lengthy sentence.

Having completed my remarks, I stepped to the prosecution table and sat down next to Kinzler as Maginnis again boldly strode to the podium.

Maginnis: There is an expression that the government indicts and the government incites, and I think basically that is what this case is all about. Every chance that Mr. Kalmansohn gets he brings out a new trick out of his bag. He talks about dreams turning sour in this case. There is no difference . . . because these victims were survivors of concentration camps [and] the lawyer in this town who settles a car accident case, puts the money in his trust account and doesn't pay his client.

I don't condone what [Kozminski] has done. He has embezzled funds from his clients. But this is not the crime of the century. This is not a child molesting; it's not a murder; it's basically money involved in this case, sweet and simple, it's what it's all about. There is no such thing as dreams come true, as Mr. Kalmansohn would have the Court believe—or dreams turn sour. . . . It's strictly a financial thing.

Now, I submit to the Court that in spite of the rhetoric we have heard from Mr. Kalmansohn, that in spite of the outbursts we have heard in court today from some of the spectators, the best thing to do in this case with regard to the future of justice of the victims . . . is to order that man seated over there in the blue jumpsuit to make restitution, not to put him in Terminal Island. . . .

So I submit to the Court that, sure, this is a difficult case; sure, it's an emotional case; sure, the government thinks it's the greatest crime in the century in the Central District of California. Some people that have been hijacked at L.A. airport might not think so, some prisoners who have been killed at Lompoc might not think so, but to this assistant, maybe it's the biggest crime he has prosecuted.

I say to the Court that what the Court should do is order him to make restitution; give him a chance; put a little carrot in front of him.

With this final plea for mercy, Maginnis was done. The arguments were completed and the matter submitted. It was time for Judge Kenyon to pronounce Kozminski's sentence.

The Sword of Justice

Without hesitation, Judge Kenyon matter-of-factly commenced reading from his sentencing order:

Judge Kenyon: Mr. Kozminski has demonstrated a clear pattern of antisocial behavior, which has really been established through years of corrupt activity toward people, to whom, perhaps even those in the most heartless, ruthless business, would feel—would be just—inclined to show some deference. It is the Court's intention to sentence in this case so that Mr. Kozminski will not be in a position during the period which he would normally be expected to be active in business to do this kind of thing to anyone else. It is not done out of retribution, although some feel strongly that that is a proper use of a sentence; it is done because it can't happen again, certainly not by Mr. Kozminski. And there is no reason to believe, none whatsoever, that Mr. Kozminski has changed or perhaps, sadly enough, is able to change, at least not in the foreseeable future, although there is always certainly hope.

Kinzler and I glanced at each other, now fully aware that Kozminski would be going to prison. The only remaining question was for how long.

Meanwhile, Judge Kenyon continued:

> Judge Kenyon: It is adjudged in Case Number 82–00540 [the mail fraud indictment] on Counts One, Three, and Six that the defendant is hereby committed to the custody of the Attorney General of the United States . . . for imprisonment on each count for a term of five years, the sentence on each count to run concurrently with each other.

Kenyon paused briefly, and Kinzler and I glanced at each other again. But before we could ruminate over our emerging disappointment, Judge Kenyon continued:

> Judge Kenyon: It is adjudged that in the same case, Number 82–00540, on Counts Seven, Nine, Ten, and Thirteen, that the defendant is hereby committed to the custody of the Attorney General of the United States . . . for imprisonment on each count for a term of five years, the sentence on each count to run concurrently with each other. The sentence on Counts Seven, Nine, Ten, and Thirteen—the sentence regarding those counts shall run consecutively to the sentence on Counts One, Three, and Six.

Kinzler and I again looked at each other, pleasantly surprised. The sentence now stood at ten years' incarceration and Kenyon was not done:

> Judge Kenyon: It is further adjudged that in Case Number 82–00620 [the bankruptcy indictment] on Count One that the defendant is hereby committed to the custody of the Attorney General of the United States . . . for imprisonment for a term of two years. The sentence on Count One is to run concurrently—pardon me—consecutively to the sentence imposed in Case Number 82–00540.

The total term of incarceration would be twelve years, a record for our district in a white-collar fraud case. Several gasps came from the spectators' section, as most of the victims assuredly could not believe their own ears.

Proceeding apace, upon our motion Judge Kenyon dismissed the remaining counts and then completed his sentence:

> Judge Kenyon: I was going to make this order: There is not much indication that the defendant will pay restitution or costs of prosecution. The court orders, however, that restitution be made by the defendant.
>
> The Court further finds that the costs of prosecution as set forth by the United States in its statement of costs are legitimate, and that the costs of prosecution in the amount of $34,771.48 be made and paid by the defendant. It is to be understood, however, that no costs of prosecution are to be paid until after and unless full restitution to any of the victims, either named in the indictment or not named, is made.

And that was it: a twelve-year term of incarceration with orders of restitution and costs of prosecution. The sentence was four years longer than the government's own minimum recommendation and two years longer than the pre-sentence officer's proposal.

Judge Kenyon's reasoning was direct and compelling. Having characterized Kozminski's conduct as "heartless, ruthless," and "antisocial," he designed his sentence *not* to deter others or for retribution, but to ensure that Kozminski himself would be unable to perpetrate similar acts during his active years.

Now formally ending the hearing, Judge Kenyon slowly turned and left the bench. The U.S. Marshals promptly handcuffed a crestfallen Kozminski and escorted him out of the courtroom while Maginnis abruptly gathered his papers and rushed past us toward the rear doors. Meanwhile, beaming with satisfaction and relief, and faces filled with emotion, several of the victims approached Kinzler and me and warmly congratulated us.

MINUTES LATER, surrounded by cameras and reporters on the steps of the courthouse, Maginnis complained that the import of the case was greatly exaggerated, suggesting, "I don't know . . . maybe we feel guilty because we should have bombed the camps or the railroads leading to the camps and tried to save some of the victims."

When asked about his immediate plans now that the case was concluded, Maginnis puckishly responded, "I'm going to go home, lie
down on my waterbed, and drink a good bottle of wine."

After Maginnis was done, we shook hands, and he bounded down
the courtroom steps in the fading afternoon light.

Shortly afterward, I stepped out of the elevators and onto the thir-
teenth floor of the Courthouse. A buzzer sounded as I proceeded
through a security door and entered the U.S. Attorney's Office.
Suzanne Conlon stood there waiting for me.

Stepping forward to shake my hand, she remarked with a broad
smile, "So, rumor has it you just sent another innocent person to
jail?"

"Yeah," I remarked, grasping her hand tightly. "And I couldn't
have done any of it without you."

All kidding aside I truly meant it, for indeed none of this would
have been possible without Suzanne.

WHILE THE FORMAL prosecution of the case had ended, we did not
intend to forget the victims, nor did they forget us. In a spontaneous
outpouring of humbling affection, Jewish holiday greetings inundated Lou Kinzler's office and mine.

Among them were a Rosh Hashanah card from Hans and Sarah
Wittner and kind greetings from Molly Schimel, who wrote, "Let
me know you received this card. Keep my best wishes together with
this card. With all my best wishes to you, and all your people around
the world, from your true friend, Molly Schimel."

Fela Fuchs graciously wrote, "May you enjoy good fortune, be
blessed with peace and have happiness."

And the Lustmans, elderly victims residing in Israel, poignantly
remarked:

> This holiday is the symbolize [sic] of *shofar* . . . the Jewish people and
> tradition to wish love [and] good health for 120 years, and luck with
> happiness. Prosperity and success to you. Oh, dearest God bless attor-
> ney Mark E. Kalmansohn with best [sic]. Your future stay in roses.

Much as these warm thoughts and heartfelt expressions of gratitude deeply touched both Kinzler and me, perhaps my most reward-

ing memory is embodied in a letter sent by Stefan Mandel a few months later, in which he graciously wrote:

> I wanted to take this opportunity to express my sincere appreciation for your handling of the Kozminski case. . . . The compassionate manner in which you conducted the investigation, and your sincere commitment to seeing that "justice" be done, was an inspiration to both myself and my wife. Since coming to this country over thirty years ago, we have always been proud to call ourselves "Americans" and our exposure to the judicial process during the Kozminski case reaffirmed our belief in this great democratic country.

This eloquent and moving testament, standing alone, made our efforts seem worthwhile and would remain with us long after the case, indeed to this very day.

BUT THESE LASTING memories aside, our task was not yet done. We were committed to taking one last crack at securing victims' funds from abroad. Further, though we hardly expected it, we would soon face Kozminski and Maginnis one final time in the courtroom of Judge David V. Kenyon.

The Swiss Vault

Because we knew that Kozminski neither spent nor deposited most of the victims' money in this country, we had continually searched for evidence of likely foreign havens. Kozminski himself once boasted to Jacob Weingarten that he deposited all his funds in Europe and would never keep any in the United States.

Several documents from Kozminski's files, including letters in his own hand, ultimately convinced us that he possessed one or more Swiss bank accounts. This conclusion was buttressed by Lucian Ludwig Kozminski's odd affinity for the Germans, who stashed untold billions in untraceable Swiss accounts during the period of the Third Reich. All signs, as a result, pointed to Switzerland.

For many months, the Swiss government had advised us to wait until conviction and sentence before pursuing Kozminski's suspected holdings. A few days after Judge Kenyon imposed sentence, therefore, we dutifully informed the Justice Department's Office of International Affairs, which promptly sent a telex to the Federal Office for Police Matters, International Assistance Section, in Bern, Switzerland, as follows:

> Certain correspondence between Kozminski and Handelsbank, N.W., Rue Du Stand 60–62, 1211 Geneve 11, has come to the attention of the U.S. Attorney's Office. Copies of this correspondence will be sent to you airmail express immediately, and a formal request for assistance under the treaty will follow within a reasonable time. Meanwhile we ask that the funds be blocked in any account existing in the name of Lucian Kozminski . . . in this bank until the rights of the victims to these funds can be established in Swiss courts. We ask that you grant this request under the "Ancillary Administrative Proceedings" Provisions of Article 1, Section 3 of the treaty.

Despite the seriousness of Kozminski's crimes and the sensitive subject matter of our case, it took the Swiss government just *one day* to provide a formal response. And the answer was a firm and resounding "no":

> We refer to your telex of [10/20/82] and inform you that we would not be able to execute your future request of assistance in the above-captioned case. According to Article 1, Section 1, Letter B of the Treaty, the contracting parties [the United States and Switzerland] undertake to afford each other mutual assistance in effecting the return to the requesting state . . . of any objects . . . belonging to it and obtained through such offences.
>
> In the present case the assets do not belong to the USA. According to Article 2, Section 1, Letter B of the Treaty, we cannot execute an American judgment in a criminal matter. Furthermore, we cannot grant this request under the ancillary administrative proceedings provisions of Article 1, Section 3 of the Treaty because we have not exchanged diplomatic notes concerning such an agreement and . . . for the present proceedings are not administrative proceedings. In this case the victims have to ask personally for an attachment for a civil court.

And so, in one simple telex message, the Swiss government refused to relinquish their vault's combination, dashing the hope of recovery by hundreds if not thousands of Kozminski's victims. We apparently had been reduced to one limited option: locating a *Swiss* victim of Kozminski who would commence a civil action in Switzerland seeking to freeze the suspected accounts.

As the Swiss government was well aware, however, the prospects were abysmal. Switzerland was a small country with a relatively small population that included few Jews, and it had technically remained neutral during World War II. It was extremely unlikely that *any* Swiss Jews departed that relatively safe haven for another destination during Hitler's reign of terror. Thus, the chance of locating a Swiss victim of Nazi Germany was very slim, and one who had been defrauded by Kozminski even slimmer.

Still livid at the Swiss government's blunt response, I turned to the press, hoping that if I publicized our search, a Swiss victim might materialize.

After my lengthy interview with a reporter, a *Los Angeles Times* headline on December 10, 1982, read, CON MAN MAY HAVE BANKED FORTUNE, followed by a story highlighting our concern, which began:

> As much as $1 million is believed to be in a Swiss bank account of a World War II Nazi concentration camp inmate imprisoned in Los Angeles for defrauding other Holocaust survivors, a federal prosecutor said Thursday.
>
> However, Assistant U.S. Attorney Mark E. Kalmansohn said the Swiss government has abruptly rebuffed his efforts to confirm that the account exists and have authorities there hold the funds so that victims may have a chance to recover their losses.
>
> And so Kalmansohn is seeking a victim from 3,000 on file who is or was a Swiss citizen, and may be able to bring a civil suit in Switzerland to attach the funds on behalf of all the victims. So far, he has been unsuccessful.
>
> "It is the ultimate in frustration," the prosecutor reported.

Responding to our plea, the Bet Tzedek Legal Services clinic graciously volunteered to assist our search. Rabbi Cooper of the Simon Wiesenthal Holocaust Center vowed to join our quest and offered to contact the Swiss consulate to "explore" its position. However, despite these generous offers and our many months of sustained effort, we could not locate a single Swiss victim or budge the Swiss government from its steadfast posture. The Swiss vault would remain secure.

It would be another fifteen long years before revelations of the Swiss banking system's complicity with the Nazis, coupled with intense international pressure, would affect the Swiss government's outlook on a variety of Holocaust claims. That, however, was fifteen years too late for the three thousand victims of Lucian Kozminski.

The Crumbling Wall

With our chances of locating Kozminski's assets dwindling, we finally decided to seek help from a highly unlikely source: Esther Kozminski. Though our hopes of eliciting her cooperation were faint, to our surprise she greeted Kinzler's call warmly and spontaneously invited him to the Kozminskis' Beverly Hills apartment.

The moment Kinzler arrived, the pleasant, black-haired woman played the gracious hostess, ushering him into the living room and offering him a cup of tea. After her guest was comfortable, she slowly sat down and fixed her gaze upon him, and even the translucent white remnant of the eye she lost in Auschwitz appeared rapt.

Yet when they began conversing, Kinzler could instantly discern something was very wrong. When he asked Ms. Kozminski directly about her husband's assets, she mumbled, "Yes, he told me about that . . . Oh, God, it was a terrible, terrible thing he did . . . I'm through with him . . . You know, I'm from Lodz myself . . . the camps . . . and, I was in the camps . . . I . . . I don't know what to do."

Each time Kinzler attempted to return to the subject, her answers were rambling and disjointed. Beneath Ms. Kozminski's veneer of charm, she appeared curiously brittle and nearly unhinged. Convinced this was not mere artifice, Kinzler knew something was seriously amiss. Owing to Ms. Kozminski's fragile condition, he decided to terminate the interview.

In the end, it mattered little, for despite her apparent eagerness to cooperate, Ms. Kozminski could provide only sketchy details. While eventually confirming that her husband accumulated substantial funds and spent little, she simply could not offer any helpful leads concerning the location or nature of Kozminski's hidden assets.

Finally, in an ironic culmination to their meeting, Ms. Kozminski

earnestly invited Kinzler to speak before a local Jewish group, pointedly noting, "I . . . I'm sure they would be interested in hearing from
the man who caught . . . my husband."

MANY HOLOCAUST survivors suffered from a common syndrome.
Emerging from the ashes of destruction, they denied the horrors of
the past and sought refuge in day-to-day existence. The painful
memory and the insulated present remained distinct and uninte-
grated until a traumatic event occurred. Then the porous wall divid-
ing these two existences would crumble, creating internal chaos.

Esther Kozminski suffered greatly in her life. Interned in several
concentration camps, she lost her entire family to the Holocaust. Her
marriage had been extremely difficult, culminating in her husband's
conviction for cheating Holocaust survivors. Finally, it now appeared
that the pressure of denial had caused the fragile wall between her
past and present to crumble spontaneously.

The Last Offensive

In moving to reduce a sentence, ordinarily the defense must show
some defect in or overriding new evidence affecting the original sentence. Focusing on neither, Maginnis's motion to reduce Kozminski's
sentence instead disputed the government's evidence that Kozminski
was an *oberkapo* at Gross-Rosen (expressly disregarded by Judge
Kenyon at sentencing) and challenged a passing media reference to
the purported operation of a Munich "cabaret-bordello" by one of
Kozminski's sons.

Maginnis's memorandum had four attachments. The first two
attachments were letters submitted by Kozminski's first wife, Janina
Liebermann. One letter starkly alleged that "U.S. Attorney Mark
Kalmansohn has been *manipulating* and *lying* about the past of Mr.
Lucian Kozminski from the beginning." Liebermann then complained about the "unprecedented *inquisition*" of Kozminski and
members of his family "[j]ust to let some *inept U.S. Attorney* get his
career off the ground!" In the same vein, she later opined, "I have

seen a lot of *low lifes* [*sic*] in my lifetime. But so far the personality of M. Kalmansohn tops everything." [emphasis added]

In her second letter, Ms. Liebermann adamantly claimed that "my ex-husband Lucian Kozminski is *totally innocent* of the *outrageous charge* made in the *Los Angeles Times* and the U.S. Attorney's Office that he was some sort of Nazi collaborator during the period of World War II." Turning to Kozminski's sentence, she tossed a pointed barb at Judge Kenyon:

> How was it that for allegedly cheating some people out of . . . *a pit-tance* . . . Mr. Kozminski received a *cruel and unusual* sentence of twelve years in prison?

Liebermann then accused me of "*debas[ing] the honor of the U.S. Justice Department* and all our constitution stands for. Behaving not like an American attorney, but more like some *Bolshevik/Soviet lowlife goon inquisitor!*" Finally, she even put Maginnis on the spot:

> You have been paid so far and received monies for some of the victims that supposedly were due money . . . from Kozminski's estate. Has all this been made clear to the court?

Though admittedly unpleasant, none of this was particularly surprising. Having prosecuted for several years, I was well aware that personal attacks occasionally come with the territory, at times as part of a deliberate defense strategy.

As Kinzler remarked upon reviewing Liebermann's letters, "Looks like we've got another Weasel. They must have made quite a couple."

Meanwhile, shifting to another subject, Maginnis's third attachment contained a purported affidavit of a Henryk Ingster from Munich, who claimed that sometime after the War:

> . . . there existed a court of honor both in the Jewish Central Committee, as well as the City Committee of Munich, which devoted itself primarily to accusations made by Jews against other Jews for having acted wrongfully toward co-prisoners during the period of persecu-

tion. . . . I did not know then, nor do I know now of any such accusations brought at any time against Lucjan Kozminski.

Even in failing to refute Shlomo Blajman's detailed sworn statements, this affidavit did not appear to bear any relevance to the original sentence.

Illuminating in an unintended fashion was Maginnis's final attachment of a power of attorney, dated November 9, 1967, in which Kozminski transferred ownership of "Scotch-Bars" in Vilsbiburg and Weilheim and a lessee interest in a "Bungalow Restaurant" to his son Januscsh. Maginnis's apparent purpose (to demonstrate that none of these "legitimate" establishments included a "cabaret-bordello") was beside the point: It was far more germane that these property transfers occurred immediately after Kozminski's spate of West German convictions and thereby apparently reflected one method he used to secrete his assets.

In the end, Maginnis's motion clearly served notice that he was mixing an incendiary cocktail of smoke, mirrors, and heat. As the hearing date approached, we braced ourselves for another clash with our adversaries.

Clash in the Courtroom

When the hearing on Maginnis's motion commenced, nearly four months after the original sentencing, he swiftly challenged my quote in the recent *Los Angeles Times* article containing a minor reference to Kozminski's son. But Judge Kenyon quickly cut him off, pointedly advising, "But [the case] wasn't tried—I generally don't even read newspapers, but if it was—I don't read newspapers generally having to do with any case that I'm connected with, not even the article."

When I then addressed the court, my remarks were unexpectedly interrupted:

Kalmansohn: [A]s the article in the *Los Angeles Times* indicated, what the government is looking for, because the Swiss government was uncooperative under the Treaty of Mutual Assistance, was a victim of Kozminski who is or was a Swiss citizen, so that a class action could be filed in Switzerland, to reveal the existence of . . . any . . . bank accounts. (*Courtroom disturbance*)

This time the proceedings were abruptly halted by one of Kozminski's witnesses, his ex-wife Janina Liebermann. Standing in the spectator section, the short, brown-haired woman gestured vehemently and shouted insults at me until Judge Kenyon finally intervened:

Judge Kenyon: Please don't do that. Wait a minute. I'm a grown man. I've been trying cases for a few years. I give everybody a fair shake. You can't sit back there and testify, shaking your hands and raising them. We're not a sixth-grade class. The point of it is, ma'am, if you want to talk—if you have something to say—the lawyers, in the first place, are representing each side.

Maginnis then revealed his intent to call Liebermann as a witness:

Maginnis: Your Honor, I would ask that she take the stand, and I think she was still thinking—
Judge Kenyon: That's fine. That's fine. But I want to explain to her that when she takes the stand that there are certain rules of the road. . . . The first thing we had when we first came in was this lady sitting back there talking when—
Maginnis: Your Honor, she has never been in a court in the United States—
Judge Kenyon: I don't think [she] should get away with anything in any other courtroom [she's] ever been in. . . . Probably gets away with more in this court than any other court.

Moments later, Liebermann took the stand. Her voice now quivering, she testified insistently that several Jews had contacted her since Kozminski's sentencing but were afraid to testify "because they're scared of Mr. Kalmansohn . . . he do [*sic*] everything in the newspaper."

Angrily dismissing evidence showing Kozminski was an *oberkapo* and contending, rather, that he saved the lives of two concentration camp inmates, Liebermann then directed her remarks toward me:

Liebermann: Either he is Jew or non-Jew; I don't care for him, because he don't know [*sic*] what's going on in concentration camp [*sic*]. . . . When my whole family was burning . . . he no help [*sic*]. His family no help my parents [*sic*]. . . . Who gave him the right to make judgment or to tell lies about someone?

In finally pleading that Kozminski's sentence be reduced, Lieber-mann referred to the curious absence of his then wife, Esther, from the courtroom:

> Liebermann: I don't know—I ask the Court please to reduce the . . . sentence. He hasn't earned that. He is a good man. He is a good man. I don't know what he did that twenty-two years . . . it's sad enough that his wife is not here . . . it's sad enough.

With those final remarks, Liebermann briskly departed the stand and returned to her seat in the spectators' section.

Now it was Kozminski's turn. Clad in blue prison garb and appearing oddly detached from the proceedings, through his interpreter Kozminski briefly addressed the Court from the podium:

> Kozminski: I am sorry for what I have done up until now. I believe that I shouldn't go—I don't belong in prison. . . . I have a good record, and I would like to return to society.

Having presented the evidence at his disposal, Maginnis boldly stepped to the podium for his argument, a final earnest plea to reduce Kozminski's sentence.

> Maginnis: Your Honor, as far as I know, as long as Mr. Kozminski has been in Terminal Island there have been no disciplinary reports filed against him. . . . He is apparently working in the kitchen, and he has been assigned duty in the kitchen.
>
> I think the court should take into account that the government in this case has really made a *political* case out of this . . . Mr. Kalmansohn . . . makes these wild outlandish statements over and over both in the courtroom and in the newspapers . . . he never once takes the stand in this case under oath; and never once files any affidavits under oath with this court that he has any proof that Mr. Kozminski was a *kapo*. Why does he do it? He wants to just make it look like a big deal in this court.
>
> We all know the powers of the United States government. If the government really thought that there was any buried secret accounts in Switzerland, they could have people like Edwin Wilson or the CIA or somebody over there checking it out. The reason they haven't done it is because there is no such account.

Well, it appears to me, your Honor, that all Mr. Kalmansohn has in mind here is, he wants to make sure that the Court does nothing in this case as far as reduction of the sentence goes, and wants to characterize this in his own mind as the crime of the century. Well, I think it's hardly the crime of the century.

The fact that the [victims] were concentration camp survivors and their pensions were taken away from them does not make this the worst crime on earth. It's nowhere near what Klaus Barbie did, the butcher of Leon, or anyone else like that, and I just think that it's remarkable that Mr. Kozminski could be *pilloried* the way that Mr. Kalmansohn has done in this courtroom without the benefit of anything under oath by Mr. Kalmansohn. . . . I think we should take into account the fact that Mr. Kozminski is *sixty-six years* old, in spite of another red herring brought up by the government that they feel he is only fifty-six and he has falsified his age. Again, they haven't proved that before this Court.

What I point out to the Court is that this man is not a hundred percent evil . . . and I think that the Court should seriously consider, as in Shakespeare's *Merchant of Venice*, the quality of mercy and consider reducing his sentence.

There was little for me to say. As I could not discern any legal reason presented by Maginnis for reducing Kozminski's sentence, I kept my statement brief:

Kalmansohn: I would like to point out just for the record, of course, that there was a sworn declaration under oath filed by the gentleman from Israel, Shlomo Blajman, to the effect, based on direct observation, that Mr. Kozminski was an *oberkapo*. That is not an issue here. It wasn't an issue at the sentencing . . . and I don't know why it's been brought up here. The government has also had a good-faith basis in documents as well as testimony for every other statement the government has made in this case, in court or out of court.

There is no new information that would justify a reduction in the sentence, your Honor. . . . The government believes . . . [that] this crime . . . which extended over thirteen years, is perhaps the best reflection of the *weakness* of the United States government. The sentence of twelve years is appropriate; that is the least Mr. Kozminski should serve to serve justice in this matter.

It now was Judge Kenyon's turn, for the last time, to confront Kozminski. Facing the defendant, who stood between Maginnis and the interpreter, Kenyon issued his final ruling from the bench:

Judge Kenyon: The most disturbing thing from the Court's standpoint is that a lot of issues are being raised here that the Court in passing sentence originally gave no consideration to, and doesn't intend to give any consideration to at this time.

The Court sentenced Mr. Kozminski because it was convinced that there had been a lengthy period of many years during which Mr. Kozminski *very selfishly* and *very cruelly, really*, without any concern for the humanities involved, *bilked* people, *lied* to people, *cheated* people, and that same attitude continued on even up until the Court became involved. There was indication that there was still dishonesty going on.

And the Court felt that for purposes of punishment, one; two, to protect the public—Mr. Kozminski apparently has shown a great amount of skill in getting people to believe in him, and yet the evidence was overwhelming, and admitted by him to a great degree, that he had and was able to persuade people that he was honest when he wasn't honest at all; he was *bilking* them. . . .

At this juncture, it does not seem to the Court that anything has changed . . . and does not feel it has any reason to change the original sentence, and it will remain.

Like the sound of silver trumpets, Judge Kenyon's eloquent summary of Kozminski and his acts ended the case. The defense's arsenal was now empty, and Kozminski's lengthy sentence would stand without further challenge.

Moments after the session ended, the U.S. Marshals handcuffed a stone-faced Kozminski and escorted him out of the courtroom while Kinzler and I turned to each other and shook hands warmly one last time.

5

REUNION, REDEMPTION, AND MYSTERY

Revelations And Recrimination

After our prosecution concluded, media comments by principal defense figures were revealing in some instances, and in others quite predictable.

Pat Maginnis continued to disparage the motives behind our prosecution as well as the magnitude of our case:

> Mr. Kalmansohn . . . tried to make this into the case of the century. I think the undertones are political. Perhaps he [Kalmansohn] is considering a run for Congress or maybe for president of the Jewish Defense League, I don't know, but this [was] ridiculous.

I have not yet filed my candidacy for either office.

Kozminski, meanwhile, was interviewed in his cell at the sprawling concrete prison known as the Federal Correctional Institution at Terminal Island, near Los Angeles. Now inmate number 76505-012, Kozminski referred to the bluish tattoo on his left arm—Auschwitz inmate number 111790—and remarked, "They make mistake first time, must make 7 into 9. Very much pain. I can never forget the Nazis."

Then he turned to those who would take satisfaction in his current predicament, flippantly reporting, "I like it here. The food is good. You'd pay $10 or $12 for the meal you get here." This was consistent with reports that Kozminski had landed a prized position in the Terminal Island prison kitchen and had insinuated himself into an elite group of white-collar fraud criminals at the prison.

Still unrepentant, Kozminski offered transparent excuses for his guilty plea, disingenuously contending, "I pleaded only to avoid the aggravation. Mine [*sic*] *heart*, you understand? I could not stand the show."

Kozminski's thinly disguised disdain toward his victims also remained evident, "I like to help mine [*sic*] peoples until they turn on me. But I love mine [*sic*] Jewish people. I am proud to be a Jew. Jews are mine [*sic*] blood."

Expounding upon why "his" people "turned on" him, he claimed, "You do not understand. The post office give [*sic*] these people [the witnesses] money to come live in hotel [*sic*] and eat. Jews say anything if you pay them."

Finally, when asked about allegations that he fraudulently stashed his victims' money, Kozminski contemptuously snapped, "If I have millions, I *buy* you [*sic*] and the court. I won't [*sic*] be in jail."

Cynical as it was, events would later indicate that this statement may have been prophetic.

Meanwhile, Kozminski's then wife, Esther, presented an entirely different perspective. Sitting on a long black sofa and wearing sunglasses to conceal her bad eye, she was interviewed well after the conclusion of the case in the Kozminskis' Beverly Hills apartment. Far more composed than during her prior interview with Kinzler, she soberly and meticulously recounted her experience with her now incarcerated husband.

Ms. Kozminski began with her first impression of Kozminski, at a pastry shop in the Lodz ghetto, "His hair was long and greased like pea soup, and girls were on either arm. I asked my friends, 'Who is this playboy?'"

Thirty years later, Kozminski married her while facing an INS order of deportation, now prompting her to conclude, "I think now that's *why* he married me. That's the only hope he had to stay."

Ms. Kozminski then succinctly characterized her difficult married life:

> Looking back on our marriage, I cannot say I was ever happy. Every month, to make him pay the rent, it was a spectacle. He wouldn't even give me a quarter for the laundry. He wouldn't buy food. There was something about him I don't understand, something about him and his money. He could never get enough. He hated even to take it out of his own pocket.

Outside the privacy of their home, however, an entirely different side of Kozminski's Dr. Jekyll–Mr. Hyde personality emerged:

> A macho man, you know? A big shot. He bought drinks for everybody, even people he didn't know. I had a secret deal with the bartenders to send him home after five or six drinks. Never have I seen a man, especially a Jewish man, to drink so much. It's like he was afraid to be sober. But he never had a hangover. He could bear any physical pain.

Ms. Kozminski noted that her husband regularly drank large volumes of Seagram's VO, Hennessey cognac, and Stolichnaya vodka, all with no apparent effect.

Perhaps offering a small clue to Kozminski's antisocial behavior, Ms. Kozminski then related one of his idiosyncrasies:

> After he finished his dinner, you had to stop, too. For some reason, he couldn't stand to watch people eat. I think maybe he had problems mentally from the concentration camps.

Finally, she responded to the government's deduction that Kozminski hid victims' money, admitting, "Maybe not $1 million, but he has *lots* of it. He had told me not to worry, that he will have money waiting when he got out of prison."

Shortly after this unusually candid interview, Esther Milich formally commenced divorce proceedings against Lucian Kozminski in the Los Angeles Superior Court.

WHILE REAFFIRMING many of Kozminski's known behaviors, these interviews did little to provide answers to deeper questions. One thing remained certain: Something was definitely askew in the complex bundle of Kozminski's character and persona, if not in his mental makeup. At once boastful as well as dismissive of other Holocaust victims, he was a confirmed alcoholic and likely severely depressed, perhaps in part from the trauma administered by the Nazis. I now wondered whether, on most occasions, he was even connected to reality at all.

Yet, even with lingering questions, my experience with this case appeared to be concluded. Time now slipped by almost imperceptibly, month after month and year after year. Though it remained deeply etched in my memory, the case slowly faded from my present consciousness, and I suspected that I would never hear or read about Lucian Ludwig Kozminski again, much less ever see him.

A Phantom Appears

After leaving the U.S. Attorney's Office, I spent a year in Europe studying for a Diploma in International Law at Cambridge University and, after my return, worked for several years at a law firm in Beverly Hills. One day during this period, in late 1986 or early 1987, an associate of mine and I went to lunch.

As we strolled south on Beverly Drive, I was startled to recognize someone approaching us. At first this person seemed like a phantom in a surreal vision from my past. But as he drew nearer, no doubt existed.

It was *Lucian Ludwig Kozminski.*

Clad in an orange short-sleeved shirt and beige pants, the bespectacled Kozminski appeared tan, trim, and well-rested. As he came within a few feet of us, he looked at the sidewalk and then quickly tossed a cigarette to the ground. Scurrying past, he showed no visible hint of recognition.

My mind was a swirl of thoughts, but one would not escape me: Somehow the parole system had thwarted Judge Kenyon's clear directive that Kozminski be incarcerated during his active years, and after just four years he was back on the streets.

While I felt an urge to turn and say something, I did not, nor would I have known what to say. I simply continued walking until, as if to confirm the reality of this encounter, I finally glanced back as Kozminski faded into the distance.

My companion, apparently noticing my startled expression, remarked, "Who in the hell was *that?* You look like you just saw a ghost!"

Ruminating briefly, I slowly replied, "It was . . . nothing. Just a defendant from one of my cases several years ago. It . . . It's ancient history."

But despite my attempt to relegate this odd encounter to the past, the memory would persist, having planted a seed of curiosity that would later flourish.

A few years later, I spoke to Steve Trott, who as deputy district attorney filed the original complaint against Kozminski in 1972, and presided over the U. S. Attorney's Office during his conviction and sentence ten years later.

Trott related that during his tenure as a high-ranking official at the U.S. Justice Department in Washington, D.C., Kozminski unexpectedly scheduled a formal appointment and, at their ensuing late-1987 or early-1988 meeting, requested a full pardon permanently expunging all convictions from his record. But Trott remembered him all too well and rejected the request out of hand, unceremoniously "kick[ing] him out" of his office. As Trott added indignantly, "that guy had some nerve."

Lou Kinzler later told me that sometime after being released from prison, Kozminski reportedly reopened his restitution business. Kinzler, however, was no longer with the U.S. Postal Inspection Service and could not verify this secondhand account.

FINALLY, while visiting me in Los Angeles in December 1991, Menahem Russek introduced me to Dr. Tony Chari, an Auschwitz survivor from Lodz. As Russek and I reminisced about the Kozminski prosecution, it emerged that Chari was a grammar-school and high school classmate of Kozminski's.

Chari recounted, "Oh, yes, I remember Lutek well. He went to school with us until high school, then I think he dropped out."

Chuckling briefly, he went on, "Maybe he just couldn't take it. From day one we all called him 'Koza'—it means 'the Goat' in Polish—as slang for Kozminski. Boy, did we give him grief."

Shortly afterward I turned to another subject, querying, "When he was sentenced, Kozminski claimed he was sixty-six years old. Do you—"

Chari interjected, "Sixty-six? In 1982? Boy, is that a laugh! He was . . . let's see, fifty-seven or maybe fifty-eight then, and he couldn't have been a day over sixty."

His curiosity sparked by our discussion, Chari obtained Kozminski's phone number from directory assistance and called him.

Moments later Kozminski answered the phone, and after remembering Chari instantly, chatted with him in Polish for several minutes.

Upon hanging up, Chari noted that after he revealed he was visiting me, Kozminski cursed at the mention of my name and railed, "Let me tell you, I was *innocent* of all charges. They *framed* me, just think of it, a poor Jew from Lodz."

An Odd Reunion

Some five years later, while waiting to make an appearance in a crowded courtroom, I worked on an early draft of this manuscript. Glancing up at a line of lawyers standing against the far wall, I was surprised to see the familiar visage of one J. Patrick Maginnis.

Time seemed to have mellowed him. His hair short and gray and his facial hair reduced to a small mustache, he presented an almost distinguished and venerable bearing.

When Maginnis's civil case was called, he identified himself in a quiet, understated tone. Toward the end of that appearance, after opposing counsel claimed his client was bankrupt, the judge asked whether either lawyer had familiarity with bankruptcy law.

Pausing momentarily, Maginnis slowly replied, "I am not a bankruptcy lawyer, and I definitely have no . . . experience in the area."

Minutes later he slipped out of the courtroom, apparently oblivious to my presence in the dense throng of spectators.

A FEW MONTHS LATER, as I sat in a Santa Monica courtroom during a recess in a trial, the sound of muffled voices was suddenly punctuated by the raucous laughter of none other than Pat Maginnis, who had just entered the room with a characteristic flourish.

When I went over to my erstwhile adversary, who stood chatting amiably with several attorneys, he immediately recognized me, wrapped his arm around my shoulder, and remarked with a big smile, "Well, speaking of the devil, Herr Kalmansohn! Why don't you sit down next to me so we can chat?"

After I obliged, we engaged in lighthearted banter and briefly exchanged war stories about the Kozminski case, during which I quietly apprised him of the nature of my work in progress.

Clearly intrigued by my project, Maginnis spontaneously stated, "Listen, I really want to hear more about this. Why don't you come over to my Malibu home this weekend? I'll be recuperating from surgery—they're removing a malignancy from my tongue—but I should be able to talk."

"That was never a problem before, was it, Pat?" I retorted.

Several days later, I entered the comfortable, spacious Maginnis house and was introduced to Pat's wife, Jeanette, and their son and daughter. A charming and gracious host, Maginnis opened a bottle of red Australian wine and then, as we sipped, began recounting the story of his representation of Lucian Ludwig Kozminski.

MAGINNIS BEGAN, "Well, it turns out, for years Kozminski I both were regulars at the noon-hour watering hole at Harry's Bar in Century City. You know, we'd down three or four hard ones and then go back to work. Well, he seemed real lively and charming, you know, usually the center of attention."

"Well, how did you come to represent him?" I queried.

"Yeah, a day I'll regret," Maginnis muttered. "So one day, I guess it was in the spring of 1982, Kozminski pulls me aside at the bar, and he gets real serious. He says he's in a 'bit of trouble' and needs a criminal defense lawyer. So like a fool I agreed."

"So then what happened?" I asked.

"Well, as soon as I looked at all the goddamn evidence you compiled, I knew he was in a more than a bit of trouble."

"What did he say?" I queried. "I mean, did he admit he was guilty?"

"Hell, no!" Maginnis retorted. "He kept claiming those 'those damn Jews' had ganged up on him. And he kept ranting that Kinzler secretly was a German Jew bent on revenge. Then, when I suggested an insanity plea, he called *me* crazy. Well, it only got worse. In all my years of criminal defense, he was my most despicable client ever."

"Oooh, that must be pretty bad," I remarked.

"Christ, what I went through," Maginnis continued. "Did you know I received death threats, I don't know from whom, maybe the JDL? And I had to represent this scumbag knowing my own mother-in-law is a Jewish survivor of the Holocaust. Yeah, it's true. She was almost killed in Lembeck, Poland, and then the Nazis put her in a death camp. I'll tell you, I could feel the glare of those Holocaust survivors every time I entered the courtroom."

"So how'd you finally persuade him to plead guilty?" I asked.

"It was a goddamn struggle," Maginnis replied. "But I finally convinced him the evidence was so strong that he'd be creamed at trial. Then when I tried to arrange some restitution for his victims, he wouldn't cough up anything. His wife, Esther, kept telling me he's got these Swiss and German accounts, but *he* wasn't talking. I guess he wanted to sit on his pile of gold."

"That's a real shame," I replied.

"Yeah, well, maybe he would've gotten a shorter sentence, but he didn't give a shit," Maginnis remarked.

"So what happened after the case?" I asked.

"Well, it hardly ended for me. The son of a bitch keeps sending me threatening letters from Terminal Island, and finally he files a formal complaint against me with the State Bar. Of course, they dismissed it out of hand."

Sipping his wine, Maginnis expressed deep regret that he ever had undertaken the task of representing Kozminski. As he ruefully remarked, a pained expression on his face, "That guy is capable of absolutely *anything*. I'm sorry I had anything to do with him."

Whispers of the Spirit

More than thirteen years after the final court appearance in our case, I set out to contact several of our key witnesses, including Hans Wittner, Theodore Seidman, Jacob Weingarten, Mordka Wolman, and Stefan and Ella Mandel. While fearing some may no longer be alive, I relished the prospect of being reunited with several of these memorable and inspiring people.

Hans Wittner

When I called the Wittner residence, an elderly woman with deeply slurred speech answered and promptly identified herself as Sarah, Hans's wife. Moments later, her voice rose in recognition of my name and we exchanged pleasantries, followed by a brief period of uncomfortable silence.

Sensing something was amiss, I tentatively asked if Hans was there, but after a short pause, her voice quivered with emotion as Sarah wistfully replied: "I . . . I'm very sorry, but Hans, well, he died of influenza in 1986."

Her words instantly seared into my intestines and wrenched them with pain while my eyes welled with tears. I thought: *not* Hans Wittner. It *could not* be true.

After all, Hans may have been in his midseventies during our prosecution, but his buoyant soul and indomitable spirit made him seem timeless and immune to the ravages of age. This was a man who escaped from Germany to Poland, England, France, Cuba, and then the United States, always remaining one step ahead of the Nazi juggernaut. It was hard to fathom that just three years after our case, he could be felled by the silent scythe of the Grim Reaper.

After gathering myself and briefly extending my heartfelt sympathies, I suggested that we meet, and Sarah eagerly concurred.

The following week, as she ushered me into her apartment, I sensed something timeless about this 82-year-old woman, as if she had risen from the canvas of an ancient Flemish or Dutch portrait. Sarah's gray hair was long and stringy, and her face was crisscrossed with fine lines, but her bluish-green eyes, yellowed with age, still beamed with the spark of life. Her speech still slurred but far easier to comprehend in person, Sarah animatedly recounted the poignant saga of her relationship with Hans.

HANS AND SARAH first met in her native Bialystok, a textile center in northeast Poland. Calling Sarah shortly after fleeing to Cuba, Hans advised her that he was sick and nearly destitute and proceeded to express his love and plead with her to join him. A joyous Sarah readily agreed.

The year was 1939, shortly before the Nazi-Soviet invasion of Poland. Although Sarah begged her parents to accompany her, after they deemed it impossible, she reluctantly departed alone for the port of Gdansk. It was the last time she ever saw them. Soon afterward, the Germans stormed into Bialystok; locked seven hundred Jews in the main synagogue, and burned them alive; wantonly butchered thousands of Jewish men, women, and children on public streets as well as in hospitals and homes; and in the midst of this surreal nightmare swiftly dispatched Sarah's parents to Treblinka, Majdanek, or Auschwitz for gassing and cremation.

Sarah took a ship to London and, shortly later, headed to France. She then boarded another ship for Cuba, which traversed treacherous, storm-tossed waters for three weeks. Finally, amid a magical string of shimmering evening lights, Sarah arrived in the port of Havana. Soon afterward, she was at last reunited with Hans, and they eventually married and lived together in America for forty-three years.

Sarah remembered the cold winter's day, in 1986, when Hans insisted on going to their cigar store for several hours. The shop's heater was broken, and Sarah feared that Hans's severe asthma would become aggravated. Sure enough, soon after his return, Hans's lungs filled up and he contracted influenza and died after clinging to life for seven weeks in the hospital. Now fighting back tears, Sarah termed these sad events *"bashert"*—or fate.

After Hans died, Sarah was devastated and felt completely alone. Submerging her grief into sixteen hours of daily work, she finally suffered a debilitating stroke. At first partially paralyzed, a determined Sarah fought her way back and, despite her slurred speech, had virtually regained full use of her limbs.

SLICING FRESH STRAWBERRIES on her living room table, Sarah turned to me and mischievously raised the knife. Eyes gleaming, she recounted how she threatened Kozminski with a butcher knife to secure partial repayment of Hans's loan, and we both laughed at her bittersweet remembrance.

Finally, Sarah said, "You know, shortly after my stroke I gave my cigar store to two employees. I think you should go over there for a visit . . . for old times' sake."

Minutes after agreeing to her suggestion and bidding her farewell, I pulled up in front of Wittner's. As I stepped into the musty store filled with the aroma of tobacco, time seemed to bend back into the past, and I could almost envision a beaming Hans Wittner stepping forward and greeting me from behind the counter.

Theodore Seidman

Upon calling the Seidman home and reaching Ted's wife, Anna, I identified myself as the federal prosecutor on Kozminski's case, prompting her excited response; "*Federal prosecutor?* Why's a federal prosecutor calling *here?*"

Anna calmed down, however, after I assured her that I no longer prosecuted and was simply writing a book about the case.

Now fearing the worst, I hesitantly asked if Ted was there and, after a short pause, was relieved to hear Anna chuckle and reply, "Well, we *are* senior citizens, you know, and he's still sleeping. He sleeps *most* of the time now." Quickly glancing at my watch with curiosity, I noted that it was 11:00 A.M. on a Monday.

The following afternoon, Ted Seidman returned my call, and several days later we met for a short walk near the beach and a casual dinner.

When the subject turned to the Kozminski case, Seidman shook his head and proclaimed he would never forget our chart, succinctly adding, "It showed all the evidence."

Seidman recounted that after the guilty plea, he met outside the courthouse with Hans Rock, Kozminski's attorney-contact on his restitution claim. Puffing incessantly on cigarettes, the wild-eyed Rock reported that he was appalled by his first sight of Kozminski, grousing, "And to think *he* called me *Herr* Colleague for all these years!"

Although Seidman's memory appeared quite lucid, the 77-year-old said he spent most days sleeping and most nights reading the newspaper, frequently until 5:00 A.M. His activities were restricted by his back injury and limp, as well as the effects of a massive heart attack he had suffered the previous year. He and his wife subsisted on just two meager Social Security pensions, thanks in no small part to Lucian Kozminski.

As our meeting drew to a close, Seidman and I hugged each other, and he quietly wished me the very best in the future. His eyes still dancing with life, Seidman smiled warmly, turned, and limped away.

So Ted Seidman, the gentle man with fiery spirit who stood tall and shook his fist at Maginnis in court, was spending most remaining moments in sleep and relative tranquillity. Shakespeare's poignant words came to mind: "We are such stuff as dreams are made on, and our little life is rounded with a sleep."

Jacob Weingarten

I then called Jacob Weingarten, earnestly hoping he still was alive. While greatly relieved when the indomitable survivor of Mauthausen promptly answered the phone, I could barely recognize his high-pitched, strained voice, interspersed with gasping breaths.

Soon after we exchanged greetings, Weingarten informed me in a plaintive tone that he was not doing well. His income was limited, his diabetes had recently worsened, and the asthma that had gone into remission twenty years earlier had resurfaced with a vengeance, requiring regular visits to doctors and expensive medicines.

Despite his impaired condition, Weingarten eagerly invited me to his apartment. Upon my first sight of Weingarten, I was pleasantly struck by his appearance. Wearing a gray beret, white slacks, and a striped shirt, he seemed alert and energetic and still exuded a distinctive European charm. Age, physical maladies, and past suffering, however, undeniably had taken their toll, for the 77-year-old Weingarten was skinny, his back somewhat hunched, and his left eyelid occasionally drooped from diabetes.

Offering fond greetings from Esther, his wife and fellow Holocaust survivor, who was away at work, Weingarten stepped into the kitchen and emerged with a tray of coffee, sweet cakes, and *mandelbrot*. For several hours, we sat together and reminisced.

Weingarten began by chastising Kozminski for keeping his entire restitution award, lamenting, "He kept *mein* money." Not content with Kozminski's conviction, he said that after our prosecution, his private attorney vigorously continued to pursue Kozminski's assets.

Eventually believing he had located a Swiss bank account of Kozminski's, Weingarten banded together with several victims and approached the Swiss government. But the Swiss would reveal nothing and again insisted that only a Swiss victim of Kozminski's could file a suit to retrieve his holdings.

Exhaling in frustration, Weingarten added, "And, you know, Mr. Kalmansohn, Switzerland was neutral during the War and *had* no victims of Hitler."

In the end, Weingarten paid his attorney $1,250 and never received any portion of his $3,747.62 restitution payment or the substantial disability pension he would have been awarded if Kozminski had not bungled his claim in the first place.

When I asked Weingarten how he would react if he were face-to-face with Kozminski, he paused and remarked, "Pick up a gun and shoot him."

At the end of our meeting, I remarked that our prosecution never could have succeeded without his determined effort and thanked Weingarten for keeping the early investigation alive and allowing us to apprehend Kozminski.

Clearly pleased, he gasped, "Thank you very much. I did my best."

He certainly did. It was a long, perilous road from prewar Czechoslovakia to this moment, but Weingarten had somehow retained the shimmering spark of life.

Mordka "Max" Wolman

Upon contacting Max Wolman, I was confident I had finally located a survivor who enjoyed reasonably good health. After all, when the case ended, he was just fifty-five years old and appeared sufficiently strong to crush Kozminski in his bare hands, as he had once threatened. My optimism, however, soon was dashed.

After greeting me warmly and fondly remembering the postcard I sent from Cambridge, England, Wolman related a fateful incident that had occurred less than two years after Kozminski's conviction.

On August 7, 1984, at 1:00 P.M., while working in his television repair shop, Wolman noticed that the room suddenly began to spin. Standing up, momentarily, he blacked out, and immediately collapsed in a heap on the floor.

Two days later, barely clinging to life, Wolman awoke in the hospital and discovered he had suffered a massive stroke, leaving him nearly paralyzed.

His life would never be the same.

Wolman sold his business and home and, dreaming of recapturing his youthful adventures on horseback in the wilderness outside Paris, moved with his wife to a rural community on the outskirts of Los Angeles.

When I went to their ranch home a few days later, I was greeted by the bearded Wolman and his charming, auburn-haired wife and partner of forty-eight years, Dyna. Wolman's forceful handshake immediately served notice that despite a severe limp and left hand curled tightly into the wrist, his strong and tender spirit had somehow revived the burly, strapping Wolman of old.

Indeed, Wolman stated, "I'm not a religious man, but I look on this [my condition] as a blessing from God. He took my father and most of my family, but he spared me." Almost to reassure me, he added, "There are a lot worse things than physical pain. I can handle that. The difficult thing is the recurring nightmares about the Germans chasing me, about my father's miserable death."

The three of us walked through the spacious house and stepped outside to the large, adjoining stable. Wolman beamed as he approached and affectionately patted his sinewy brown mare, Cognac. Turning toward me, he recounted that after years of physical therapy, struggles, and setbacks including a fierce bout with cancer, he eventually learned to work with his disability.

At the beginning, Dyna and four others would regularly lift Wolman out of a wheelchair onto his beloved Cognac, and he would ride with the strange sensation of a body "dead on the outside" and "alive inside." Continually training his "existing brain cells" to compensate for the "dead ones," he graduated to crutches and then dispensed with them entirely, ultimately forging his way back to relative health.

All along, Wolman's inspiration remained those rare, unguarded moments on horseback, the wind streaming against his face, when he felt free and uninhibited by mere mortal restraints, pain, or suffering.

Shortly before departing, I asked Wolman what he would do if he were face-to-face with Kozminski right now. Without hesitation, he responded just as Jacob Weingarten had, "I would pick up a gun and shoot him." After a long pause, Wolman added, "It has nothing to do with the money. It's what he did to the survivors."

Stefan and Ella Mandel

When I called Stefan Mandel, he greeted me with effusive warmth and remarked, "It's funny you called. I have thought about you many times, especially recently." Reporting that Ella, his son, and his daughter were all reasonably well, he tenderly added, "And my three grandchildren are the joys of my life."

Chuckling briefly, Mandel related a casual and unexpected encounter years after Kozminski's conviction and sentence. While walking in the Fairfax District, he was astounded to see Kozminski, a free man, approaching. Stefan went right up to him and asked, "What are *you* doing here?"

Startled, Kozminski winced during a curious and uncharacteristic moment of silence and, after regaining his composure, sarcastically retorted, "And what are *you* doing here?"

A few minutes later, Mandel turned serious and recounted that several years before, he spoke to Esther Milich, Kozminski's ex-wife, who revealed that during their marriage, Kozminski often beat her "like an animal." But her dread did not end with divorce, as she remained terrified of Kozminski, fearing he would exact revenge for her cooperation with several victims of his scheme.

Upon hearing this somber account, I asked Mandel if he might prevail upon Esther to meet with me, and he readily consented.

The next week, Mandel called and hesitantly advised me that

Esther would be unable to meet. As confirmed by several Holocaust survivors, as well as an official publication of the American Congress of Jewish Survivors of Concentration Camps, she had passed away five years earlier, on June 7, 1991. Her long period of suffering, only compounded by her ex-husband's cruel deeds, apparently ended quietly and in relative obscurity.

Several days later, I met with Stefan and Ella, who had just returned from her trip to Turkey with a university group. While Stefan greeted me cordially, Ella was far more restrained. She simply could not recall our prior meeting, asked if I was Jewish, and repeatedly questioned why I would write a book about Kozminski rather than someone who performed "good deeds."

As Ella queried me, I had a distinct sense of déjà vu from fifteen years before, when the Mandels were initially reluctant to cooperate with our investigation. Sensing the same feeling, Stefan briefly joked about it, but Ella still seemed perplexed.

Now slowly turning directly toward her, I replied that sometimes the vision of white becomes clearer when contrasted with tones of black and gray and explained that my depiction of Kozminski was meant to serve this purpose. Ella still remained silent, but her sad eyes seemed to acknowledge my objective.

As the evening continued, Stefan and Ella began to recount their experience as survivors. Stefan succinctly remarked, "You know, to me the War was a prior lifetime, entirely separate from my present existence. Somehow I managed to survive through good fortune and a strong body, but now I've placed it all behind me. I really don't think I've had any other choice."

The balance remained more delicate for Ella. She quietly stated, "I think I survived because of hope—hope that after the War ended my family would . . . magically reappear. But when they didn't . . . when that dream was shattered, I started to feel guilt. Guilt about Zosia's death and, I guess, guilt about surviving."

Stefan and Ella remarked that some survivors simply dwelled in the past, citing Esther Milich as one notable example. While she reportedly participated in several Holocaust survivor groups, volunteered as a docent at the Simon Wiesenthal Holocaust Center, and aided an assortment of Jewish charities, that was just part of the story.

The Mandels showed me advertisements Esther placed in survivor publications seeking "information" on the "whereabouts" of her sister Hena and her brother Daniel. Far from "lost," however, these siblings had perished in the Holocaust fifty years before and continued to exist only in the mind of Esther Milich, for whom the past and present had merged.

Before I departed, Ella showed me several prewar photographs of her family. I was particularly struck by the photos of Ella's mother, a striking, dignified brunette woman. In her sad brown eyes, I could see Ella's, and in Ella's I could see hers. In the end, while studying these yellowed remnants of the past, I shuddered at the thought that Ella's mother, father and sisters were systematically murdered for the purpose of "cleansing" the human race.

I SENT LETTERS to German restitution agencies on behalf of Sarah Wittner and Jacob Weingarten, describing Kozminski's fraud and pleading for belated relief.

Several weeks later, I received responses. The Berlin Restitution Agency reiterated that the Wittner claim had been denied and the period for filing further appeals had ended. Similarly, the Stuttgart Restitution Agency replied that despite Kozminski's embezzlement of Jacob Weingarten's restitution payment, it was precluded from issuing another one. The agency wrote, however, that Weingarten's existing claim for "injury" would be submitted to the survivors' Claims Conference for possible issuance of future benefits.

I also reached the U.S. Department of Justice, which confirmed that any request under the Treaty of Mutual Assistance with Switzerland would be futile. Soon afterward, I contacted the Swiss Banking Association and initiated the laborious process of searching for the existence of Kozminski's assets in Switzerland.

AFTER MY REUNION with these survivors, I realized why I had delayed writing this book for so many years. It assuredly was not because the materials were voluminous or details would be difficult to recall. Rather, it was because of my denial of the enduring hidden pain—both the survivors' and my own.

Indeed, when the case ended successfully, I dispelled a gnawing feeling of irresolution and considered our task complete. Justice was apparently served and the survivors vindicated. The time was ripe to move on to new cases, challenges, and conquests, preserving this experience as a conclusively pleasant memory. But the ensuing period exposed quite a different reality.

As the years passed, I sensed the evaporation of the false confidence of youth, with the unstated assumption that life should proceed on a purposeful, ascending, and positive course.

I was confronted with the illusion of security in employment, commitment, constancy, and even love. I experienced the unsettling notion that, in a fleeting nightmarish moment, the most cherished and revered things in life can be ripped from the deepest bonds of one's heart and soul without warning or choice. I learned the consequences of having existed as a mere extension of others, who disappeared as a source of love and support when I simply lived my own life, or revealed my own human frailties during times of trouble or need. Finally, I felt the eerie and elusive sensation of rapidly escalating time enshrouding the fragile state of our own brief existence.

Like life itself, even these experiences and realizations were bittersweet and engendered greater personal insight. I admit it did not come easily.

Thrust onto a winding path that was unplanned and uncharted, and in some respects undesired, I navigated only by confronting my pain and struggling to grow with it and through it. In finally emerging from this personal ordeal, I came to recognize my own vulnerability and mortality, the source of inner strength and identity, and the elements of real and enduring love and commitment.

With the benefit and clarity of this awareness, the stark reality became clearer. Through my own searing, occasionally gut-wrenching pain, I comprehended that virtually nothing we experience in our ordinary lives can compare to the suffering and anguish of Holocaust survivors. Years later, I fully appreciated that our case could not undo *any* of the wrongs perpetrated by the Nazis, nor erase the survivors' agonizing past; heal their injured bodies; restore their shattered emotions, families, or lives; or mend the hidden hole of grief that still existed in each of them.

Yet even this sad truth bore the seeds of inspiration, for I also realized that despite their travails, these people would not and did not die. Rather, through spirit and sheer force of will, they rose above despair and infirmities and lived.

It was only in the end, for some, that the painful inner hole finally conspired with the failing body, reducing their spirit to a barely palpable whisper. That spirit, however, still exists and will endure within their souls and in others.

Of Visions, Flight, and Death

Though my meetings with the survivors were illuminating in several respects, they only confirmed the dark, mysterious shroud engulfing Kozminski.

It all started during my first telephone call with Stefan Mandel, when he related that more than a year before, his wife, Ella, had conversed with Janina Liebermann, Kozminski's first wife.

"And you know what Ms. Liebermann told Ella when the subject of her ex-husband came up?" Stephan recounted. "She said, 'Oh, you didn't hear? Lucian [Kozminski] suddenly and . . . unexpectedly died in 1993. And we quickly buried him in a local cemetery.'"

For a moment Stefan's words did not register, as I struggled with this jarring and bewildering news, straining to comprehend that one simple account apparently ended a long and complex tale. My visceral instincts told me otherwise, pulling at my senses, warning that this ending was too neat, too offhand, too inconspicuous, and, indeed, too anticlimactic. But the cold reality nevertheless seemed undeniable: Lucian Ludwig Kozminski, at long last, had been laid to rest. He was dead and the story was done.

Apparently left with little choice, over the next few days I slowly attempted to release my doubt and integrate the report of Kozminski's passing. Again and again during this process, my mind wandered to Hans Wittner. In an odd way, I eventually felt some comfort that Kozminski had finally joined him in death, knowing that if our spirit truly lives on, then surely Wittner would chase his tormentor around the metaphysical universe for eternity.

But my nagging doubt persisted as closure would not be reached so easily. Deciding to contact Jacob Weingarten, I discovered that I would be propelled into an uncharted territory of exploration and mystery.

It took only moments for Stefan Mandel's news to elicit a reaction from Weingarten. Vehemently scoffing at the word of Kozminski's death, he said, "I don't believe it for a moment. I think Liebermann spread a false report to protect herself, Kozminski, and their sons. You know, Mr. Kalmansohn, many of Kozminski's victims still were after him, and so, I hear, was the government, including the IRS. I think this—what did you call it, 'sudden death'?—was a way for him to escape."

But Weingarten was far from done. He thought for a moment and continued, "And you know, Mr. Kalmansohn, I hear things from the other survivors. One of them, Isador Lando, told me that he saw Kozminski less than two years ago [well after the date of his reported death], strolling on Fairfax Avenue with a girlfriend and smoking a big cigar. Later, Lando heard Kozminski ran away to Mexico."

As I listened rapt, he went on, "But I heard other things, too. One survivor told me a black inmate stabbed Kozminski to death in a Kentucky prison. A few others told me that Kozminski's own girlfriend said he had been killed. Personally, I think he ran away to Mexico."

Upon Weingarten's suggestion, I contacted Regina Weinstock, of Los Angeles, for further clues concerning this riddle. Soon after I announced my purpose, the affable white-haired woman said, "I think I can be of some help. But first let me tell you how about my own experience with Mr. Kozminski."

And with that brief but promising introduction, she turned to the harrowing journey that eventually lead her into the clutches of Lucian Kozminski.

In 1939, with the Nazi vise tightening, Weinstock fled Danzig, Poland, aboard a Jewish refugee ship bound for Palestine. When the ship finally arrived at its destination, the British summarily fired upon it and forced a hasty retreat. But there was nowhere else to go. All local ports barred the refugees.

While the ship languished for the next four months off the Greek coast, many of the famished passengers took ill, others died, and some went insane. This hellish near-oblivion finally ended when the ship managed to slip past the British blockade and anchor offshore at Gaza, Palestine.

The perilous odyssey to the Promised Land at last over, the Jews slowly waded ashore. But their greeting was less than hospitable, as a band of armed Arabs promptly swooped down from the Gaza hills and attacked them, stealing all their possessions and leaving them shivering, emaciated, and half-naked in the remote desert.

Weinstock eventually left Israel and moved to Los Angeles. Shortly after the West German government announced a substantial restitution award for her loss of liberty and education, she had the distinct misfortune of meeting Kozminski. Promising he would obtain an even greater award, Kozminski extracted more than $2,000 for "fees" and then managed to botch her claim. In the end, Weinstock was awarded no restitution and when I met her, subsisted on meager Social Security payments.

Drawing a deep breath, Weinstock quietly added, "So you can see, I was one of his victims, too." Pausing momentarily, she turned to the matter at hand in a steady voice and confident tone. She revealed that a close acquaintance, the recently deceased Henry Fisher, ate breakfast with Kozminski "nearly every day" in the Fairfax District until sometime during 1994. Then the regular breakfasts abruptly and inexplicably stopped. Fisher had not seen him again.

Weinstock had heard nothing about Kozminski's "death" from Fisher or anyone else, only that he had suddenly "disappeared." She concluded by remarking with certainty, "I'm sure those breakfasts continued into 1994. And I can tell you another thing: If Kozminski died, I or the other survivors in this community *definitely* would have known."

BUT THAT ASSUREDLY was not all. I later contacted Molly Schimel, who sadly reported that her husband, Henry, had passed away the previous month after a long battle with cancer. When we turned to the present mystery, Schimel's somber mood dissipated and her eyes lit up as she remarked: "Kozminski, dead in 1993? That's *impossible*.

I just saw him, maybe one and a half years ago [in late 1994 or early 1995] on the sidewalk in front of the Glendale Federal Savings in Beverly Hills. I went right up and tried to talk to him, but he looked very worried. Then he waved his hand, like to brush me off, turned away, and went inside the bank."

Molly wagged her finger while continuing, "And let me tell you something else. I've heard from several survivors that he fled the country and went to Germany, Argentina, Poland, or Mexico. I don't know where he is, but I'm sure he's somewhere."

Now both intrigued and confused, and not knowing whom or what to believe, I turned to several likely sources. Ella Mandel was convinced Kozminski was buried in one of two local Jewish cemeteries, either Mt. Sinai or Hillside. I soon discovered, however, that neither cemetery possessed any record of his death or burial. The same was true with Chevra Kadisha (which handles Jewish "pauper" graves and services all Jewish cemeteries), five other Jewish mortuaries, and two national survivors' organizations. A routine check on Kozminski's Social Security number similarly revealed no record of his death. Finally, a variety of other sources either could not locate or were unaware of any information relating to Kozminski's passing.

It therefore appeared that despite Ms. Liebermann's unequivocal report, Lucian Kozminski had neither died nor been buried in Los Angeles or elsewhere in the United States. Rather, it seemed that sometime about two years earlier, sometime in 1994 or early 1995, he suddenly and mysteriously had "fallen off the edge of the earth."

THESE VARYING accounts of Kozminski's fate evoked the continuing controversy over three other Holocaust-related figures: Adolf Hitler, Josef Mengele, and Raoul Wallenberg. For years disputes raged over reports of Hitler's death in his Berlin bunker in 1945, Mengele's drowning in Brazil in 1979, and Wallenberg's death in a Soviet prison in 1947. Particularly as to Wallenberg, and less so Mengele, these matters remain unresolved and the subject of ongoing debate.

In a chillingly similar vein, I contemplated: Did Kozminski commit the supreme con by propagating false stories about his own death and secretly absconding when the heat was on? Was he enjoying the good life, living grandly on his own victims' blood money? Or, if Ms. Liebermann had related the truth about his passing, had a Kozminski myth convinced his victims he could cheat even death? Was his corporal existence important for their hope of ultimate retribution? In the end, was Kozminski nothing more than a living phantom, like one of *Macbeth*'s ghosts, intoning to the world: "Be bloody, bold and resolute; laugh to scorn"?

The Valley of Dry Bones

Rather than leave Kozminski's mystery in the hands of time and fate, I initiated a final effort to unravel it. This new excavation into the past would presumably unearth one of three things: the dry bones of death, a flesh-covered living pariah, or an enduring mystery.

Several incentives spurred me on. Fresh on the heels of my reunion with the survivors, I was inspired by the prospect that *if* Kozminski could be found so could his assets, which could finally be seized and returned to their rightful owners. Then, too, regardless of whether Kozminski or his assets could be located, I also knew the victims would simply want to know the truth about his fate. My intellectual curiosity and even the thrill of a challenging mystery, particularly one involving death itself, further encouraged me. Last, I retained the lingering sense that my business with Kozminski was not done, that some unknown and unforeseen challenge still remained.

SEVERAL WEEKS after my victim interviews, I received a preliminary report from Frank Coonis, head of a local private investigative outfit.

Upon placing a call to me at my office, Coonis remarked in his gravely voice, "So, Mark, are you hanging onto your hat?"

"Yeah, Frank," I responded playfully, "that's what I *always* do when I'm sitting here in my office."

Ignoring my aside, Coonis went on, "Good, 'cause here goes. First, according to a statement submitted to the Secretary of State on December 23, 1992, it looks like your Kozminski fellow was the

named president of an active Beverly Hills 'public benefit' corporation called the Prisatarium Institute."

"Huh?" I replied, "That's just three weeks before he . . . died.
Well, you know, whatever he did."

"Right," Coonis stated. "And two of his sons also run their own
local corporation, named the Munich Group, Incorporated."

"Munich, huh?" I queried. "That's where Kozminski lived for
several years."

"Well, that's just the beginning," Coonis remarked. "Local court
filings show that one of his sons, Adam Bigwood, was sued along
with Kozminski's ex-wife, Janina Liebermann, in two separate civil
actions. In one, they were accused of reneging on a real estate loan
and causing damages to the lender."

"Mother and son?" I remarked. "That's sort of interesting."

"You think that's interesting?" Coonis continued. "In the second
case, they were sued by the owners of Kelbo's restaurant."

"Geez," I replied. "That's the place Kozminski tried to buy *fifteen
years* ago."

"Yeah," Coonis noted, "well, somebody must have been pissed off
when that deal fell through. Because the complaint charges that this
Bigwood guy fraudulently converted $400,000 in loan proceeds from
the restaurants' elderly owners, diverted part of it toward purchase
of two Mercedes, and later threatened to *kill* the plaintiffs as well as
his own business associates and their children."

"Geez, this guy sounds a little unstable, Frank," I remarked.

"Unstable?" Frank retorted. "You ain't heard nothing yet. So it
also seems this Adam Bigwood was a named defendant in two other
cases. One of them arose from a dispute over a forfeited deposit on a
property lease."

"Sounds pretty tame to me—" I noted.

"Tame, my ass," Coonis interjected. "Based on the conclusions of a
handwriting expert, the complaint charges that Bigwood distributed
fraudulent notices to pay rent or quit to the landlord's tenants, as well
as false circulars announcing an Aryan Nation meeting at the offices
of the landlord's Jewish attorney."

"*Aryan Nation* meeting?" I queried, now intrigued and utterly
confused.

"Yeah," Coonis remarked. "A regular skinhead. Well, these circulars also stated that 'Auschwitz never happened . . . the Jews are all liars and we can prove it. . . . kill the Jewish babies.' Then they say that the 'male prostitute [attorney] that was hired by that bitch [landlord] to fuck him in the ass . . . is HIV positive.' As if that weren't enough, the lawsuit also claims Bigwood threatened to off the landlord."

"Wow, what a piece of work!" I remarked. "This guy almost sounds like a . . . bad caricature of his own father. And that's . . . pretty bad."

"Right," Coonis replied. "And don't forget the old lady Liebermann. She's the one who first reported Kozminski's so-called death. Let me ask you: Would you buy a used car from her?"

"Well, certainly not a real estate loan," I retorted.

My thoughts were swirling as we rang off moments later. But as we continued our exploration into the unseemly morass enveloping Lucian Kozminski, we soon discovered that the more evidence we acquired, the more confusing the picture became.

Baffling new facts about the term of Kozminski's federal custody emerged, duly reported by Mike Flagor, the Bureau of Prisons official responsible for responding to my Freedom of Information Act request. Upon reaching me at my office, Flagor noted, in a slow Southern drawl, "I'm going to fax you the records, but here's what they show. This Kozminski fellow was incarcerated at Terminal Island until October 1988. Then, beginning in April 1989, he was imprisoned for four more months in the Oakdale federal facility in Louisiana before being released to INS custody. Two months later, in September, he made his first visit to the U.S. Probation Office to register for a mandatory supervision program."

"Wait!" I exclaimed. "That's *impossible*. I mean, how could he have been incarcerated from 1982 to late 1989 when he walked right past me in 1986?"

"I can't explain that, sir," Flagor responded.

"And how could he have met with Steve Trott in Washington, D.C., *before* Trott's appointment to the Ninth Circuit in April 1988?" I queried.

"Look, I can't answer that," Flagor drawled. "But these are the official records."

"Well, let me ask you," I responded, "do you have fingerprints or a photo . . . any identifying information on the prisoner at the time of release?"

"Why, no," Flagor answered matter-of-factly. "All we know is a body went in during 1982 and a body was released in late 1989. It really could've been anyone."

"Oh, my God," I muttered.

Moments after ringing off, I ruminated on this new turn of events and wondered: Did a gap exist in Kozminski's term of incarceration that Bureau of Prisons' records failed to reflect? Or was something truly corrupt at play, even something that related to Kozminski's strange, decades-long maneuverings with the laws and officials of two governments, dating from the Allied Expeditionary Force Military Government?

Ever more mysterious, I then discovered that on January 21, 1993, Adam Bigwood reportedly sent the U.S. Probation Office a death certificate for Lucian Kozminski, which promptly closed Kozminski's federal file and terminated his supervision. Yet this flatly contradicted indications that Kozminski was alive after that date. Indeed, no fewer than four eyewitnesses claimed to have seen him during 1994 and confirmed that his sudden disappearance occurred later that year.

As a result, regardless of Kozminski's present status, this new evidence raised the macabre specter that fifty years after Nazi doctors' falsification of death certificates at Auschwitz, he may have fabricated his own death certificate. If this were true, the submission of that document to the U.S. Probation Office represented several violations of federal law.

In the final analysis, if Kozminski truly feigned his own death, he was assuredly at the center of a cleverly designed plot to displace him from the federal system and expunge all accountability to the government and his victims. Faced with this sinister prospect, I dug even deeper, obtaining the name of the mortuary reported on Kozminski's death certificate and then the certificate itself.

The Gold Cross

Once I ascertained the name of the funeral director on Kozminski's death certificate, the irony was self-evident. The body of the man who figuratively crucified the hopes of Holocaust survivors on a "cross of gold" was purportedly brought for final handling to the Gold Cross Mortuary.

After contacting a mortuary employee and matter-of-factly requesting the death certificate, I received and reviewed a faxed copy with keen interest. The certificate reflected that, on January 10, 1993, Kozminski entered Century City Hospital with pneumonia, contracted adult respiratory distress syndrome five days later, and died of cardiopulmonary arrest on January 19, 1993, at 3:05 P.M.

It went on to state that Warren L. Roston, M.D., became Kozminski's physician on the date of admittance and "last [saw him] alive" on January 18, 1993, at least fifteen and perhaps as many as twenty-nine hours before the recorded time of death. The document also attested that without any autopsy or report from the coroner, Kozminski's body was cremated and his remains transported to a "residence."

The certificate was signed by Dr. Roston, and a stamp at the bottom showed that it was filed with the Department of Health Services on January 21, 1993. The certificate was replete with oddities, exaggerations, and outright falsehoods. It listed Kozminski's date of birth as July 5, 1916, despite compelling evidence that he was born years later, perhaps as many as ten. Under "Full Maiden Name of Mother," the document said, "Unknown."

While accurately reflecting that Kozminski was born in Poland and "stateless," the certificate wrongly stated that he resided for "75 years" in Los Angeles County and falsely listed his occupation as a "banker" involved in "financial" business for "45 years." The named Social Security number, moreover, was entirely different from that reported on Kozminski's federal income tax returns and otherwise associated with him. Finally, the "Informant" (next of kin) was listed as Adam Bigwood, Kozminski's son, who provided a mailing address identical to the "Place of Final Disposition" of Kozminski's remains.

In the end, Kozminski's death certificate appeared susceptible to two divergent interpretations. On the one hand, it may have reflected a hurried and careless attempt to dress up the last chapter of an unsavory and disreputable life, clumsily wrapping Kozminski within his own shroud of fraud in the grave. On the other hand, like the forgery of the letter on Hans Wittner's claim fifteen years before, it may have embodied something far more sinister: the culmination of a deliberate and cunning plan to deceive and evade the government, the survivors, society, at large and even death itself.

AWARE THAT ONE of his earliest schemes in Germany entailed the fraudulent "refurbishing" of nonexistent gravesites, I sought to determine the purported ultimate location of Kozminski's own remains. On a sunny Saturday afternoon, I set off for 8424-A Santa Monica Boulevard, the death certificate's reported address for both Adam Bigwood and Kozminski's place of "final disposition." Along the way, I checked several known signposts for clues.

First stopping at Kozminski's last documented residence, a stately Beverly Hills apartment building on a serene block of South Crescent Drive, I observed that another party was listed on the mailbox for his unit. Having confirmed that Kozminski no longer resided there, I moved on, leaving the secrets of his final days undisturbed, like the placid and silent trees fading in the distance behind me.

Heading next to the official mailing address for the Munich Group, the corporation run by two of Kozminski's sons, rather than finding a listing for company "President" Patrick Graf-Bleiberg, I discovered a simple apartment building with a mailbox for Adam Bigwood, the company's designated "agent," reportedly located at a different address on the same block.

After I ventured to within some forty feet of Bigwood's apartment, a shadowy figure appeared, standing directly behind a closed screen door at the apartment entrance. A man in his late forties of average height, he seemed to be grasping a shiny object, perhaps a letter opener or a kitchen knife. Unwilling to take any further chances at this critical stage, I nonchalantly turned and swiftly departed, knowing that this discovery raised intriguing questions about what might be found at 8424-A Santa Monica Boulevard.

Minutes later, I arrived at that location but observed only a small

storefront mailbox center called Mail Boxes and Things. Because the
entire strip mall appeared fairly new, I surmised that Bigwood may
have relocated an office or second residence after Kozminski's death
and concluded that an "undercover" visit to Gold Cross Mortuary
might shed light on the matter.

Stepping into a nearby phone booth, I called the number listed
with directory assistance for Gold Cross and was greeted by a young
woman stating, "Gold Cross. May I help you?"

When I asked for the mortuary's address, presumably a routine
inquiry, she retorted with curiosity, "Who *is* this?"

I remembered that as Kozminski's former prosecutor my name
could raise a red flag and proceeded to provide my law partner's
name.

But the woman persisted, asking, "Why do you want the
address?"

While struck by this unexpected query, I nonchalantly answered,
"Just to see the location before I make any . . . final decisions."

After a long pause, the woman claimed, "Well, I'm just the
answering service and I don't have their address. You should call
back tomorrow between nine and four and ask for Nathan."

After this odd conversation, I called directory assistance and asked
for the address of Gold Cross Mortuary. The operator reported no
such mortuary listing, advising merely that a "Gold Cross" was
located at 5970 Santa Monica Boulevard.

Now somewhat befuddled, I hopped in my car and headed
directly to that location. Shortly afterward, I drove alone through the
rusted gates of the ancient Hollywood Memorial Park, a dilapidated
cemetery in the shadows of Paramount Studios. Slowly circling the
silent, deserted graveyard, going past hundreds of worn tombstones,
many of them askew, unkempt, and casting long shadows in the late-
afternoon sun, I wondered whether this journey might reveal something as concrete as the final resting place of Lucian Ludwig Kozminski.

As I approached an office with a bare sign reading, MORTUARY, I
observed it was closed and saw no posting for a "Gold Cross Mortuary" anywhere. My skepticism now growing, I decided that a return
visit to the mail center could prove illuminating.

When I pulled out of the cemetery moments later, I noticed in my rearview mirror that one of the few other cars traversing the grounds had pulled onto Santa Monica Boulevard a hundred yards or so behind me. Studying the rearview mirror more closely in the afternoon glare, I could now see a black sedan with a lone male occupant.

As I continued block after block, so did the black sedan, now directly behind me.

Perhaps in a fleeting moment of paranoia, I now wondered whether someone had become aware of my discreet inquiries, of my grave suspicions about the fate of Lucian Kozminski. My mind raced to Kozminski's four-decade record of duplicity, and perhaps even complicity with an agency or official of the U.S. government, as I muttered to myself, "Is it possible that someone knows? Could this even be a tail?"

Concluding that discretion was the better part of valor, I decided to put this to the test. Turning my steering wheel sharply, I made a sudden change into the left lane. But moments later, the sedan slid over into the lane right behind me.

A few blocks later, I abruptly changed into the right lane. For a moment the sedan did not react, but then it smoothly followed suit.

Several minutes later, I approached an intersection just as the light turned yellow. Gunning my engine, I raced through while quickly glancing in the rearview mirror. Slowing for a moment, the sedan followed me again, speeding up through the intersection and gliding directly behind me.

Finally, having crossed some twenty-five blocks, I approached the intersection where Mail Boxes and Things was located. I slowly slid over into the left lane. The sedan stayed in the right lane for several seconds but then abruptly changed lanes and once again remained positioned behind me.

I now moved into the left-turn lane and slowed to turn in to the small shopping center. While I studied my rearview mirror intently, the sedan appeared to hesitate, lurched slightly to its left, and then slowly continued on past me.

Before turning in to the parking lot, I peered to my right, straining to catch a glimpse of the car's rear license plate. But the orange afternoon glare clouded my vision as the car drove into the distance and faded from sight.

To this day, this brief encounter is a mystery: I remain unaware whether I had just experienced one of life's many forgettable, trivial coincidences—or something immeasurably different.

Now relieved that my secret apparently remained secure, I pulled in to the parking lot and, moments later, stepped into Mail Boxes and Things. There I briefly met with the owner, a young dark-haired man of Middle Eastern descent named Frank.

Frank reported to my surprise that his business had opened in 1989 and had been located at the same site for the past seven years. In response to my further inquiry, he advised me that while he could not disclose customer records, his files apparently reflected no listing for Adam Bigwood, Patrick Graf-Bleiberg, Lucian Kozminski, or a Munich Corporation.

Hence, this strange and surreal picture suddenly became more focused, as two more entries on Kozminski's death certificate appeared quite peculiar, if not extraordinary. Regardless of whether Adam Bigwood ever possessed a box there, for some unknown reason he provided a mail drop address as his official "locating information" on a public document. Even more unusual, he reported the same location as the final resting place of his father's cremated remains.

For the next several nights, I tossed and turned fitfully, acutely aware that I was the only one alive who had unearthed these curious secrets surrounding Kozminski's "death." Already having discovered layer upon layer of apparent deception, I vowed to continue cutting into this mystery like it was a raw onion until I reached its core or my own limited utensils failed me.

The Sun Stands Still

Time almost seemed to stand still as the resolution of this perplexing mystery stood in the balance. I knew that over the next several weeks, I would need to act quickly to minimize the risk that Adam Bigwood would hear about my expanding inquiry. At least based on allegations against him, Bigwood appeared entirely capable of destroying evidence or even perpetrating physical violence, a concern that was only compounded by a mysterious, anonymous message left on my office voice mail that weekend.

On Sunday morning at 10:00, when I rang Gold Cross hoping to reach "Nathan," the answering service picked up my call and reported that "they [the mortuary employees] should be coming in a little later." But no one answered my calls at 1:30 p.m. and 2:10 p.m., and when I finally reached the answering service again at 3:00 p.m., they tersely advised me to call the next day.

This singular inability to reach any mortuary employee on a Sunday only increased my deepening suspicions about Gold Cross's operation. I resolved that I would attack this wall of intrigue on four separate fronts, probing for any opening or point of weakness. First, I would attempt to elicit records from Gold Cross relating to Kozminski's purported cremation. Second, I would discern whether any data could be traced to the new Social Security number on Kozminski's death certificate. Third, I would seek to discover whether Kozminski was a patient at Century City Hospital during January 1993. Finally, I would approach Dr. Warren Roston to confirm whether he treated Lucian Kozminski and signed his death certificate.

On Monday morning, my trustworthy and persuasive paralegal, Anita Stephan, finally reached "Nathan" at Gold Cross and, in short order, cajoled him to fax the mortuary's "Authority to Cremate" for Kozminski's body.

Carefully reviewing the document, I noted its vague allusion to disposition "in accordance with [Adam Bigwood's] instructions in GOLD CROSS files." Though reference to any Social Security number was conspicuously absent, all other entries matched the death certificate's except for one new piece of information: a mailbox number at the 8424-A Santa Monica Boulevard address.

Armed with this evidence, my sources soon confirmed that an "A. A. Bigwood," in fact, retained a mailbox there from October 1992 to October 1993.

After a physician acquaintance of mine vouched for Dr. Roston's professionalism, another piece of the puzzle slipped into place, as I realized that fraud may have been cut and pasted around the doctor's otherwise legitimate entries on the death certificate.

Scrutinizing the document more closely, this time I observed that the horizontal line above the decedent's Social Security number was partially obliterated and that all typing above the line, including Kozminski's name, birthplace, and birthdate, appeared different and more faded than the rest of the certificate. Vividly recalling the fraudulent postscript that had led to our search warrant fifteen years before, I concluded that the new Social Security number on this document was probably not Kozminski's at all.

A few hours after consulting with Frank Coonis Investigations, I learned the odd and disturbing truth: The Social Security number in question belonged not to Lucian Kozminski but to Claire H. Comiskey, a former resident of West Los Angeles who reportedly died on January 13, 1993.

This evidence appeared both profound and momentous. The striking similarity of Comiskey's name to Kozminski's coupled with the date of her passing, just six days before Kozminski's "death," seemed all too convenient and no mere coincidence or haphazard mistake.

In the end, this revelation only appeared to confirm the stench of fraud engulfing Kozminski's death certificate, thereby enhancing the bizarre prospect that Lucian Ludwig Kozminski might be raised from his shallow grave and resurrected both in body and spirit.

The Pillar of Cloud

Days passed with no news as I awaited belated reports from several sources, and the entire investigation seemed to fall into an eerie state of suspended animation. Then a smattering of additional evidence began to dribble in.

In response to our request, the *Los Angeles Times* formally advised us that no obituary notice or death announcement had been submitted for Lucian Kozminski. This unequivocal report weighed decisively in favor of a finding of fraud. Whereas Kozminski's family should have wanted to announce his actual death to dissuade the government and survivors from continuing their relentless pursuit, public announcement of a *feigned* death could have generated dangerous speculation or even investigation, possibly resulting in exposure, apprehension, and further criminal charges. Another small piece of the puzzle slipped into place, and I anxiously awaited the arrival of more telltale evidence.

It would arrive in short order and from, of all places, a crematorium.

My assistant had elicited from Gold Cross that during 1993, they contracted out all cremations to an East Los Angeles–based concern named Heritage Cremation.

Now, several days after we had submitted a formal inquiry, a Heritage Cremation employee called and said, "Well, we've conducted an exhaustive search of our files. We checked for payments, records of the body going in, the body going out, and an assortment of other papers that should've been generated. And there are none."

"None?" I queried.

"None," he responded. "And since we handled all of Gold Cross's cremations during that period, I don't think this guy was cremated. By anyone."

Coupled with the absence of an obituary, this stunning news of Kozminski's noncremation began to form a clearer picture of the larger puzzle. But many critical pieces remained outstanding, their shape and size undetermined. Several days later, still awaiting the official Kozminski and Comiskey death certificates from Los Angeles County and other crucial data, I decided to inspect the last known residence of Claire H. Comiskey. Little could I have expected the results of this short but illuminating trip.

Upon arriving at the West Los Angeles apartment complex, I noticed that despite Comiskey's death, three and a half years before, a J. Comiskey was listed on the mailbox for her unit. Sensing that the Kozminski mystery was destined to deepen, I tentatively approached the Comiskey residence.

Shortly after I rang the apartment doorbell, a gray-haired man in his early sixties opened the door and faced me.

After identifying himself as Jim Comiskey, Claire's divorced husband, he responded to my inquiry by emphatically denying any relation to the Kozminski family. Convinced that Comiskey was absolutely truthful, I advised him that as an attorney representing several private individuals, I had a few questions regarding the circumstances of Ms. Comiskey's death.

While confused by my purpose and understandably circumspect, Mr. Comiskey directly answered several private and probing queries. Much to my surprise, however, virtually all his responses contradicted the medical and related entries on Lucian Kozminski's death certificate.

Mr. Comiskey matter-of-factly reported that though the fatally ill Ms. Comiskey was treated by a staff doctor from Century City Hospital, the primary physician definitely was a female. Ms. Comiskey's place of death was the Ocean View Convalescent Home, not the hospital. Her cause of death was Alzheimer's disease and throat cancer, not pneumonia and cardiopulmonary failure, and her body was brought to the Pierce Brothers' Westwood Memorial Park, not Gold Cross.

A long moment of silence passed as I anxiously attempted to integrate this bewildering new evidence. Finally, stumbling over my words I remarked, "Thank you, thank you very much for your cooperation, Mr. Comiskey. In a few weeks, I hope to shed some more . . . light on all of this. If I do, I'll be sure to give you a call."

As I walked away from the Comiskey residence, my head virtually spun as I pondered the latest jagged pieces thrown into the mix, none of which seemed to fit. Did someone research local obituaries and select the name of a person similar to Kozminski's who died just six days before him? If the medical entries on Kozminski's death certificate did not even correspond to Ms. Comiskey's, then why was her Social Security number expropriated? And, if the "Kozminski" decedent's medical entries were cut and pasted from another death certificate, then just who was Dr. Roston's patient and who died?

The next day, this surreal picture became even more confusing, as I finally received the "official" Kozminski and Comiskey death certificates filed with Los Angeles County.

The entries on Ms. Comiskey's death certificate were as I expected. The document contained her valid Social Security number, identical to that listed on Kozminski's certificate, and reported her date of death as January 13, 1993, six days before Kozminski's passing. No other entry bore any similarity to Kozminski's death certificate except that her doctor, Jeanne E. Bishop, was then on the Century City Hospital staff and maintained an office just four floors above Dr. Roston's.

Kozminski's death certificate was another matter. It was nearly identical to the copy I had previously received, but with one glaring exception: The line above the Social Security number was not obliterated and the entries for "Decedent's Personal Data" appeared to match the typing on the rest of the form.

This new evidence, therefore, cast doubt upon the notion that Kozminski's certificate was cut and pasted, and I speculated whether the top portion of my duplicate simply suffered from poor photostat quality.

Although admittedly confusing, none of this came as a surprise. I had learned long before as a federal prosecutor that sorting out a reputed fraud was like shadowboxing with two phantoms. While flailing away and absorbing hits, you often remain unaware, at any given moment, whether you are making headway against the suspect or your own theories. In short, while assuredly closer to *reaching* the truth, I seemed even farther from *discerning* it.

Several days later, I met for lunch with an unexpected and welcome visitor from Northern California: Lou Kinzler. Sporting a beard and mustache, the lanky, silver-haired Kinzler had aged well and, relieved that his loving wife, Olivia, was recovering from cancer, appeared to be in good spirits.

Kinzler and I hugged each other warmly, reminisced for a time, and then turned to the familiar subject of Lucian Kozminski.

Carefully reviewing some of our recently acquired evidence, Kinzler became convinced that Kozminski was still alive but remained baffled by his tactics and motive, repeatedly asking in consternation, "*Why* would Kozminski use Claire Comiskey's Social Security number? And *why* would he apparently concoct this body-laundering scheme?"

Yet even as Kinzler posed these disturbing inquiries, I retained the distinct feeling that further answers would be forthcoming, somehow sensing that his surprise visit meant the wheel may have come nearly full circle.

The Twilight Struggle

The following day, surprising evidence seemingly confirmed one of my hunches as to why Claire Comiskey's Social Security number may have been expropriated. Once again the bearer of news was Frank Coonis.

Reaching me at my office, he jokingly queried, "OK. Are you hanging onto your hat?"

"Oh, God, are we going to go through *this* again?" I playfully replied.

"All right," he responded. "If you *really* don't want to, then I'll just give you the goods. Seems like your dead man was receiving Social Security payments through direct bank deposits for several years after he kicked the bucket. It's all there under his name and . . . valid Social Security number."

"Wow, that's amazing," I responded. "But let me ask you, could someone *else* actually have received these payments?"

"Oh, sure," Coonis replied. "And, tell me, who's buried in Grant's tomb?"

WE HAD AT LAST found our first concrete evidence that Kozminski survived his "death" and still may have been alive.

Yet even with this provocative development, my options continued to dwindle. Realizing one of the few that remained was a face-to-face meeting with the enigmatic Dr. Warren Roston, I cast aside my reluctance and sought him out.

Shortly after leaving a message identifying myself as an author seeking to "verify information concerning a decedent," I received a return call from Dr. Roston. From the beginning, it was evident that he would adopt a guarded posture toward this entire matter.

Dispensing with formalities, Roston brusquely queried, "Now, tell me again, why did you want to meet with me?"

Though put off by his tone, I calmly repeated my voice mail message, "To verify some information concerning a . . . decedent."

Roston then tersely replied, "Well, unless you give me more information, I'm not going to meet with you."

Faced with no other choice, I responded, "Well, I'm investigating a man who was convicted of cheating thousands of Holocaust survivors. His name happened to appear on a death certificate that you signed, a certificate that I believe is fraudulent."

The line fell silent. I continued, "Our sources also report the absence of any . . . record of cremation for the decedent. And since this guy's presumably dead, I don't believe the doctor-patient privilege would apply."

After a long pause, Roston queried, "And just what is the name of this man?"

Drawing a deep breath, I replied, "Lucian Ludwig Kozminski."

The phone fell silent. Then Roston finally spoke, uttering in a hushed tone, "OK, I'll meet with you. But only for a few minutes."

Shortly afterward, I stepped into the medical building next to Century City Hospital and approached Dr. Roston's suite. Immediately upon entering, I saw Roston leaning against a counter intently perusing the contents of an open folder and noticed that the short, bald man in his late forties bore a slight but noticeable resemblance to Kozminski.

Grasping the file, Roston looked up, briskly walked into the outer office, and sat next to me, tersely stating, "Well, let's see what you've got."

Reaching into my briefcase, I showed him a newspaper article from Kozminski's prosecution, and though Roston was apparently Jewish, the depravity of his reported crimes elicited no change of expression or other response. I displayed two photographs of Kozminski, but Roston responded that he would not recognize the patient after having administered treatment for just one week.

I next handed Roston the Kozminski and Comiskey death certificates, pointing out Comiskey's date of death and the fraudulent use of her Social Security number. Roston bluntly responded, "I've never heard of Claire Comiskey and don't recall ever treating her. And I certainly have no idea how her Social Security number got on his [Kozminski's] death certificate."

Roston quickly slipped a copy of Kozminski's death certificate out of his folder and compared it to my certified copy. Remarking that "they looked the same," he nonchalantly queried, "OK. Is there anything else?"

Briefly ruminating on Roston's almost flippant responses, I decided that I had collected enough information and said, "No. That should be it for now."

Upon hearing my reply, he abruptly stood and quickly headed back toward his inner office. Stepping several paces away, Roston suddenly stopped, turned toward me and uttered, "You know, whoever died was very sick when I first treated him."

He silently looked at me, almost seeking some sort of reassurance. But I purposefully ignored his comment and instead requested that he keep this entire matter quiet, prompting Roston's almost smug reply, "You bet I will."

Moments later, when I offered to leave a business card for future reference, Roston quickly snapped, "That won't be necessary. I don't *want* your number."

And with that last offhand dismissal, he hastily turned and stepped into his inner office, disappearing from sight.

So AFTER OUR five-minute encounter, my meeting with Dr. Roston was done. As I closed the door and departed his suite, again confounded by the twists and turns of this investigation, I realized that only three options remained.

One possibility was that *no one* died on January 19, 1993. This option was supported by the apparent absence of cremation records for Kozminski, the furnishing of a mail drop as the place of "final disposition" of his cremated remains, Ms. Liebermann's contradictory report that Kozminski was "quickly buried," the fraudulent use of Comiskey's Social Security number, and other duplicity associated with Kozminski's death certificate.

This theory, however, meant that Dr. Roston and perhaps other medical and hospital personnel may have been directly implicated in a conspiracy to feign Kozminski's death. While the magnitude of this prospective plot seemed too far-fetched to be plausible, I was more inspired than ever to obtain hospital records relating to the mysterious decedent.

The second prospect was that an unidentified person died on January 19, 1993. This version would be entirely consistent with the evidence in support of the first option as well as Roston's story, particularly because he did not recognize Kozminski and never saw the decedent until nine days before death.

Yet this theory also raised a host of troubling and perplexing questions. Was Kozminski admitted in the first place? What happened to the body? And most profoundly, how did Kozminski arrange to pull a complete identity and body switch with a dying person? Did he pay the decedent's family? Was this person a paid double for an even longer period of time?

The third option was that Kozminski died on January 19, 1993. This theory, however, was riddled with gaping and inexplicable holes. For example, if Kozminski had truly died, then why did the Social Security number for a recent decedent end up on his death certificate? So that an unidentified third party could continue to obtain Kozminski's monthly Social Security benefits? And if Kozminski had truly died, where were the records of cremation, and why was the rest of his death certificate replete with fraud?

Unaware of any of the answers to these troubling questions, I resolved to foreclose no option. After one last attempt to link the Kozminski and Comiskey death certificates, my primary attention shifted to the trail of Kozminski's Social Security payments, as I now hoped this difficult search into the present would yield lasting answers about the cryptic past.

Aware that the *only* apparent connection between the Kozminski and Comiskey death certificates was that both treating doctors then were on staff at Century City Hospital, several days later I managed to find Dr. Jean Bishop, who had relocated in 1993 to Syracuse, New York.

Immediately acknowledging that she treated Claire Comiskey and signed her death certificate, Dr. Bishop was appalled by my account of Kozminski's brazen swindling of Holocaust survivors.

When I asked how Ms. Comiskey's Social Security number could have materialized on the death certificate of Lucian Kozminski, a convicted felon, Dr. Bishop replied, "Well, I distinctly recall that Ms. Comiskey suffered from respiratory failure, pneumonia, and lung cancer. I'm not a specialist in that area, so I brought in a consulting pulmonologist. And that doctor certainly would have had direct access to her Social Security number."

I responded, "Do you remember who that doctor was?"

She reflected for a moment and remarked, "Oh, it would have been one of two doctors. Definitely. Either a Dr. Ralph Potkin or . . . more likely, a Dr. Warren Roston."

After thanking Dr. Bishop profusely for her candor and cooperation, I contacted Dr. Potkin's office. His assistant for the past nine years advised me, "I can absolutely confirm that Dr. Potkin never treated a Claire Comiskey."

Based on this discovery, it appeared that despite his ostensible failure to recognize Claire Comiskey's name or condition when I displayed her death certificate, Dr. Warren Roston was a treating physician for both Kozminski and Comiskey and the only known link between them.

One week later, new evidence irrefutably confirmed Roston as a bridge between the Kozminski and Comiskey death certificates. Directed by Dr. Bishop to Century City Hospital's Geriatric Center, with Jim Comiskey's approval I received a "consultation report" from Claire Comiskey's file prepared by none other than Dr. Warren Roston.

In his three-page memorandum, dated December 16, 1992, Roston noted that Ms. Comiskey "experienced a code blue" that afternoon at the Granada Hills Community Hospital and was transferred to the intensive care unit at Century City Hospital. Roston's detailed evaluation included a diagnosis that the patient was suffering from carcinoma of the lung, among other evidently terminal conditions.

His memory jogged by this latest evidence, Jim Comiskey called me to advise that he recalled *speaking* to Dr. Roston sometime in early to mid-December 1992.

Comiskey remarked, "He was very grim and very . . . specific. Dr. Roston noted Claire's critical condition and her recent seizure and bluntly concluded, 'I think she's only got about one more week to live.'"

Though she would manage to rally over the ensuing few weeks, Ms. Comiskey died less than one month after Roston had spoken with Jim Comiskey, penned his consultation report, and delivered it to Dr. Bishop.

Thus, while Roston presumably engaged in no intentional wrongdoing, this startling evidence placed the opportunity for expropriating Claire Comiskey's Social Security number squarely in his hands or those of his staff or other hospital personnel and further revealed that he (and presumably others) knew Ms. Comiskey was about to die well in advance of Kozminski's purported death, leaving more than a month for a plot to be hatched.

As I approached the penultimate stage of the investigation, I sensed an alignment of forces engaged in a grim life-and-death struggle over the result.

On the one hand, a determined and sustained effort was slowly wrenching Kozminski from the twilight of death, virtually resurrecting him piece by piece. On the other hand, a complex array of defenses strained to preserve him, like the deceased Polonius in *Hamlet*, as a "counsellor . . . most still, most secret, and most grave."

Alternately pulled toward life and pushed toward death, Kozminski lay in the throes of this fierce tug-of-war, with one fist now seemingly clutching a wad of blood-soaked dollars.

The Resurrection Mirage

Before finally presenting our evidence to the U.S. attorney's office, I decided to make one last effort to trace the trail of recent Social Security payments issued under the name of Lucian Kozminski. For assistance in this quest, I contacted the U.S. probation officer who closed Kozminski's file after receiving the fraudulent death certificate, assuming she would be eager to make amends. But I could not have been more mistaken.

After detailing the apparent fraud on the face of the certificate, I asked, "Considering that the file was closed under . . . suspicious circumstances, do you think you may be able to place an inquiry concerning these recent Social Security payments?"

Kozminski's former probation officer, however, would hear nothing of it and snapped, "I'm afraid that's impossible. . . . Look, I'm just an employee here. That file's been closed, there's nothing I can do about it . . . and nothing I want to do about it."

But I had better luck with another government worker, who upon hearing our evidence of fraud, agreed to call the Social Security Administration. While that agency was initially unmoved by his report that two federal agencies had been defrauded, my contact persevered and finally elicited critical and illuminating facts.

We learned that in May 1991, Kozminski instructed the Social Security Administration to remit all future Social Security checks to his Bank of America savings account, located at 460 North Beverly Drive in Beverly Hills. The Social Security Administration thereafter forwarded monthly checks of $425, less $73.80 for Medicare, directly to Kozminski's account. This continued until March 3, 1995, twenty-six months after Kozminski's reputed death, when a check was mysteriously returned to the Social Security Administration, which suspended future payments.

Aware that the duration of these payments was entirely consistent with several sightings of Kozminski in 1994 and early 1995, we turned to the critical period between Kozminski's reported death and the termination of payments some two years later. In seeking the nature, timing, and extent of withdrawals, as well as locating information on the notorious account holder, we hoped to receive further clues to his elusive fate after "death."

But it was not meant to be. Initially informed that Kozminski's account had been designated "dormant" and officially closed, we were later tersely advised that absolutely none of the account data could be accessed without a formal subpoena.

We had hit a brick wall. Our last available line of inquiry had been stymied.

AND SO, with this last development, my patchwork investigation foundered at the edge of a final, cathartic revelation. Having tapped all available options in my informal inquiry, I was still left with the ultimate mystery.

A critical phase of a long journey had apparently ended, one that began in the Lodz ghetto, traveled through the Auschwitz and Gross-Rosen concentration camps and postwar Germany, continued through the U.S. federal court and prison system, and ended in a present-day cemetery, mortuaries, and crematoriums. The past had truly been unearthed. Along with it, Kozminski had nearly been resurrected. But at least for the present, that haunting and almost life-like vision remained a mirage.

THE TEACHER, a son of King David, advises in Ecclesiastes: "[T]he race is not to the swift or the battle to the strong . . . but time and chance happen to them all."

This was surely the case in the near-exposure of Lucian Ludwig Kozminski's apparent scheme to cheat death. Plodding along for many hours, week upon week, and lacking the authority of an assistant U.S. attorney or even the subpoena power of a civil action, I was neither the swiftest nor the strongest.

Driving me onward were a host of compelling motivations. Most noteworthy were my inspiration from the courage and dignity of the Holocaust survivors and my continuing fascination with and repulsion toward Kozminski. All along, I remained intrigued by Kozminski's essential mystery and complexities: the braggadocio shrouding layers of insecurities, fears, and torments; the apparent talent to persuasively entice, evade, and rebut; and the chameleon-like ability to adapt and survive, regardless of the implications or consequences.

At the same time, I remained repulsed by this Jew who had turned on other Jews—fellow Holocaust survivors, at that—in the camps, in postwar Germany, and in the United States, by his sheer embrace of dark and forbidding impulses and his brazen failure to assume responsibility for his acts.

Though I will never be certain, perhaps in the end this reflected my continuing fascination and repulsion with the human condition itself, with the daily internal struggles we all face, and the personal battles we have all won and lost.

The Scales of Justice

Possessing evidence of a major criminal fraud, I could have chosen to continue pursuing Kozminski on my own. That course, however, would have been fraught with pitfalls. My tools would have remained severely limited, my investigation unduly prolonged, and the specter of retaliatory threats or even violence largely undeterred.

The time, therefore, had come to offer the proverbial baton to the U.S. Attorney's Office. The prospective benefits were readily apparent. If federal prosecutors could be prompted to initiate a formal inquiry, they would immediately gain access to extensive investigative resources, far beyond those available to me.

In a matter of mere weeks, prosecutors could obtain hospital, medical, mortuary, cremation, and bank records, as well as telephone tolls for Adam Bigwood, Janina Liebermann, Gold Cross Mortuary, and Dr. Roston. Enlisting the aid of Interpol and other authorities to track down Kozminski and arrange for extradition, they then could order the arrest of others implicated in this apparent fraud, eventually calling all conspirators to justice in federal court. Finally, they could formally request that the Swiss government locate and freeze Kozminski's holdings, possibly leading to the belated restoration of victims' blood money to its rightful owners.

Grasping at our best remaining hope, I was referred to Rick Drooyan, Chief of the Office's Criminal Division, who had worked alongside me at the U.S. Attorney's Office years before. Struck by the import of the apparent plot to feign Kozminski's death, Drooyan requested a written summary of our proof.

The next day, I forwarded our documentary evidence and a comprehensive letter, putting the fate of the entire matter in the hands of the U.S. Attorney's Office in Los Angeles.

My guarded optimism proved to be short-lived. Just two weeks later, I spoke to Richard Robinson, Assistant Chief of the Frauds Section, who had been assigned the matter for routine preliminary review. Unimpressed with our evidence, Robinson clearly wanted no part of a new investigation of Lucian Kozminski's most recent activities or whereabouts. Bypassing any informal exchange, Robinson peppered me with a series of pointed inquiries.

Most notably, with a distinct edge in his voice, he asked: "How do you *know* the use of Ms. Comiskey's Social Security number on Kozminski's death certificate was not attributable to clerical error?"

"Why would anyone *possibly* want to fake Kozminski's death when just two years of his U.S. parole supervision remained?"

And "Even if he were alive, wouldn't Kozminski be too old to prosecute?"

Question after question. All generated from the same perspective. By the time our brief, strained conversation ended, I knew that Robinson's investigation of Kozminski would never materialize. It was already dead in the water.

WHEN I CALLED Robinson four months later, my instincts were confirmed. Once again formal and taciturn, he dispensed with any personal greeting or exchange and quickly advised me that he was putting the "finishing touches" on a detailed memorandum recommending declination of any formal investigation. After he briefly outlined his findings, I knew there was nothing I could do or say. The die was cast: The government would not commence any further investigation of Lucian Kozminski.

Though discouraging and even understandable considering their daunting workload, the response of the U.S. Attorney's Office was somewhat predictable and, indeed, oddly reminiscent of the three failed initial investigations of Lucian Kozminski. The reasons were strikingly familiar: The victims are too old, the evidence is too stale or weak, and resources would be better spent elsewhere.

Yet even with the doors of opportunity slamming shut, I retained faith that all was not lost. Inspired by this flicker of hope, I vowed to resume my private hunt for the solution to the Kozminski conundrum undeterred, attempting to track a virtual shadow and prove negative.

Did I know for a fact that Kozminski had died on January 19, 1993? No. Did I know for a fact that Kozminski was still alive? No. And that was the rub. For even in the end, Kozminski remained, in Winston Churchill's words, an enduring "riddle inside a mystery wrapped within an enigma."

SUMMARY CHART FOR PRESENTATION TO UNITED STATES ATTORNEY

†LUCIAN (LUCJAN) LUDWIG KOZMINSKI: TIMELINE OF FRAUD AND DECEPTION†

1916
Claimed Birthdate; Actually Born Between 1922–1926, Turek, Poland

1943–1945
Interned In Four Camps During WWII; Admits He Worked In Auschwitz SS Kitchen; Eyewitness Later Identifies Him as "Oberkapo" Or Nazi Collaborator At Gross-Rosen Camp

1963–1967
Convicted Of 6 Criminal Offenses In West Germany, Including For Defrauding Holocaust Survivors By Falsely Claiming He Would Refurbish Graves Of Relatives In Poland

1968
Arrives In U.S. On 90-Day Nonimmigrant Visa; Fraudulently Fails To Disclose German Convictions Or Existing Probation

1969
Starts Operation Of Restitutions Office In Los Angeles; Continues Until Arrested in 1982

1970's
Ordered Deported By INS On Two Occasions But Remains In US; LAPD, D.A.'s And Postal Inspectors' Investigations All Fold

December 17, 1981
Search Warrant For Kozminski's "Wiedergutmachungs" Office Executed By Postal Inspectors

June 28, 1982
Kozminski Indicted On 15 Counts of Mail Fraud For Cheating Holocaust Survivors Out Of Restitution; U.S. Estimates 3,000 Victims Worldwide, $1 Million Or More In Losses

July 25, 1982
After Discovery Of Bankruptcy Petition (4/28/82), Kozminski Indicted For Bankruptcy Fraud; Evidence Also Reveals Tax Fraud And Social Security Fraud

August 31, 1982
Kozminski Pleads Guilty To 8 Counts Of Mail Fraud And Bankruptcy Fraud Before Trial

October 12, 1982
Judge Kenyon Sentences Kozminski To Twelve Years In Federal Custody: Switzerland Rebuffs U.S. Attempts To Locate Victims' Monies

July 1982–July 1989
Kozminski *Reportedly* In "Continuous" Federal Custody (Terminal Island And Oakdale). But Kalmansohn Sees Him In Beverly Hills In *Late 1986, Early 1987*, And Kozminski Seeks Pardon In *Meeting With Steve Trott In Washington, D.C. Before April 1988*

January 1993
Kozminski's Son Reportedly Submits Death Certificate To USPO Showing Kozminski Died On 1/19/93 And Was Cremated Under Auspices Of Gold Cross Mortuary; Federal Supervision And INS, IRS, And Victims' Pursuit Immediately Terminated

July–December 1996
Kalmansohn Obtains Death Certificate, Identifies Many Items As False And Gathers Evidence That Kozminski, His Son (Adam Bigwood), Dr. Roston, And Gold Cross Mortuary May Have Conspired To Feign Kozminski's Death Through "Body Switch" Involving *Claire Comiskey*, DOD, 1/13/03; Kozminski's Social Security Payments Continue To 3/95 [Sec. 18/USC §§ 494, 1001, 1341]

Days of Judgment

It was time to act. The only formal recourse left was a civil lawsuit filed on behalf of one of the victims. Once a lawsuit was filed, I could issue subpoenas for documents that could provide further clues to this mystery. And if we could somehow manage to obtain a judgment against Kozminski, we would possess proof that his death was faked. But as I knew all too well, it would not be easy.

The first step was selecting a victim who would stand as plaintiff in our civil action. I did not have to look very far. As with several other victims, I had enjoyed a warm rapport with Max Wolman from the moment we met. He had always been extremely cooperative and gracious. And there were no nuances in his claim against Kozminski: Years after West Germany had issued an award of restitution and directed payment to Kozminski, Wolman had heard and received nothing from Kozminski. He would have been unaware of any restitution payment but for our search of Kozminski's offices.

And so, in late 1997, I contacted Wolman about my plans. Though he offered to pay for costs of the prospective action, I insisted it be handled on a pro bono basis and that my law firm would charge no fees. As the chance for any real dollar recovery was slight, I was not about to encourage any of Kozminski's victims to throw good money after bad.

Only reluctantly conceding the point, Wolman gave me the green light to file an action against Kozminski, adding, "Nothing is too late. Not as long as I'm still alive."

Striving for simplicity, I prepared a complaint containing just two claims: fraud and declaratory relief. The fraud claim was straightforward, laying out Kozminski's pilfering of Wolman's restitution. The declaratory relief claim, however, was somewhat more ambitious. Building step by step, it requested no less than a formal declaration by the Court that Kozminski had faked his death.

As I explained to paralegal Anita Stephan, who helped assemble case materials, "I tried to hedge our bets on this claim, giving the judge several opportunities to find in our favor . . . even without going all the way with us."

Perusing the document, Anita queried, "What do you mean?"

"Well," I replied, pointing at the first paragraph of the proposed declaratory relief judgment. "See, there we contend that Kozminski's death certificate was 'false or fraudulent in one or more material respects.'"

"Yeah, I see that," Anita responded. "You should get that granted just with the use of Ms. Comiskey's Social Security number."

"Right," I concurred. "And that finding alone would be huge. But we don't stop there." Pointing to the next paragraph, I added, "Now, here we allege that Kozminski did not die on or about January 19, 1993, if ever, 'as otherwise purported by the . . . death certificate.'"

"Oooh," she responded. "So now you go from the death certificate being false to Kozminski's death being faked. It's a big step you slipped in there, but I think you should get this one from your evidence, too."

"Well, I sure hope so," I responded. "And if we can just get these first two findings, our friend Kozminski is a dead duck."

"Or, more accurately, a live one," Anita retorted.

"Good point," I replied, baring a slight grin. Pointing to the next section, I continued, "And here we allege that the body of Kozminski was not cremated in or about late January 1993, if ever, 'as otherwise purported by the . . . death certificate.'"

"Yeah," Anita replied, studying the document. "So now it's no death *and* no cremation. I think you've proved this one through Heritage Cremations' records. That is, the absence of any records."

"OK. Next," I continued, gesturing at the next paragraph, "we ask the court to find that the place of final disposition of any remains of Kozminski 'was and is *not* located at 8424-A Santa Monica Blvd., West Hollywood, CA [Mail Boxes and Things], as otherwise purported by the . . . death certificate.'"

"Well, he's sure not in a mail drop," Anita replied.

"Let's hope, for his sake," I concurred.

"So, let's see," Anita said. "Now you've got findings on a false death certificate, a faked death, no cremation, and no burial place. Looks pretty tight to me."

"Yeah, and then we get to the final section," I added. "It says that 'Defendant Kozminski may be alive today at an unknown location.' Since we don't know for sure he's alive—and didn't die between January 1993 and today—it's just about the strongest statement we could make that he's still around . . . somewhere."

"I like it," Anita remarked. "You give the judge some options and sort of nudge him on to the end. I hope it works."

NOW IT WAS time to prove our case.

I filed the action, served Kozminski "by publication" (by publicizing the lawsuit in a local publication), and issued a host of subpoenas seeking to uncover additional evidence. Soon it was time for a status conference before the assigned judge, Los Angeles Superior Court Judge John Ouderkirk.

Ouderkirk, a former state prosecutor, was known as a fair and no-nonsense judge. I felt very comfortable with his selection.

In early 1998, I faced him in court. Ouderkirk was a pleasant-looking man with a poker-faced expression, brown hair and mustache, and rimless glasses. After our case was called, he asked me what the case was about.

When I finished describing Kozminski's fraud and the claim that the death was faked, Ouderkirk gazed at me for several moments, smiled ever so slightly, and dryly remarked, "Well, I'll tell you one thing. You better present me evidence *demonstrating* that if you want *this Court* to issue a judgment."

Undeterred, I responded, "That is exactly what we intend to do, your Honor."

It would take eleven long months from the filing of the complaint for me to compile my evidence and declarations. It was no easy task, but finally all the pieces fell into place.

The most interesting new evidence was from Century City Hospital. I learned that Kozminski (or someone purporting to be him) had been transported by Beverly Hills paramedics to the hospital, where he had complained of a stomachache and was administered Tylenol some ten days before his death.

The patient presented no picture identification upon admittance, merely an FHP card bearing the name Lucian Kozminski. Though the patient could not pay for the hospital's services, Dr. Roston waived the fee requirement and allowed "Kozminski" to be treated there.

Whoever was admitted was listed at six-two—a full ten inches taller than Kozminski's five-four—in at least two hospital documents. The patient's condition was so befuddling that one doctor speculated he might have Legionnaires' Disease or some other rare affliction. The patient's mysterious condition rapidly worsened and developed into pneumonia within three days. A week later he was dead. Records reflected that after the patient's demise, the body was released to Gold Cross Mortuary with just three personal items, one of them a shirt and one an unidentified pendant.

Several inches thick, Kozminski's hospital file created more questions than it answered. I wondered: Who was admitted in the first place? Could it have been Kozminski? And who really died? Could it also have been Kozminski? And yet, if Kozminski had died, how could all the ensuing evidence of fraud be explained?

Tempting as it was, this was no time to notice depositions of Dr. Roston or Kozminski's other doctors, Adam Bigwood, Janina Liebermann (who claimed Kozminski had been "quickly buried"), or anyone else who could tip Kozminski off if he remained alive. This was no time to reveal what we knew. So I maintained my focus on completing a paper trail that would prove our case. We would have to show that more likely than not we were right—a "preponderance of evidence" standard that I was increasingly confident we could meet.

Methodically preparing our request for entry of default judgment, I attached three hundred pages of exhibits and ten sworn declarations detailing all our evidence against Kozminski, from his underlying crimes to his recent deeds. I completed an assortment of other pleadings required for a judgment of default against a defendant who has been served but never answers a complaint.

Finally, the whole stack was ready for filing. But, as plaintiffs seeking default judgments often experience, much of the challenge remained. As is required, our request for default was filed with the defaults section in the Superior Court, not Judge Ouderkirk's department. Weeks later, the whole batch was returned to us, evidently because we had overlooked two technical requirements out of some thirty on the default judgments checklist. We corrected these items and returned the entire pile.

But in the meantime, we received notice that by some strange circumstance and without any warning, Judge Ouderkirk had dismissed our case!

Shocked at this turn of events, we found the culprit: A "miscommunication" between the defaults section and Judge Ouderkirk's department had led the Judge to conclude we had never filed for a default and had failed to prosecute our action.

Days later I was in court detailing the bureaucratic foul-up and, much to my relief, Judge Ouderkirk reversed his ruling.

Then it was time to wait. The weeks slowly went by, and the case nearly slipped from my daily consciousness. But the lingering hope and expectation remained, along with the abiding concerns. I wondered: Could our papers have been more persuasive? And even if Judge Ouderkirk found our papers persuasive, would he really have the gumption to issue a ruling that Kozminski's death had been faked?

Finally, it arrived in the morning mail. Three years after first reviewing Kozminski's death certificate, and some one and a half years after commencing a civil action against him, I opened an envelope containing the Court's judgment.

When I read it, I could hardly believe my eyes: In my hands was a formal judgment issued in favor of Max Wolman against Lucian Kozminski, stamped March 1, 1999, signed by Judge Ouderkirk.

But that was not all. Not a single word had been deleted or changed from our proposed judgment: In a bold if not courageous act, Judge Ouderkirk had adopted *all* our contentions concerning Kozminski's faked death. And the judgment he had issued could be enforced throughout the United States and most jurisdictions abroad.

Looking at the document almost in disbelief, I felt a huge burden lift from my shoulders. I no longer felt like a lawyer pushing this matter all alone; a distinguished and experienced judge had formally validated my efforts.

Moments later I closed my office door and put my head on my desk. And I cried. Tears of joy, tears of relief, tears for Max Wolman, and tears for the work and the result. And the memories flooded back. Nearly seventeen years after Kozminski had first been convicted, another judgment had been issued against him. A loop had been connected, almost like a wormhole in time. And I was inside.

Shortly later, when I called Max Wolman, there was a long silence on the other end of the line. I could almost feel him pondering, the memories flooding into his mind, including those reaching back long before Kozminski.

And then, his voice slightly quivering, he remarked simply, "Thank you for everything."

NEARLY ONE YEAR LATER, on April 10, 2000, a nearly identical default judgment was entered in favor of Jacob Weingarten against Lucian Kozminski. This second conclusive finding that Kozminski faked his death, issued by Los Angeles Superior Court Judge Morris B. Jones, reinforced Judge Ouderkirk's bold ruling and insulated it from any claim of mistake or overreaching.

At Pat Maginnis's suggestion, the case had commenced some ten months before as a class-action suit seeking damages and accrued interest of more than $10 million on behalf of all three thousand of Kozminski's victims. But absent timely production of the files of Kozminski's victims by the government, we had pared it down to an action prosecuted individually on behalf of Weingarten.

The day after we received this second judgment against Kozminski, Esther Weingarten answered when I called and quietly listened as I briefly recounted the favorable outcome of her husband's action. Her voice filled with emotion, Esther remarked, "I'll be sure to tell Jack right away." She paused, then added, "Just in time for Passover."

LIKE DÉJÀ VU, I turned to Switzerland. Determining that Kozminski's former bank (Handelsbank) was now the Coutts AG Bank, I enlisted the help of a local Jewish attorney active in Holocaust restitution efforts. The attorney's informal inquiry—placed through a well-positioned bank insider—swiftly revealed that no evidence presently existed of a Coutts AG account in Kozminski's name but could not eliminate the prospect of accounts at other banks. Our contact surmised that while Swiss government authorities would find our judgments against Kozminski "most interesting," they would not enforce them or permit access to any accounts without a new lengthy and expensive civil action in Switzerland.

We had come down a long road, but our efforts were not over. I awaited the INS's production of Kozminski's extensive and likely illuminating file in response to my nearly two-year-old Freedom of Information Act request. I explored the prospects of refiling a class-action suit. And I planned to make further inquiries regarding Kozminski's suspected foreign accounts.

But as none of these avenues seemed particularly promising, I reached what would prove to be a fateful decision: After four long years, it was time to go public. The decision was not difficult. I no longer needed to be concerned about disrupting a criminal prosecution, which had been declined, or our civil cases, which had ended favorably. While we could drive a still-extant Kozminski further underground or prompt some sort of violent reaction from one of his relatives, the risk of these occurrences appeared slight.

And I could not discount the potential benefits. For the palpable prospect existed that by going to the public, we could receive leads concerning Kozminski's fate, whereabouts, or assets. We could elicit answers to some very troubling questions. And one way or another, perhaps we could finally put this entire matter to rest. So I prepared a press release and issued it to the media.

All the while, the mystery of Lucian Ludwig Kozminski endured. For if he did not die as claimed, and if he survived the intervening years, then he and his ill-gotten assets were yet to be found.

The Pandora's Box

The Los Angeles Times

One day slowly passed, then another, and still another. There was only silence. As the hours ticked by, it seemed that the Kozminski mystery might simply fade away, a minor, unsolved footnote on the ash heap of history.

But my musing was broken by a welcome surprise, a phone call from Ann O'Neill of the *Los Angeles Times*. Ann was no stranger to me or my firm. A dedicated, hardworking reporter on the court beat for the *Times*, she had written articles on several of our noteworthy cases. And now she was on the line, eager to talk.

"Hey, Mark!" she exclaimed with a burst of energy. "That's *quite* a press release. Tell me—did you *really* get two judgments that this guy faked his death?"

"Yeah, somehow, believe it or not," I replied.

"Well," Ann stated with conviction, "this is going to be a feature article, and the *whole world* is going to know about it."

"I really don't know what to say—" I began.

"Believe it," Ann snapped. "I'm *on* it. Now, when can you meet?"

And with that the process was set in motion. Like a whirling dervish, Ann would dive into the evidence in our bulging Kozminski files, scurry about town meeting with witnesses, and pepper me with regular calls, always probing, questioning, and seeking greater insight.

One evening Ann and I met with Jack and Esther Weingarten to hear their firsthand account of Jack's perilous wartime existence and Kozminski's swindle. Days later, on a sunny, blue-skied Saturday, we ventured to the home of Max and Dyna Wolman, who imparted their vivid memories while everyone munched on homemade French pastries.

Events seemed to accelerate as Ann attacked the case with unbridled energy. The story quickly coalesced in her mind, and soon she began putting pen to paper. And then her article was done and submitted to her editors. Everything suddenly lurched to a stop, and now it was time to wait.

But it also was time for internal politics at the *Times* to surface.

"I don't know about these guys," Ann lamented in frustration. "It's all about turf over here. I really don't know when the article's going to be printed, what section they'll put it in, or how much they'll chop it down."

First she assumed the article would be printed in July, then early August, and finally she despaired that it may never see the light of day.

But Ann was not to be denied.

On Friday, August 18, 2000, she called and excitedly exclaimed, "Mark, it's running this Sunday! The headline of the Metro section, no less. I'm not thrilled with some of the editing . . . but it's going to be *big*."

The next day was a tranquil, lazy Saturday. Everything seemed quiet and still, and the minutes slowly passed like sifting sand through an hourglass. My feelings remained mixed. This was the day before an important step in our journey. But unknown consequences might ensue.

The next morning, I awoke to the Sunday paper on my doorstep and opened it with great anticipation. Flipping to the Metro section, I saw a headline splashed across the top, SWINDLER OF HOLOCAUST SURVIVORS LEAVES A TRAIL OF MYSTERY. Below was a detailed and gripping story of the Kozminski saga, with poignant references to the plights and perseverance of Max Wolman and Jacob Weingarten.

A wave of jumbled feelings passed through me. I had a sense of great appreciation for Ann O'Neill and her tireless work, vindication for the survivors' dogged attempts to achieve justice, and exhilaration for the exposure our efforts had received.

But my prevailing sentiment, oddly enough, was relief. At long last, the Kozminski story had reached a level of public awareness that would bring other forces to bear, perhaps alleviating the frustration of my prolonged and lonely pursuit.

Dateline and *America's Most Wanted*

The pace of events generated its own momentum. Amid calls of encouragement from friends, family, and professional acquaintances, I was contacted by producers of *Dateline NBC*, *Sixty Minutes II*, and *America's Most Wanted*. Each had read the article and was keenly interested in producing a feature segment about Kozminski.

Meetings ensued with producers Peggy Holter and Jeannie Hedden of *Dateline* and *Sixty Minutes II*'s Andy Battag, who arrived from New York with impressive dispatch. Both *Dateline* and *Sixty Minutes II* adopted the same posture: Do what you want with *America's Most Wanted*, but you *cannot* commit to both *Dateline* and *Sixty Minutes II*. You must choose one or the other.

The choice was easy. I remained impressed by Andy Battag's enthusiasm, command of the facts, and genuine personal interest. *Dateline*, however, stood prepared to offer a firm commitment while *Sixty Minutes II* wavered. And with that, the wheels were set in motion for a nearly full-hour *Dateline* story on the infamous Lucian Kozminski.

Not to be outdone, *America's Most Wanted (AMW)* also jumped aboard, committing to produce a segment featuring survivor inter-

views and carefully constructed reenactments of Kozminski's nefarious activities.

It became like the proverbial story of the hare and tortoise.

Barely missing a beat, *AMW* moved full steam ahead. Spurred by
a former sports producer named Charles Stark, an amiable, sympathetic man in his fifties, the cameras were soon rolling. Stark interviewed me in my office, and shortly later the effervescent Molly
Schimel and Max Wolman were interviewed separately.

Molly Schimel gloried in her moment before the camera, dramatically recounting both her sufferings during the War and the later
decades of frustration at the hands of Lucian Kozminski. Excitedly
describing her sighting of Kozminski in 1995, she assuredly brushed
off any doubt about her recollection of date or location.

Max Wolman was another story entirely. His interview was at once
gripping and poignant, as he described his father's miserable death at
Auschwitz and Kozminski's brazen theft of the restitution payment
for this grievous loss.

But Wolman did not relish his moment in the sun. Weeks later he
called and said sheepishly, "Mark, I *tried* to bury all this. But ever
since the interview, I cannot sleep. I dream about my father freezing
in that chamber, then about that snake Kozminski. It has all rushed
back into my mind, and it all seems *so real*."

"Max," I replied. "I'm truly sorry . . . I never expected that—"

"Now," Max interjected, "my doctor says my blood pressure is too
high, so I'm sorry, but I just can't do any more interviews."

"I understand completely, Max," I responded, taken aback by the
physical toll the interview had exacted. "And you have my word:
There will be no more interviews."

Meanwhile, preparation of the *AMW* segment moved forward.
According to Charles Stark all that remained was editing of existing
interviews and inserting a few historical reenactments.

But it soon appeared that the Wolman interview, like the Schimel
interview, would never see the light of day. Though *AMW* possessed
ample footage for a powerful segment, within a matter of weeks
something had changed. Charles Stark was off the production. The
segment was placed in suspended animation. And for more than two
long years it would remain in the proverbial can, unknown and
unseen by the general public.

Yet, as fate would have it, shortly before publication of this book, *AMW* reemerged in the picture. Expressing a renewed interest and enthusiasm, *AMW* producers vowed to complete production of the segment quickly and broadcast it within a matter of weeks. The effects on our pursuit of Kozminski from this national broadcast remain to be seen.

The tortoise signified by *Dateline* was another matter. Peggy Holter, an intelligent, experienced professional with an engaging sense of humor, embarked on a lengthy production of a Kozminski segment for *Dateline*. Before it was over, Kozminski's son, Jakob Janusch, would be interviewed in Munich, Adam Bigwood would be tracked down and enticed to appear on-camera in Los Angeles, and even Kozminski's former neighbors would be canvassed for post-death sightings.

Delayed indefinitely by the terrorist attacks of 9/11, swamped by other duties arising from cutbacks at NBC, and often caught in a political crossfire between her Los Angeles office and NBC corporate headquarters in New York, Peggy Holter continued to persevere, meticulously piecing together her story. Peggy had made a commitment, and one way or another, she was going to abide by it.

Throughout, she remained undaunted. When the traumatic effects of Max Wolman's *AMW* interview did not subside, Peggy substituted Molly Schimel. When Jack Weingarten declined an interview out of fear that "Hungarian Fascists" would exact revenge, she replaced him with Ted Seidman. Slowly but surely, it all fell together, and after nearly one and a half years the segment at last was completed.

In January 2002, Peggy Holter advised me that the *Dateline* segment was slotted to run on March 3. But two days before the scheduled broadcast, she called again, this time with angst in her voice, and reported, "I'm sorry, Mark, but they just told me that the broadcast has been suspended indefinitely. Apparently it's a New York thing, trumping an L.A. segment with one of *theirs*. . . . Now I just don't know when it's going to run—or even if, God willing, it's *going* to run."

Several months passed without a word. And then Peggy suddenly called again, this time offering good news, "Mark, you're not going to believe this, but July seventh is *the* date, and it's etched in stone.

The story's running—that is, so long as those damned terrorists don't strike again."

A FEW WEEKS BEFORE the scheduled broadcast of the *Dateline* segment, I received a phone call and instantly recognized the genial voice on the line. It was Tom Tugend, an accomplished author and veteran freelance writer for several prominent Jewish publications. Tom had written articles on the Kozminski prosecution twenty years earlier, and his interest had been piqued by news of the upcoming *Dateline* broadcast.

"Seems like old times, huh?" Tom mused. After pausing for effect, he added, "So the guy's dead and *still* you can't give him a rest?"

"That's right," I replied. "If *I* can't rest, then *he's* not going to, either—even if he *is* dead as a doorknob."

We both laughed heartily, pleased to have renewed our long-dormant acquaintance. We would catch up several times during the ensuing weeks, as Tom pieced together his *Jewish Journal* story.

A short while later, he advised me that the article was about to run. But Tom added a note of disgruntlement, remarking, "Remember those photos of you and Kozminski that I asked you to submit? Well, I told our editor we must use Kozminski's photo to help *find* the son of a bitch when this gets picked up by the wires. But the damned guy just ignores me, so guess what? They're only using *your* photo. Some kind of sense that makes!"

Just two days before the broadcast of the *Dateline* segment, Tom's story ran in the *Jewish Journal*. Oddly enough, a headline reading, MAN OF MYSTERY was placed just above *my* black-and-white photo while Kozminski's photo was nowhere to be seen.

I later remarked to Tom, "I'm sure some of my acquaintances would consider me a man of mystery, but it really seems off-subject here." Tom laughed lustily, fully appreciating the levity in this editor's unintended joke.

Tom's article was a succinct, suspenseful account of the hunt for Kozminski, fueled by my "obsession," which "only intensified after meeting with several Holocaust survivors in Israel." It was revealing to see this in print, for despite my lengthy pursuit of Kozminski, I had never really considered it an obsession. I realized that Tom was correct, but this remained one obsession I had not and would not come to regret.

AND, FINALLY, July 7 arrived. A nearly hour-long segment on Kozminski was about to be broadcast over the airwaves.

Shortly before the broadcast, a trailer ran for the upcoming segment featuring a clip of Ted Seidman. His familiar visage gripped me instantly, and tears welled in my eyes. I realized that at long last, it would be a time for joy and a time to weep. Ted Seidman was about to tell the world his story.

The well-crafted segment, titled "Final Betrayal," began moments later and moved along at a brisk pace. Along with riveting passages from the vivacious Molly Schimel and the somber Ted Seidman, several cuts contained Adam Bigwood, his head shaved, limbs fidgety, and bulging, saucerlike eyes darting about.

At one point Bigwood conspicuously stumbled when asked where his father had been cremated, replying, "I can't . . . recall that right now."

Shortly afterward, he recounted the final disposition of Kozminski's ashes, "He [Kozminski] liked to go on walks at Franklin Canyon with the swans . . . no, not swans . . . ducks. And I sprinkled his ashes at the lake there."

Near the end of the segment, Jakob Janusch Kozminski impassively remarked with an ever-so-faint twinkle in his eyes, "God bless him [Kozminski] if he's alive. That's *all* I can say."

And then the story abruptly ended without resolution, for the mystery of its subject still endured.

New Victims and New Sightings

The heightened level of public awareness generated by the *Los Angeles Times* article, as well as the *Jewish Journal* article and *Dateline* segment two years later, spawned several new reports of recent Kozminski sightings.

Was the late Lucian Kozminski alive? We would soon discover that even if he were, he remained just out of reach, a slippery, elusive quarry.

One indication of fresh tracks was made by Abe Hecht, the middle-aged son of Harry Hecht, a documented Holocaust survivor and Kozminski victim.

Ringing me up in the summer of 2000, Hecht first established his bona fides, remarking, "My father and I met several times with Kozminski on my father's claim. Let me assure you—I know *exactly* what he looks like."

After pausing for effect, Hecht continued, "And I'll tell you this: I've seen him *many* times in the Fairfax District over the past three years. In fact, I saw him twice just eight months ago [in early 2000] right on Beverly Drive in Beverly Hills. I mean, the guy walked right by me."

"Right by you?" I queried excitedly.

"Yes," Hecht replied firmly. "But that's not all. The second time, I followed him on foot several blocks to—"

"To where?" I asked.

"To 137 South Crescent Drive. And then he slipped inside the building and disappeared."

Hecht's account sounded credible: 137 South Crescent Drive was the last known address of Kozminski before his death in early 1993.

More Kozminski sightings were revealed during the taping of the *Dateline* segment. They were uncovered by a tireless investigator, Arlene Friedman, a brown-haired woman with alabaster skin in her early fifties who had eagerly signed on with our case long before the *Dateline* airing.

An experienced veteran of several high-profile investigations, including the search for the hidden gold of Ferdinand Marcos, Friedman proved an invaluable source of support and strategy. It was a continuing relief to know that my efforts were supplemented by this upbeat, dedicated professional.

On her initial assignment, Friedman threw herself with charm and aplomb into canvassing Kozminski's former neighborhood. Bearing a "birthday gift" for a friend in the neighborhood whose address she had "misplaced," she managed to pry open locked doors and hitherto sealed recollections.

Casually flashing a photo of Kozminski, Friedman elicited no fewer than five affirmations of recent sightings between mid-2000 to the summer of 2001. Some witnesses pointed at Kozminski's former building; a few at buildings directly across the street.

Yet the riddle grew only more perplexing, as we confirmed without doubt that Kozminski no longer resided at 137 South Crescent. Did the sightings indicate Kozminski had the temerity to return to his former neighborhood to visit acquaintances? Was he checking in on valuable possessions left with a friend for safekeeping? Or was a Kozminski look-alike in the area, unwittingly playing a cruel joke on all of us?

A New Twist on Kozminski

What was to be believed? Another report would only heighten the mystery.

On July 11, 2002, I received a call from Howard Winkler, the son of Martin and Magda Winkler, who were known victims of Kozminski in our criminal prosecution twenty years earlier.

Launching into his story, Winkler recounted Kozminski's incessant lulling of his mother, Magda, stating, "For years he promised she would get $200,000 in restitution. But he *always* demanded more and more fees. She kept paying him and paying him, and in the end she got nothing."

He added, "She was in Auschwitz, you know, where her legs froze in the winter. The pain *still* kills her."

Kozminski had also defrauded Howard Winkler's father, Martin.

As Winkler recounted, "My dad was in the Jewish Underground, fighting against the Nazis, but was captured and tortured several times. Later, Kozminski filed a claim through a German attorney, Karl Pokorny. He assured us my father would get $40,000 and monthly payments."

Howard Winkler still possessed records showing the deposit of his father's restitution monies directly into Kozminski's bank account, payments Martin Winkler would never receive.

Laying the foundation for his recent Kozminski sightings, Winkler began, "I know this man all too well. My parents and I met with him several times—too many times—through the years."

Winkler continued in an unequivocal tone, "My father *saw* Kozminski less than two years ago, in the summer of 2000, walking near the corner of Gardner Avenue and Third Street. He got a good look at him—"

"Is he *sure*?" I interjected, acutely aware of the fallibility of witness identifications, especially among the elderly.

"No doubt about it," Winkler snapped. "And I *knew* he was right because *I* had seen Kozminski one or two months before on Beverly Boulevard. He was walking on the sidewalk, and when I veered my car over and yelled out at him, he cursed and spat at my car window."

When I probed his recollection as to time frame, Winkler shot back, "There's just no doubt at all. I *know* what car I was driving. And it's the *same* car that I got rid of less than two years ago. Believe me, I had to wipe Kozminski's spit off my car."

Winkler's account appeared concrete, detailed, and convincing. But his story was not over. Winkler went on, saving the best for last, "I'll tell you something else. I know that SOB better than you may think."

After inhaling deeply, he continued, "So I used to have an office right down the hall from Kozminski, just above the King David Bakery. And guess what I saw, again and again?"

"I don't know," I responded, my mind whirring with possibilities.

"Well, that little slime used to pick up male prostitutes right from the street and bring them back to his office. And boy, would they get it on! They used to create such a racket with their grunts and groans that I had to blast classical music in my office."

Winkler paused in reflection. "Yeah, I'm telling you, that guy was *quite* a character. A very strange man."

Winkler's riveting account had disclosed a revelation that peeled another layer from the onion of Kozminski's character.

In the days that followed I would ponder: One's sexual persuasion should be his own business, but did these encounters have greater meaning? Did they in some way relate to Kozminski's mode of survival in five concentration camps, where he was interned as a mere youth? Were they a factor in his self-loathing, his bouts with alcoholism and depression?

Once again the tantalizing questions were many, and the answers all too few.

An Old Twist on Kozminski

I would soon unexpectedly be reminded of Kozminski's better known mode of survival during the War.

Shortly before completing this book, I met with Steven and Ella Mandel in their home, along with their friend and fellow survivor Bill Deutsch. As I entered, Steven waved his hand and motioned to me to join him at a table.

It was then that I observed he was sitting in a wheelchair. I would soon learn, much to my dismay, that several months earlier, a stroke had felled this man of such remarkable courage and impressive physical strength.

But after surviving years of grueling forced labor at the hands of the Nazis, Steven was not about to relent. He had slowly fought his way back, was walking with assistance, and appeared clear-eyed and alert.

Steven and I were joined at the table by Deutsch, an energetic bespectacled man in his seventies with an air of calm intelligence. Moments later Ella entered the room and greeted me warmly, a transcendent look of sadness nonetheless apparent in her large brown eyes.

After Ella approached and sat next to Steven, Deutsch matter-of-factly remarked, "So, I hear you've come to talk about Kozminski? . . . I know him well."

"*Really?*" I responded with surprise.

"Yes," he continued, not missing a beat. "You see, near the end of the War, I was incarcerated at an outpost camp of Gross-Rosen named Wüstgiersdorf, in Germany. Lutek was very well known there."

"You mean, because he was an—" I replied.

"Yes, an *oberkapo*," he interjected. "He wore an armband that said

OBERKAPO. The prisoners . . . the prisoners were filthy, starving, and miserable."

Deutsch raised his arm and whipped his wrist down as if grasping a stick.

"But I often saw Lutek chase and beat them with a large black truncheon. It was terrible. Believe me, I will *never* forget it."

A moment of silence ensued.

"Yes, that Kozminski," Steven remarked. "He's *quite* a character."

After renewing my acquaintance with Steven and Ella awhile longer, I departed, still startled by the firsthand confirmation of Shlomo Blajman's account some twenty years earlier. No matter how distant in time and place his conduct, new disclosures about Kozminski seemed to be emerging with uncanny regularity.

Adam Bigwood: New Revelations and Encounters

Startling revelations were by no means limited to Lucian Kozminski. Owing largely to Arlene Friedman's efforts, our strange and unsettling portrait of Adam Bigwood became at once clearer and even more confounding.

New evidence solved the mystery of Kozminski's phantom "third son"—Patrick Graf-Blieberg. Rather than Graf-Bleiberg residing in an apartment across the street from Bigwood, we learned that he lived in Bigwood's apartment itself: The two were, in fact, one and the same person.

As it turns out, Patrick Graf-Blieberg was just one of many aliases (and Social Security numbers) adopted by Adam Kozminski through the years, among them Patrick Adam Graf-Bleiberg, Patrick A. Bleib, Patrick A. Bleiberg, P. Graf Blieberg, Patrick A. Graf, Patrick A. Grafbleiberg, and, of course, Adam Bigwood.

Several of these aliases were revealed in Bigwood's newly discovered rap sheet, a litany of criminal charges including perjury, subornation of perjury, forgery, violation of probation, altercation with a police officer, driving with a suspended license, and providing false information to a police officer.

Bigwood may have been a cipher to the outside world, but court files now revealed that his own *mother* and *stepmother* had identified him as a culprit. First to file an action was Bigwood's stepmother, Esther, who sought judicial relief in November 1990, just seven months before her death.

Esther's startling account led to the swift issuance of a temporary restraining order barring Bigwood from approaching her residence. According to Esther, it all began on August 29, 1990, when she was standing on a street corner in Beverly Hills waiting for a ride to take her to temple:

> Suddenly a car drove up. I was about to get in when I heard my [then estranged] husband [Lucian Kozminski] say, "We're going to do away with you." . . . Then I heard [Bigwood say] . . . "I'll get your *fucking* wife." . . . My husband [Lucian Kozminski] then said, "We'll get her some other place," and the car drove off.

Esther continued, "The police questioned my husband [Kozminski] . . . [and] he told [them] that [Bigwood] wanted to *do away* with [me] and that my husband could not restrain [Bigwood's] actions. I am terminally ill with cancer. . . . [Bigwood] knows that I am dying and extremely weak."

We would later learn this incident was no idle threat, for Bigwood reportedly had waved a gun at Esther from the car and threatened to fire it.

Not playing favorites, Bigwood also prompted his mother, Janina Liebermann, to obtain a temporary restraining order in December 1996. Lieberman's application alleged that just days before, Bigwood had come to her residence and demanded money, leading to the following exchange: "When [I] refused he started to scream and rant and kicked [me] with his foot."

Yet this assault, according to Liebermann, was anything but isolated:

> Adam Bigwood has been coming to [my] residence almost every day where he constantly demands money and almost always becomes violent and abusive. From 1990 to date [I] have given Adam . . . approximately $350,000. He constantly abuses [me] . . . and on numerous occasions threatened to kill [me] as well as [my] friends . . . He has forged [my] name and social security number on many documents. . . . It is strongly believed that Adam Bigwood is addicted to drugs.

As if his criminal acts and threats to his family were not enough, we also discovered that Bigwood was President and Secretary of the Poopie Scoopie Corporation, the website for which featured a graphic animation of a dog emitting a stream of urine.

These latest findings lent some bold brush strokes to an odd and chilling portrait. The implications were clear: Adam Bigwood was definitely a force to be reckoned with.

I would not have to wait long. Shortly after the *Los Angeles Times* article ran (long before the *Dateline* segment), I received a voicemail from a man identifying himself as Adam Bigwood. I hesitated to return the call, but in the end I had little choice: Like it or not, Bigwood's story had to be heard.

I slowly dialed the phone and waited as it rang several times. He answered in a slightly accented middle-aged voice. After we briefly identified ourselves, Bigwood quickly interposed, "Mr. Kalmansohn, I remember you *well* from the U.S. Attorney's Office and, as I recall, your studies afterward at Cambridge University."

It was mildly discomfiting that he distinctly recalled me from many years before. But I had little time to dwell on this concern. Bigwood rapidly introduced the matter at hand, "I didn't actually read the whole thing, but I *heard* about the article in the L.A. *Times.* Now, I don't want to threaten you . . . but I trust we've heard the last of this subject."

Fully aware that Bigwood had just issued a threat, I matter-of-factly replied, "No, I'm *sure* you don't want to threaten anyone, Mr. Bigwood."

And then he was off, launching pell-mell into an often meandering, peculiar and strained account of the life and death of Lucian Kozminski.

Bigwood first sought to dispel the mystery surrounding Kozminski's "death": "I have to tell you, there's no doubt my father died," he began, with a note of urgency.

As Bigwood recalled, "I still can remember the day in 1990 . . . or 1991 . . . or somewhere thereabouts. I was in his hospital room and he died in my arms. Right then and there, suddenly he was gone."

As it turns out, this was just one of several accounts of Kozminski's fateful day offered by Bigwood. Days later Bigwood would advise Ann O'Neill that his father had died while "I sat in a chair facing him" and still later would tell *Dateline* that he first learned of Kozminski's death in a terse phone call from the hospital.

Bigwood went on, addressing the issue of Kozminski's phantom ashes: "You see, Century City Hospital has a service where you come and pick up the ashes of the dead. That's what I did, and after I picked up the ashes I spread them on the lake at Franklin Canyon where my father liked to walk."

When I queried why a mail drop was listed on the death certificate as Kozminski's "place of final disposition," Bigwood answered with an uncomfortable silence, and then moved on. Continuing to spin his tale, he turned to Kozminski's activities during the War: "My father was a real hero. You know, he snuck out of the ghetto every night and always returned with food!"

Bigwood would later embellish this story on *Dateline*, claiming that Kozminski often came back armed with "pounds and pounds of hams," which indeed was a strange repast for the Orthodox Jewish denizens of the ghetto.

Still Bigwood went on, remarking, "And after the War, my father broke up a ring of Eastern Bloc Communist spies in Schwandorf (outside Munich). I'm telling you, you've got this man all wrong. He was a *real* hero."

Now he turned to the subject of Kozminski's incarceration, saying, "You see, my father was released from federal prison in San Pedro in 1990 or 1991 and was sent to Louisiana for deportation. But some top-secret evidence was presented to the judge. And instead of being deported, my father got his green card *and* Polish citizenship back!"

"Really?" I replied reflexively.

"Oh, yes," Bigwood continued. "This was the *only* time that an order of deportation of a released prisoner was reversed. And I'd like to . . . but I can't tell you why it happened."

With a tone of reassurance, Bigwood added, "You can call the FBI or anyone you want to verify this."

After pausing for effect, he went on, "So I'm *not* threatening you. I really just want to clear this up."

"I appreciate your clarification," I responded.

"And listen," Bigwood concluded, "my father *never* was the type to hide. He was a courageous man. And he didn't end up with any money, either. Believe me, his sons would be the *first* to know. So please, let us live in peace and let us be left alone."

Moments later he rang off. I would not hear from him again.

My surreal and strange encounter with Adam Kozminski, a.k.a. Adam Bigwood, had ended. But the impression he left was a lasting one. In his own words, tone, and inflection I could sense the very person who had emerged in our composite portrait. It was not a flattering vision, and that would only be reinforced by later events.

Several months after the *Los Angeles Times* article ran, Arlene Friedman reported that she had received a mysterious call at home. A man with a gruff voice had said, "I understand you're looking for my father—*stop!*"

Before Arlene could respond, the dial tone abruptly sounded.

Meanwhile, during the taping of Bigwood's interview with *Dateline*, I received an anxious call from Peggy Holter, a note of distress creeping into her usually composed voice. Almost in a hushed tone, Peggy remarked, "This guy Bigwood is *such* a strange bird. I think he's on drugs . . . he's so fidgety, you wouldn't believe it. He keeps sniffing and rubbing his nose, and his eyes dart around wildly. Thank goodness he's gone."

Inhaling deeply, she continued, "So get this. Our interviewer asks Bigwood, 'What is the first thing you thought about when your father died?' And you know what he answers? He says, 'I thought about *killing* that former prosecutor, *Mr. Kalmansohn.*'"

A long pause ensued before Peggy resumed her account. "Well, we were all stunned. Meantime, Bigwood looks into the camera with sort of a blank expression, his eyes gazing like a trapped animal. And then, realizing his predicament, he mumbles, 'But, of course, that's against the law. I mean, I didn't actually *do* anything about it.'"

For a moment Peggy and I both were silent, as Bigwood's threat from months before quickly replayed in my mind. Then she quietly added, "I just thought you'd like to know . . . and take any appropriate precautions."

After another moment of pregnant silence, I sought to shed the best light on this distinctly ominous report. "Well, thanks for the heads-up, Peggy. I guess the *good* news is that *all* of America is going to watch him *say* this."

We both took great consolation in this. But much to our chagrin, this part of Bigwood's interview would be excised, a casualty of a *Dateline* internal policy decision.

Return of the Native Son?

The *Dateline* segment provided intriguing clues about Kozminski's mindset before his fateful encounter with the Grim Reaper.

In his on-camera interview, Bigwood's brother Jakob Janusch recalled a curious meeting with his father in Los Angeles in January 1993, just one week before Kozminski's reported death:

> My father told me [President] Lech Walesa had invited him to visit Poland. He said he intended to enter into a major deal with Visa there regarding a security card he had invented. My father said he was looking forward eagerly to starting his new life.

However unusual and grandiose, Lucian Kozminski's story of an imminent trip to Poland and "starting a new life" was entirely consistent with Bigwood's earlier allusion to Kozminski "regaining" his Polish citizenship.

This apparent match between two jagged pieces of an odd puzzle led me to wonder: Could Kozminski have made some sort of a verbal slip, a subconscious hint to his two sons? Was Poland the true final destination for Lucian Kozminski?

The Safe Deposit Box

Shortly after the *Dateline* segment ran, I received a voicemail from a woman identifying herself as an Arizona-based investigator "who had some important information about the Kozminski case."

When I returned the call, a pleasant-voiced woman answered and promptly began her story, "Mr. Kalmansohn, I'm a private investigator who'd very much like to remain . . . anonymous. I want you to know that the *Dateline* segment really inspired me, so I decided to see if I could help your efforts."

"I really appreciate that—" I began to respond.

"Anyway," she interjected, "I spent several hours on the Net, and I think I've found something of . . . interest."

"Oh, really?" I responded, assuming it was some strand of evidence with which we were all too familiar.

"A safe deposit box . . . in *his* name," she continued. "It used to be at the Bank of America, but it 'escheated' to the Controller's Office of the State of California."

"You mean—" I replied.

"They've got it," she continued. "The State *has* the box. If you execute on one of your judgments, *you* can get your hands on the contents."

Moments later she was off the phone, barely after I could mumble thanks to this Good Samaritan for a most startling find.

With a few quick keystrokes I found the website she identified. Soon afterward her report was confirmed: The State of California possessed Lucian Kozminski's Bank of America safe deposit box as officially "unclaimed property."

I tried to remain on an even keel and restrain my imagination. But for several minutes my mind darted about, contemplating the nearly infinite possibilities.

I now wondered: Was Kozminski in such a rush to depart that he would leave the contents of this box behind? Or could he have just forgotten the box was there?

And, most important, what was *inside* the box? Documents relating to his current location or identity? Numbers identifying a Swiss bank account? Cash, bonds, or jewelry that could be distributed to his victims? Or merely some vestige of valuables once stored, like a joker card dashing our hopes of gaining a winning hand?

There was only one way to find out: file for a writ of execution on one of our civil judgments and then deliver the Court-issued writ to the Sacramento Sheriff's Department for service upon the State Controller's Office. Wasting little time, I filed the required papers with the Los Angeles Superior Court. Now it was time to wait.

We had embarked on a new adventure with the tangled web of

government bureaucracy. As we would learn once again, the wheels of justice in this system move on their own time. They know no sense of urgency, fading opportunity, or the fragile existence of many aging and infirm survivors.

NEARLY ONE MONTH LATER, the court-issued writ arrived in a simple envelope and with no fanfare. We had achieved one critical step.

The same day, we sent the writ to the Sacramento Sheriff's Department. Again it was time to wait.

Days, then weeks, passed until at last, nearly six weeks later, we received a response. Rather than enforcing our writ, however, the Sheriff's Department had returned it as "defective." The court clerk, it seems, had neglected to place an official court seal on the executed writ. Absent that formality, the Sheriff's Department was not about to budge.

Back to court we went, this time with a new application and a declaration of defective writ. Again we waited. Several more weeks passed before we received a new writ bearing a prominent court seal.

Hoping that this Kafkaesque bout with the State had come to an end, I delivered the new writ to the Sheriff's Department in Sacramento. But they were not about to relent. Back it came several weeks later, now rejected because we used the P.O. box listed for the Controller's Office on its own website, rather than a street address.

So, incredibly, it was back to court again, this time with a further application for a writ of execution providing a street address for the State Controller's Office.

With one simple, routine task, we had lost precious months. It undoubtedly would take weeks to receive the writ from the Court, and then weeks more to hear our fate from the Sacramento Sheriff's Office.

Now firmly enmeshed in a tangle of red tape unleashed by the Superior Court and the Sheriff's Office, two stolid pillars of our labyrinthine judicial system, I had abundant time to ponder a growing concern: Would we *ever* enforce this judgment and lay our eyes on the hidden contents of Kozminski's secret box?

The Silent Grave

Trapped in a no-man's-land on the verge of uncovering one of Kozminski's final secrets, I decided to close a personal chapter on another furtive and mysterious existence: the life and death of Dr. Josef Mengele.

The notorious "Angel of Death" who commandeered the "selection" process at Auschwitz, directing arriving inmates to swift death in the gas chambers or slow death by forced labor and starvation, Mengele had greeted many of our victim-witnesses and their relatives at the portals of hell. The parents of Menahem Russek, the Israeli investigator who greatly assisted Kozminski's criminal prosecution, were among those ushered to immediate extinction. Russek spent decades hunting Mengele and later seeking to prove that his death had been faked.

A traveling phantom after the War, Mengele briefly was a prisoner of the U.S. Army in Germany but slipped through their grasp by assuming the identification of another doctor. Almost certainly aided by the surreptitious "Vatican Tunnel" escape route for former Nazis and their cronies, Mengele slithered into the friendly confines of several sympathetic military regimes. First it was Argentina. On the heels of a West German order of extradition, he fled to Paraguay. Tracked by Israeli agents, he moved again, this time to Brazil.

On January 7, 1979, while living near São Paulo, Brazil with a German family, the reclusive Mengele reportedly went for a swim in the ocean near Enseada de Bertioga, suffered a severe stroke, and drowned. He was 68 years old. Mengele was secretly buried in the nearby cemetery of Embu under the name of Gerhard, his most recent alias. Records would later reflect that the real Wolfgang Gerhard had died in Austria the year before.

When the secret of Mengele's purported death leaked years afterward, a firestorm erupted. Many scoffed at the revelation and demanded an exhumation of the body. Finally, in 1985, the "Gerhard" body was exhumed from the Embu cemetery. On June 21, Mengele's alleged bones, skull, and other remnants were placed before an international group of observers at the São Paulo police station.

Forensic experts explained that the skeleton's height, the broken left finger, the gap between the two front teeth, and other telltale physical markers provided a perfect match with Mengele's known medical records. The mysterious corpse, they definitively concluded, must be Mengele's.

But the controversy still lingered. Seeking to staunch the festering doubt nearly seven years later, Mengele's son Rolfe finally agreed to submit to a test comparing his DNA to the "Mengele" remains now held in Germany. According to several British DNA experts, the results were a perfect match. The corpse was Mengele's, and the mystery at last was solved. Or was it?

Now, on a hot late-December day, the air dripping with humidity, I approached the Embu cemetery with three municipal tourist guides tasked with "escorting" me through the graveyard.

We joined a line of locals and tourists meandering through a gaggle of stalls in a Sunday craft market. The entire area was a mélange of bright colors splashed against a cloudless blue sky, exotic aromas, and a hubbub of voices in the pleasant-sounding lilt of Portuguese.

Then, in a matter of a few yards, the scene suddenly shifted, and the crowd melted away as if on cue.

We had arrived at the Embu cemetery, also known as Cemíterio do Rosario.

A rundown concrete wall marked the entrance. The cemetery was notably compact, with no more than a thousand graves scattered beneath a jumble of headstones and crosses, most of them askew, faded, and unkempt.

As I stepped inside the cemetery alongside my guides, we were given a sudden start by an ear-piercing explosion.

A wisp of smoke wafted in the air a short distance beyond the cemetery's walls, and my eyes instantly locked with those of one of the guides. But our expressions relaxed in the same moment, as we both realized that this diversion was nothing more than the premature launch of a New Year's firecracker.

Returning to the business at hand, I walked a short distance to the caretaker's office and stepped inside. A diminutive couple, both in their late forties or early fifties, greeted our entourage with some apprehension. The man, a high-pitched fellow with one brown eye fixed at an abnormal angle, peered at me quizzically.

Introducing myself as a writer, I explained to him that I was looking for the former grave of Josef Mengele. I added, "I believe it is grave number 321, marked under the name of Gerhard."

A long pause ensued, and then a look of recognition crossed his face. He muttered something to the woman, who sat before an old ledger at a small wooden table. She quickly flipped through the ledger and identified a grave.

Bounding out of the office, the caretaker motioned for me to follow. We walked for about twenty yards and then we were there. It was a grave marked GERHARD with a simple headstone. The rest of the grave was dirt, smooth and bare. Next to the headstone lay what appeared to be a large, slightly ajar black mollusk. Flies buzzed about the unsightly decoration, and I wondered if this was someone's notion of a fitting tribute to the evil doctor.

The sun beat down and the air grew very still. I nearly expected to hear something, perhaps an anguished cry from one of his victims or a last guttural sound of defiance and denial. But in the end it was only silence.

The caretaker studied me carefully, as if trying to ascertain whether I had seen enough and my mission was done. "You know," he said, "the remains are not here anymore. They took them away."

"Yes, I've read that," I responded. "But just for my records, could I examine the ledger and make sure this was the Mengele grave?"

The caretaker snapped, "You're not with an *official* Jewish group, are you?"

When I shook my head no, he continued, "Well, then you *can't* see it." And before I could respond, he was gone, slipping into the shadows of his cemetery office. My side trip was over. There were no more secrets to be uncovered here, no more truths to be found.

I had seen the temporary resting place of another man whose life and death were shrouded in mystery, false identity, and flight, a most evil existence that for one moment in a sprawling camp of despair likely crossed paths with the unseemly and tortured journey of Lucian Kozminski.

The Final Journey

As the plane home dipped over the glistening snowcapped peaks of the Andes Mountains, a stark realization set in: I had traveled thousands of miles only to return to my very point of departure.

There we still remained—dangling on the precipice of a decisive breakthrough or the final dead end.

Despite the emergence of new Kozminski sightings, none led us to his doorstep, and the trail grew cold. Our efforts to track him in Poland proved fruitless. Kozminski's sons were on the record denying knowledge of a scheme to fake his death. His Swiss bank accounts remained sealed and hidden. Our Freedom of Information of Act request for his extensive Immigration and Naturalization Service file still foundered five years later, mired in the black hole of an agency under siege. We would generate no tips from a high-visibility *AMW* segment that would never air.

Our entire quest now hinged on the uncertain outcome of a single undertaking.

The secrets of the safe deposit box remained tantalizingly within reach but still firmly outside our grasp. I feared they would become nothing more than a buried remnant of the recent past.

THE SILENCE WAS deafening. An extended period had passed without word from the Sacramento Sheriff's Office on the disposition of our writ of execution. Sensing valuable time slipping away, I decided to make a call.

Prodded out of its bureaucratic malaise, the Sheriff's Office immediately searched its pending files. Within minutes I was matter-of-factly advised that the writ, in fact, had been served on the State Controller's Office nearly one month earlier.

At long last, we had cleared this exasperating and daunting hurdle.

Greatly relieved, I wasted no time in calling the Controller's Office to ascertain the status of the matter. While the attorney who fielded my call proved unfamiliar with the file, he promised a written response in short order. It arrived later that day in the form of a letter faxed from Ronald Placet, a Senior Staff Counsel at the State Controller's Office.

In his letter, Placet began by apologizing for the month delay in responding to our writ. He then turned to the matter at hand, dryly contending that "unclaimed property held by . . . this office is *not* subject to a writ of execution." Placet explained that "the funds you seek to have levied 'escheated' to the State under the provisions of the Unclaimed Property Act." Therefore, he concluded, "*title* to the property [is] 'vested' in the state of California . . . and is *not* . . . property of a judgment debtor [Mordka Wolman]."

With one swift wave of its imperious hand, the State had brushed off our judgment like an irksome diversion: The funds in Kozminski's safe deposit box were now held and *owned* by the State, and that is where they would remain.

Miffed at this cavalier response, I placed a call to Ronald Placet. Moments later he was on the line. After briefly introducing myself, I noted, "Mr. Placet, you probably are unaware that the *only* known income generated by the defendant was through cheating Holocaust survivors. *These* are the funds that the State now claims it owns. It is nothing less than blood money from years of suffering at the hands of the Nazis."

After an uncomfortable silence, Placet muttered, "Oh . . . I didn't know that."

"Well," I continued, "I hope this will cause you to reevaluate. I know that the policies of the Controllers' Office *and* the Governor's office generally have been . . . sympathetic toward Holocaust survivors. And I would *hate* to see your office come out on the wrong side here."

"OK," Placet stated. "So what would you like us to do?"

"First," I began, "we'd like to know the contents of the safe deposit box. Second, we want *all* items in the box returned to us, including any funds."

"I understand," Placet remarked quietly. "I'll see what I can do."

SEVERAL DAYS LATER, I called Placet for a status report. "Oh, yes," he replied with instant recognition. "I was about to call and give you my findings."

"OK, I'm ready," I responded, realizing the moment of truth was at hand.

"Well, here's what I found out," Placet remarked in a neutral tone. "The safe deposit box was delivered to us sometime during 2000. At the time it contained two empty yellow envelopes, two receipts stapled to three papers, and . . . and there was a key. To what, we don't know."

"And the funds?" I queried in anticipation.

"Yes," Placet continued. "In one white envelope there were three one-hundred dollar bills and two one-dollar bills. A total of three hundred and two dollars."

"That—*that's it?*" I asked, surprised at the paltry sum.

"Yes," Placet replied. "Though I *should* add that the holder of the box owed eighty-five dollars in additional rental charges."

"The items, I mean other than the money—" I began.

"Oh, yes," Placet remarked matter-of-factly. "On July 18, 2002, *all* of the materials in the box that did not have a value—meaning everything but the three hundred and two dollars—were destroyed by the state."

"*Destroyed?*" I queried, chagrined.

"Yes, destroyed. They're gone. There's nothing left but the money."

"You mean, even *the key*—" I stated.

"Gone," Placet interjected. "It's history. Nothing left but the money."

After ruminating briefly about this intriguing yet disappointing report, I finally muttered, "I appreciate your . . . cooperation. I . . . I know the funds are meager, but I'd still like to disperse them to a few of the survivors."

His voice dropping to a hush, Placet stated, "I understand. I'll see what I can do."

T HE SECRETS of the box had at last been revealed, but the mystery was only compounded. The questions were dizzying and seemed to lead nowhere.

What was in the two yellow envelopes? What were the two receipts and the three papers to which they were attached? Why would someone rent a safe deposit box and stash just $302 in cash inside? Did Kozminski remove nearly all valuables before implementing a fake death scheme? Did he deliberately leave behind a few meager traces of a "natural death"?

And what *was* the key? Why was it there? Could it have been a key to *another* safe deposit box in an unknown Swiss bank? Was it a key to a personal safe that would remain forever sealed?

Amid the many perplexing questions, one sobering truth emerged: We now knew that our prolonged attempt to retrieve the box had been doomed from the start.

The timeline was unmistakable. The *Dateline* segment had been broadcast on July 7, 2002. Soon after viewing the story, an Arizona investigator discovered the existence of the box at the State Controller's Office. Despite her prompt report of this find, the outcome was preordained, for the box's contents were destroyed on July 18, just eleven days after the *Dateline* airing.

It may be said that nothing is too late. Yet in this instance, critical pieces of the puzzle had faded into oblivion before our efforts even commenced.

While the end now seemed at hand, I vowed that our work would not cease. So long as a shred of hope remained, our hunt would continue.

At least for a time, the mystery of Lucian Ludwig Kozminski would endure.

Reflections: The Mirror of Anti-Semitism

Looking back on the several criminal and civil proceedings against Lucian Ludwig Kozminski, I have come to learn that none of these cases was about the defendant. Rather they were about dedicated investigators, including a German-born postal inspector who toiled ceaselessly in pursuit of elusive evidence. They were about a trio of judges who examined facts impartially and dispensed justice calmly and fairly. They were about many Holocaust survivors who ennobled our system of justice with their courage and humanity. And they were also about something deeper, a thread that connected all of us to the Holocaust and beyond, to the possibility of the triumph of the human spirit.

Nevertheless, recent developments have only compounded the lingering questions still swirling about the man in the vortex, as we are left to ponder whether Kozminski:

> stands isolated in a . . .
> witness stand of glass,
> a cage, where we may view
> ourselves, an apparition
> telling us something he
> does not know.

Admittedly, one could dismiss Kozminski as a mere sociopath, an inadequate person utterly devoid of character or empathy. We could simply presume that regardless of what transpired before his internment in the camps, having lived like a trapped animal, he somehow emerged without common decency or morality. Though a tempting and seemingly adequate rationale, it cannot explain why Kozminski's prey were fellow Jews and, worse, survivors of the Nazi Holocaust.

It is Kozminski's special activities in the camps, not the mere fact of his internment that may offer the best explanation. For unlike countless other survivors, Kozminski became a member of the small Jewish elite tasked with supervising other camp inmates, a notorious group that actively collaborated with the Nazis through a mixture of "greed, corruption, nepotism and violence."

Likely owing his very survival to this unholy assignment, Kozminski appears to have sunk into the dark passage of self-hatred. Once having entered, he continued his descent and unconsciously vowed, as in George Elliot's words, "I wish I had not been born a Jew, I disown any bond with the long travail of my race, I will outdo the Gentiles in mocking at our separateness."

Ultimately coming to identify with and imitate his Nazi oppressors, he continued to oppress and vilify Jews for decades. Yet in this case, it was not just any Jews but Holocaust victims—the living embodiment of his own enduring self-hatred—who became his quarry.

Like Kozminski, these victims had survived. But unlike him, they had done so without renouncing their own religion, own people, and humanity itself.

Epilogue

A voice called. I went.
I went, for it called,
I went, lest I fall.

At the crossroads
I blocked both ears with the white frost
And cried
For what I had lost.

        —Hannah Senesh, Caesarea 1942

Since the reunification of Germany, restitution programs remain in place. To date, more than $60 billion has been paid to Holocaust survivors, and some 130,000 survivors continue to receive regular monthly pensions.

Prompted by the U.S. government, several major German corporations have established a $5 billion Holocaust fund for payments covering slave labor, forced labor, unpaid insurance policies, looted property, and other Jewish assets that were "Aryanized" by the Nazi regime.

A $1 billion program providing for a onetime grant of $3,250 or a $325 monthly pension has been enacted for Jewish survivors in the former Soviet Union with annual incomes of less than $15,000. Hampered by abysmal records left in the former Soviet Union, the vast majority of the estimated 90,000 applicants are unlikely ever to receive any restitution.

Finally, while the German Finance Ministry recently instituted a program for the approximately 20,000 Nazi victims residing in Eastern Europe, opposition leaders characterized the budgeted sum of $50 million as meager and "morally indefensible."

LIKE A BIOPSIED CELL from a malignant tumor, my failure to obtain any information on Kozminski's presumed Swiss accounts denotes a virulent and larger cancer. Continuing to this very day, Europe has been rocked with disclosures of Switzerland's stashing and laundering of incalculable quantities of Nazi loot stolen from Holocaust victims, conversion of tons of victims' seized gold as recompense for foreign "expropriation" of Swiss assets, and cavalier rebuffing of efforts to identify and repossess valuables that desperate victims deposited with Swiss banks.

Turning their ire and indignation upon the victims, the former Swiss president bluntly characterized demands for a fund to compensate Holocaust survivors as "blackmail," while the Swiss Ambassador to the United States warned that "you cannot trust most of [our] adversaries" and called for "waging war" against Jewish groups and other vocal critics, fueling a storm of protest that led to his resignation soon afterward. Stung by a tidal wave of criticism, a few months later the Swiss government announced a $4.7 billion fund for victims of the Holocaust, "poverty, catastrophes, genocides and other grave violations of human rights."

These events, in turn, have prompted the scalpel to slice even deeper, revealing an ever more pervasive disease. Symptoms include the Austrians' and Hungarians' hoarding for half a century of millions of dollars' worth of victims' artwork and other stolen assets, French expropriation of Jewish-owned property in Paris and elsewhere, European insurers' denial of claims made on insurance policies purchased by Holocaust victims before World War II, the Tripartite Commission's stowing of a two-ton cache of gold containing melted fillings and wedding rings of Nazi victims in the Federal Reserve of New York's underground vault, and the Allies' failure to account for all one hundred tons of survivors' bullion seized from a Merkers potassium mine, among other Nazi treasures unearthed after the War.

Yet neither the exploratory surgery nor the diagnosis has been completed. Areas that remain to be fully examined involve the complicit role of anti-Semitic Polish Gentiles including the Polish Underground (Armia Krajowa and Armia Ludowa), who eagerly witnessed the humiliation and mass deportation of their Jewish neighbors while refusing desperate pleas for assistance from the Jewish Resistance, most notably during the Jews' battle with Nazi tanks during the destruction of the Warsaw ghetto in April 1943; the curiously ambivalent role of neutral Sweden, which fueled the Nazi war machine through shipments of iron ore while providing safe haven for fleeing Danish and Finnish Jews; the insidious conduct of a cabal of collaborators and "quislings" throughout Western Europe before and during the Nazi occupation; the Vatican's issuance of passports to Nazi war criminals seeking to evade justice after the War; and the refusal of Argentina, Paraguay, Bolivia, and other South American countries to ferret out former Nazis for more than five decades. As one member of the Israeli Knesset succinctly remarked, "The Germans murdered, the Swiss inherited and the world kept silent."

In the end, the least that we can do for the millions of victims of the Holocaust, both alive and dead, is to treat this cancer with its only cure: the unremitting, bright, radiating light of exposure. While even this remedy cannot heal the grievous wounds or alleviate the untold suffering, it may promote the awareness needed to recognize the true depth of our loss and to realize that the Holocaust ultimately represents not just a tragedy for Jews but also one for all humankind.

ASIDE FROM THE many insights I gained during my investigations of Lucian Kozminski, my personal connection with the Holocaust and its aftermath has continued to evolve over the years. After the criminal case, I traveled to Germany on several more occasions. In 1983, I visited one of my close acquaintances from Cambridge University at his family's home in Königstein, near Frankfurt.

One evening we met with a group of young Germans, most of them recent university graduates. In a discussion about events in the Middle East, I was shocked to hear one of them liken Israel's recent invasion of Lebanon to the Nazi invasion of Western Europe. I chastised the comparison as absurd, but words could not capture my consternation. I later wondered whether this perverse analogy reflected a subconscious attempt to evade second-generation German guilt over the Holocaust.

Several years later, I returned to Germany for the wedding of my friend. The evening before the ceremony, I attended an intimate dinner with the groom's family and close friends, including two *Wermacht* veterans of World War II. One of them was my friend's gracious father, Mannfred, whose arm was shriveled from a severe wound he suffered during the War.

IN APRIL 1983, I visited Israel for the first time. Menahem Russek, then about sixty, a short, beaming man with a big heart, warmly greeted me at the airport and quickly ushered me past the tight Israeli security.

For several days, Russek graciously escorted me around Tel Aviv, Caesarea, and Jerusalem, where we visited several memorable sights, including the Chamber of the Holocaust on Mount Zion and, at the Yad Vashem Holocaust Memorial, the matching sculpture of gnarled, emaciated Holocaust victims that Lou Kinzler and I had seen at Dachau, Germany, a year earlier.

During our time together, Russek and I developed a close bond that continues to this day. Despite his having lost his beloved Rose many years ago, his two sons and nine grandchildren have helped keep his spirit eternally buoyant.

Later in the trip, I had the pleasure of meeting with the irrepressible Shlomo Blajman and his wife, Lola, in their Tel Aviv apartment. Ever the gracious host, Blajman was clearly thrilled that I had accepted his invitation to visit Israel. When I called him in Israel thirteen years later, I found that despite his heart condition and Lola's serious illness, at eighty-two years of age, he sounded as spirited and lively as ever.

IN APRIL 1993, after being married under the *huppa*, my wife and I were greeted by Menahem Russek on our honeymoon in Israel, where, coincidentally, Holocaust Remembrance Day and the anniversary of that nation's birth were both being commemorated.

A few days later, on a cool blustery night, I went with my bride to the Western Wall in Jerusalem, the lone remnant of the destruction of the Second Temple. Though my marriage would prove ethereal, as we stood there ringed by Israeli soldiers and flags while a military band played the *Hatikvah,* the past, present, and future merged. For one brief moment, the jagged edges of life seemed to fit.

FINALLY, in late November 1996, I visited the United States Holocaust Memorial Museum in Washington, D.C. At the entrance, I was given an identification card for a real person who lived during the Holocaust. The card bore the name of a Kalman Kernweiss, an interesting happenstance, as my last name literally means the "son of Kalman."

The enclosed biography noted that Kernweiss, born in Kupno, Poland, in 1920, escaped from a Glogow labor camp and hid in nearby forests with other Jews during the Nazis' annihilation of Polish Jewry. Sometime in 1944, however, Kernweiss ventured back to Kupno and was quickly ambushed by several Polish Gentile neighbors. He was found dead the next day with a pitchfork stuck in his chest.

Dachau

Afterword

After the Kozminski case ended, Lou Kinzler rose rapidly through the ranks of the U.S. Postal Inspection Service, landing a senior position in Washington, D.C. He later moved to France for several years to work in a prestigious Interpol post. Kinzler is now retired and lives with his wife, Olivia, in the San Diego area. They have one son and one daughter, both of whom are married. Lou and I remain in occasional contact.

A few years after the case, Suzanne Conlon was appointed a Federal District Court Judge for the Northern District of Illinois. We still remain dear friends.

In 1988, Steve Trott left his senior post at the U.S. Department of Justice and joined the Ninth Circuit Court of Appeals, where he currently sits.

Former U.S. Attorney Andrea Sheridan Ordin is a partner in a major Los Angeles firm and, as ever, continues to promote justice and equality in the community. I remain both an acquaintance and admirer.

Menahem Russek is alive and well in Israel and enjoying retirement and special moments with his many adoring grandchildren.

Shortly before completing this book, I met again with several of the principal survivors in our cases, including Jack and Esther Weingarten, Max and Dyna Wolman, Steven and Ella Mandel, and Molly Shimel. Though several are hampered by serious physical ailments, all remain as indomitable as ever, and enduring testaments to survival with a noble spirit of grace and dignity.

In late August 2003, Ted Seidman passed away. He will be sorely missed, but his memory will live on.

Just before this book went to press, I was advised that Adam Bigwood had died on April 21, 2003, a little over ten years after his father's alleged death. The circumstances of Bigwood's reported death remain unknown.

Bibliography

Abraham, Ben, *Mengele—The Truth Exposed,* Sherit Hapleita (Association of the Jewish Nazi Survivors of Brazil), São Paulo, Brazil (1995).

Askenasy, Hans, *Hitler's Secret,* KNI, Inc., Anaheim, Calif. (1984).

Associated Press Report, "Swiss Probers Find Evidence of Bank Crimes," *San Diego Union-Tribune,* San Diego (December 21, 1996).

Barnavi, Eli (editor), *A Historical Atlas of the Jewish People—From the Time of the Patriarchs to the Present,* Alfred A. Knopf, New York (1992).

Bartov, Omer, "Inside, Outside," *The New Republic,* Washington, D.C. (April 10, 2000).

Ben-David, Calev, "Outsider at the Top," *The Jerusalem Report,* Jerusalem (July 11, 1996/Tammuz 24, 5756).

Ben-David, Calev, "World's End," *The Jerusalem Report,* Jerusalem (November 28, 1996/Kislev 17, 5757).

Braun, Stephen, "Bitter Secrets and a Cache of Gold," *Los Angeles Times,* Los Angeles (November 24, 1996).

Brinton, Crane, John B. Christopher, and Robert Lee Wolff, *A History of Civilization,* third edition, Prentice Hall, Upper Saddle River, N. J. (1967).

Camus, Albert, *The Myth of Sisyphus and Other Essays,* Vintage Books, New York (1955).

Carmichael, Joel, *The Satanizing of the Jews—Origin and Development of Mystical Anti-Semitism,* International Publishing Corporation, New York (1992).

Carroll, James, *Constantine's Sword,* Houghton Mifflin Company, Boston (2001).

Charlesworth, James (editor), *Jesus' Jewishness—Exploring the Place of*

Jesus in Early Judaism, Crossroad Publishing Company, New York (1996).

Cohn, Marta (translated), *Hannah Senesh—Her Life & Diary,* Schocken Books, New York (1972).

Crankshaw, Edward, *Gestapo—Instrument of Tyranny,* Da Capo Press, New York (1956).

Dahlburg, John-Thor, "Switzerland Unveils Plan for $4.7 Billion Victims Fund," *Los Angeles Times,* Los Angeles (March 6, 1997).

Dawidowicz, Lucy S., *The War Against the Jews: 1933–1945,* Bantam Books, New York (1975).

Dimont, Max I., *Jews, God and History,* Penguin Books, New York (1994).

Dobbs, Michael, "A New, Disturbing Chapter Emerges in Holocaust History," *International Herald Tribune,* New York (November 11, 1996).

Dobroszycki, Lucjan (editor), *The Chronicle of the Lodz Ghetto: 1941–1944,* Yale University Press, New Haven, Conn. (1984).

Flannery, Edward H., *The Anguish of the Jews—Twenty-Three Centuries of Antisemitism,* Paulist Press, New York (1985).

Frank, Anne, *The Diary of Anne Frank,* Pan Books Ltd., London (1954).

Friesel, Evyatar, *Atlas of Modern Jewish History,* Oxford University Press, New York (1990).

Gilbert, Martin, *The Holocaust—A History of the Jews During the Second World War,* Henry Holt and Company, New York (1985).

Gilman, Sander L., *Jewish Self-Hatred,* The Johns Hopkins University Press, Baltimore (1986).

Goldhagen, Daniel Jonah, *Hitler's Willing Executioners—Ordinary Germans and the Holocaust,* Alfred A. Knopf, New York (1996).

Goldhagen, Daniel Jonah, *A Moral Reckoning—The Role of the Catholic Church in the Holocaust and Its Unfulfilled Duty to Repair,* Alfred A. Knopf, New York (2002).

Goldhagen, Daniel Jonah, "Motives, Causes, and Alibis—A Response to Critics of the Author's Book *Hitler's Willing Executioners: Ordinary Germans And The Holocaust,*" *The New Republic,* Vol. 215, Number 26, Issue 4,275, Washington, D.C. (December 23, 1996).

Gribetz, Judeah, *The Timetables of Jewish History—A Chronology of the Most Important People and Events in Jewish History,* Touchstone, New York (1993).

Gutman, Israel, *Encyclopedia of the Holocaust,* Macmillan Publishing Company, New York (1990).

Hass, Aaron, *The Aftermath—Living With the Holocaust,* Cambridge University Press, Cambridge (1995).

Henry, Marilyn, "Germany Will Offer DM 20m. a Year to Nazi Victims in E. Europe," *The Jerusalem Post,* international edition, Jerusalem (November 30, 1996/Kislev 19, 5757).

Hilberg, Raul, *The Destruction of the European Jews,* second edition, Holmes & Meier, New York (1985).

Hitler, Adolf, *Mein Kampf,* Reynal & Hitchcock, New York (1939).

Horlick Levin Advertising, *Journal of Liberation—1945–1995,* Los Angeles (1995).

Jahil, Leni, *The Holocaust,* Oxford University Press, New York (1991).

Johnson, Paul, *A History of the Jews,* HarperPerennial, London (1987).

Johnson, Paul, *Modern Times—The World From the Twenties to the Nineties,* revised edition, HarperPerennial, New York (1991).

Langmuir, Gavin I., *History, Religion, and Antitsemitism,* University of California Press, Berkeley (1990).

Levertov, Denise, *Poems 1960–1967,* New Directions, New York (1966).

Levin, Nora, *The Holocaust,* Thomas Y. Crowell, New York (1968).

Levy, Alan, *Nazi Hunter—The Wiesenthal File,* Carroll & Graf, New York (2002).

Lifton, Robert Jay, *The Nazi Doctors—Medical Killing and the Psychology of Genocide,* BasicBooks, New York (1986).

Marrus, Michael R., *The Nazi Holocaust—Historical Articles on the Destruction of European Jews,* Meckler, Westport, Conn. (1989).

Mead, Walter Russell, "Long After War, Taint of Nazis Remains in Europe," *Los Angeles Times,* Los Angeles (November 3, 1996).

Montalbano, William D., "The Jews in Hitler's Military," *Los Angeles Times,* Los Angeles (December 24, 1996).

Morse, Arthur, *While Six Million Died,* Random House, New York (1968).

Mycio, Mary, "In Ukraine, Many Survivors of the Holocaust Still

Await Recompense," *Los Angeles Times,* Los Angeles (December 15, 1996).

Nicholls, William, *Christian Antisemitism—A History of Hate,* Jason Aaronson Inc., Northvale, N. J. (1995).

Pagis, Dan, *The Selected Poetry of Dan Pagis,* translated by Stephen Mitchell, The University of California Press, Berkeley (1996).

Posner, Gerald L. and Jolen Ware, *Mengele: The Complete Story,* First Cooper Square Press, New York (2000).

Prager, Dennis and Joseph Telushkin, *Why the Jews?,* Simon & Schuster, New York (1983).

Rosenbaum, Alan S., *Prosecuting Nazi War Criminals,* Westview Press, Boulder, Colo. (1993).

Reuters News Service, "Swiss Report Urging 'War' Over Jewish Assets Fuels Controversy," *Los Angeles Times,* Los Angeles (January 27, 1997).

Segev, Tom, *The Seventh Million—The Israelis and the Holocaust,* Hill & Wang, New York (1993).

Simon, Stephanie, "Proof of Suffering Is Price of Holocaust Reparations," *Los Angeles Times,* Los Angeles (June 4, 1996).

Smith, Marcus J., *Dachau—The Harrowing of Hell,* State University of New York Press, Albany (1995).

Times Wire Services, "Swiss Leader Assailed for Views on Holocaust Assets," *Los Angeles Times,* Los Angeles (January 1, 1997).

Times Wire Services, "Swiss Bank Helped Launder Nazi Gold, Documents Show," *Los Angeles Times,* Los Angeles (January 13, 1997).

Times Wire Services, "Swiss Envoy Quits Amid Holocaust Controversy," *Los Angeles Times,* Los Angeles (January 28, 1997).

Traverso, Enzo, *The Jews and Germany,* University of Nebraska Press, Lincoln (1995).

Tsur, Batsheva, "Swiss Apology for 'Blackmail' Remark Opens Way for Renewed Talks," *The Jerusalem Post,* international edition, Jerusalem (January 25, 1997/Shvat 17, 5757).

United States Holocaust Memorial Museum, *Historical Atlas of the Holocaust,* Macmillan Publishing USA, New York (1996).

Vermas, Geza, *Jesus the Jew—A Historian's Reading of the Gospels,* Fortress Press, Philadelphia (1973).

Watson, Alan, *Jesus and the Jews—The Pharisaic Tradition in John,* University of Georgia Press, Athens (1995).

Weinstein, Henry, "Insurers Reject Most Claims in Holocaust Cases," *Los Angeles Times,* Los Angeles (May 9, 2000).

Weinstein, Henry, "U.S., German Leaders Near Pact on Holocaust Claims," *Los Angeles Times,* Los Angeles (May 22, 2000).

Werbell, Frederick E. and Thurston Clarke, *Lost Hero: The Mystery of Raoul Wallenberg,* McGraw-Hill, New York (1982).

Wiesel, Elie, *The Night Trilogy,* Hill & Wang, New York (1985).

Williams, Carol J., "Germany OKs $5 Billion for Nazis' Slave Laborers," *Los Angeles Times,* Los Angeles (July 7, 2000).

Wylen, Stephen M., *The Jews in the Time of Jesus,* Paulist Press, New York (1996).

Wyman, David S., *The Abandonment of the Jews,* Pantheon Books, New York (1985).

Index

About the Author

Mark Kalmansohn is a partner in the entertainment firm of McPherson & Kalmansohn. He received a B.A. from UCLA (1974), where he graduated Phi Beta Kappa and summa cum laude and was awarded a University of California Regents Scholarship. He later received a J.D. from UCLA, and Diploma in International Law from Darwin College, University of Cambridge. From 1977 through 1983, Mr. Kalmansohn served in the U.S. Department of Justice, including four years as an Assistant U. S. Attorney (Criminal Division) in Los Angeles. A former partner at the entertainment firm of Cooper, Epstein & Hurewitz, he served as the Motion Picture Association of America's Director of North American Anti-Piracy Operations (1987–1991). The author of several published articles, Mr. Kalmansohn has appeared as a commentator on CNN's *Burden of Proof* and in a *Dateline NBC* segment (July 7, 2002) titled "Final Betrayal" on the subject of this book. He currently resides in Santa Monica, California.